DISPATCHES FROM THE WORLD

Sir Percival Phillips, 1922 (Daily Mail, London)

Also by William R. Black

Non-fiction

Railroads for Rent: The Local Rail Service Assistance Program

Transportation: A Geographical Analysis

Sustainable Transportation: Problems and Solutions

Mitigating Circumstances: The United State of Americas vs. Robert Black

Fiction

Greenhouse Effects

DISPATCHES FROM THE WORLD

*The Life of Percival Phillips,
War Correspondent*

WILLIAM R. BLACK

authorhouse®

AuthorHouse™
1663 Liberty Drive
Bloomington, IN 47403
www.authorhouse.com
Phone: 1-800-839-8640

© *2012 by William R. Black. All rights reserved.*

No part of this book may be reproduced, stored in a retrieval system, or transmitted by any means without the written permission of the author.

Published by AuthorHouse   10/09/2012

ISBN: 978-1-4772-6465-2 (sc)
ISBN: 978-1-4772-6466-9 (hc)
ISBN: 978-1-4772-6467-6 (e)

Library of Congress Control Number: 2012915942

Any people depicted in stock imagery provided by Thinkstock are models, and such images are being used for illustrative purposes only.
Certain stock imagery © Thinkstock.

Because of the dynamic nature of the Internet, any web addresses or links contained in this book may have changed since publication and may no longer be valid. The views expressed in this work are solely those of the author and do not necessarily reflect the views of the publisher, and the publisher hereby disclaims any responsibility for them.

For Donna

TABLE OF CONTENTS

List of Illustrations xi
Preface xiii
Acknowledgments xvii
Chapters:
   1. Introduction 1
   2. "Four Miners Shot" 19
   3. First Wars 29
   4. The Move To London 43
   5. The *Daily Express* And Another War 59
   6. A Very Short Engagement 69
   7. Between The Wars 75
   8. A Revolution, A Riot And A Little War 87
   9. Coronation Durbar In New Delhi And The Balkans 93
  10. War Is Declared With Germany 101
  11. Covering The Western Front 111
  12. Espionage 123
  13. Troubles In Ireland 131
  14. Back To The Front 139
  15. War's End And Its Aftermath 151
  16. Prince Of Wales Tour Of The Far East 171
  17. With The *Daily Mail* 177
  18. Far Vistas 197
  19. India And Gandhi 207
  20. With The *Daily Telegraph* 219
  21. The "Scoop" And Ethiopia 227
  22. The Spanish Civil War 245
  23. The Final Days 253
Afterword 269
Selected Bibliography 271
Newspapers 279
Index 281

LIST OF ILLUSTRATIONS

Sir Percival Phillips, 1922 (*Daily Mail*, London)
Southwestern Pennsylvania
Advertisement of Dr. Hibbard S. Phillips, father of Percival Phillip
Percival Phillips Passport Application of 1894 (National Archives, Washington, D.C.)
Percival Phillips (right) with George S. Reinoehl, a fellow war correspondent, in Cuba during the Spanish American War, 1898 (*The Telephone News*)
Percival Phillips at the time of the Russo-Japanese War, 1904
The British Sector of the Western Front (1916)
Press Camp during the Great War, 1916 (front row is Percival Phillips, Colonel Hatton Wilson, Beach Thomas, Captain A.G. Stuart, back row Basil Clarke, Perry Robinson and Percival Gibbon (William Heinemann, Ltd.)
Chateau Rollancourt, 1918 (front row is Perry Robinson, Percival Phillips with dog, and Henry W. Nevinson, Beach Thomas is sitting behind Nevinson and Frederic Palmer is standing at the far right) (James Nisbet & Co., Ltd.)
Correspondents at the Hohenzollern Bridge with Cologne Cathedral in the background, December 16, 1918. (Percival Phillips, Perry Robinson, Philip Gibbs, and Beach Thomas) (Chapman & Hall, Ltd.)
Sir Percival Phillips sitting for a portrait by Phillip Ledoux (*Daily Mail*, London)
Ethiopia and neighboring countries and colonies (1935)
Sir Percival Phillips working in his rooms, 1934 (*Daily Mail*, London)

PREFACE

Journalists are often capable of developing a huge following of viewers, listeners, and readers if they are perceived as courageous, honest, objective and worthy of our trust. In terms of television one must say that Walter Cronkite held such a position of trust in America during the Vietnam War and afterwards. A quarter of a century earlier Edward R. Murrow held such a reputation as he brought the bombings of the London blitz during World War II into American living rooms by radio. During the First World War, before radio was popular and long before television, news of the wars or other events came into our homes with the daily newspaper and the pen-pictures of the correspondents that covered these and what they wrote had no less of an impact. Percival Phillips was one of these correspondents.

Phillips was one of five war correspondents given permission by the British government in 1915 to report the events of what was called the Great War. Oddly enough he was not British. He was an American, born in Brownsville, Pennsylvania, who after holding positions with numerous newspapers in the U.S. moved to England to be a correspondent, or more specifically to be a war correspondent. Being such a correspondent was his dream. Europe with its various nations and segregated ethnic groups seemed far more likely to have wars than North America, and England would be close to such conflicts if they occurred.

Phillips' parents were teachers. His father went on to become a medical doctor shortly before divorcing Phillips' mother. The boy was nine years old when that occurred. A few years later he dropped out of school and by the time he was sixteen he was working for the local newspaper as a writer.

By 1914 Phillips had already covered five wars: the Greco-Turkish War, the Spanish-American War, the Russo-Japanese War, the Italian-Turkish War in Tripoli, and the First Balkan Campaign in

Bulgaria. He may have been the first reporter to bring a typewriter to these combat situations; he carried it in a bulletproof case. He was trained in the early 1890s as a typist, or as a 'typewriter' as typists were referred to at the time. It was said that he introduced typing to the London news establishment in 1901, which may or may not be true.

Following the Great War he traveled the world for the news, continuing to cover wars, as well as royal tours, coronations, rebellions, the Olympics, elections, and all of the other events that fill the daily newspaper. His final wars were the Italian invasion of Ethiopia and the Spanish Civil War.

This is the first biography of Percival Phillips. Unlike most journalists of his day he did not write an autobiography, nor did he write a memoir that covered a significant portion of his life. He did not keep a diary. But the absence of these is not sufficient grounds for ignoring the life of a man, who was outstanding as a journalist, or for ignoring his contributions and accomplishments.

This biography relies to a large extent on newspapers and the few things that were published or available outside of that medium. Biographies and memoirs of other correspondents who worked with him from time to time were very helpful. A few files and letters were found in archives of the U.S. and U.K. These have also been very useful. Because he became somewhat famous there was a kind of celebrity to his life, and as a result those who knew him at various points in that life did not hesitate to write about him or offer interviews about the Percival Phillips they knew. In addition he was seen as an expert on world affairs and he was often interviewed and asked for his views on events of the day. These personal views were often different from the philosophical position of the newspapers that he worked for over the years and they reveal more about the man.

I have organized most of what appears here in a more or less chronological fashion and I've focused on his writing to a large extent. His early writing was for nearly a dozen different newspapers in Western Pennsylvania and New York. He then moved to London and worked sequentially for the *Daily Express*, the *Daily Mail*, and finally the *Daily Telegraph*. However, his byline appeared in newspapers throughout the English-speaking parts of the world. I am impressed with some of the writing that he did, and where these pieces are relatively brief I have included them, or portions of them, in the chapters.

The book you hold is the result of the effort I undertook to research and write the life story of Percival Phillips, and in so doing to introduce him to the contemporary world. I trust you will find the man and the book of interest.

William R. Black
Bloomington, Indiana

ACKNOWLEDGMENTS

Several individuals and organizations have been of assistance as I researched the various facets of Percival Phillips' life. These individuals include: Lou Malcomb of the Herman B. Wells Library of Indiana University; Richard Jones and Rachel Swanston of the *Daily Mail*, London; Catherine Souch of the Royal Geographical Society in London; Suzanne M. Johnston of the Senator John Heinz History Center in Pittsburgh; Bruce Kirby of the Manuscript Division of the Library of Congress, Washington, D.C.; National Archives and Records Administration, Washington, D.C.; Clare Freestone of the National Portrait Gallery, London; Anthony Richards of the Department of Documents, Imperial War Museum, London; Mick Lidbury, *The Daily Express*, London; Parliamentary Archives of the United Kingdom, London; Marcus Risdell of the Garrick Club, London; Bob Burke, Managing Editor, Valley Independent, Monesson, PA; Christian Algar, British Library Newspaper Library (Colindale), London; Kate Colligan and Wendy Plug, Manuscript Collection, Darlington Memorial Library, University of Pittsburgh; the Register of Wills for Fayette County, Pennsylvania; the Prothonotary's Office of Washington County, Pennsylvania; and, the staff of the Pennsylvania State Library, Harrisburg.

The author would also like to acknowledge his appreciation to London's *Daily Mail* for permission to use several of the photographs included here. Similar appreciation also goes to John M. Hollingsworth of Indiana University for preparing the three maps used here.

CHAPTER 1

introduction

Sir Percival Phillips sat across the room from Francis McCullagh. They had a friendship that went back more than thirty years, having met in Tokyo in 1905 when they were covering the conflict that came to be known as the Russo-Japanese War. The men were sitting in Percival's room in the *Gran Hotel* in Salamanca, Spain, which during the winter of 1936 was not quite as grand as the name might imply, nevertheless it was a large rather elegant room. The Spanish civil war had drawn the two war correspondents to this place. The government of Spain was trying to maintain its control over the country as the rebel forces of Francisco Franco were trying to overthrow it. The two correspondents were discussing the progress of the civil war and the general situation in Spain.

Percy (as he preferred to be called later in life) was not feeling all that well and he was now worried. He had covered the rebellion from Franco's side since late in the summer and he had sent out dispatches describing the events as accurately as he could. This had caused Franco's rebel forces to become somewhat hostile toward him and he was beginning to feel as though it was time to leave. He expressed his concerns to McCullagh. "I'll feel easier in my mind when I get across the frontier," said Percy. "These Spaniards would be capable of doing anything to prevent news from leaking out. They would be capable of having me murdered." He added, "At any rate they would be capable of keeping me here for months if they thought that I got hold of important military secrets."

Eager to leave Spain, Percival requested a *salvoconducto* (papers guaranteeing a safe passage) from the rebel authorities, but this was denied. Nevertheless, within a few days he managed to cross the border into Portugal. From there he went to Gibraltar and later sailed across the Straits to Tangier in Morocco. In less than a month he was back in London. Within a few days after his arrival newspapers throughout the English-speaking world were breaking the news of his unexpected death.

Southwestern Pennsylvania

Percival Phillips was born on July 2, 1877, in the town of Brownsville in Western Pennsylvania, which is a little less than half way between Pennsylvania's southern border with West Virginia and the city of Pittsburgh, on the Monongahela River. The town had been the jumping off point for those who took the National Road to the west during the first half of the nineteenth century. The road ended in Brownsville and for several years migrants heading west boarded boats there that would take them down the Monongahela and Ohio Rivers to reach the western lands of Kentucky, Indiana, and beyond. Later the road was extended to Wheeling, Virginia (West Virginia today) and Brownsville lost much of its status.

Percival's parents were Hibbard Samuel and Anne Cochran Miller Phillips and they were descended from Pennsylvania families that had lived in the state for generations. Although his formal name was Leslie Percival Phillips, he used Leslie only on rare occasions early in his life and by 1898 he had ceased to use it entirely, preferring to be called Percival or Percy Phillips. He was the second of four children, all boys, born to Hibbard and Anne Phillips.

Percival's father, Hibbard, was born on April 9, 1845, on what was called the Rocky Hill farm; this was in Cecil Township in the northern part of Washington County, Pennsylvania. This county is the next county west of Brownsville on the National Road. Hibbard was the son of Samuel and Sarah (Fulton) Phillips, a farming couple from that area. It was said that Sarah was a descendant of Robert Fulton of steamboat fame, but this is not very likely since this Robert Fulton had only one son and he died at an early age. Many individuals sorely wanted to be related to someone of note in the 19th century and Sarah Fulton Phillips was no different from the others. Perhaps this was some way of laying claim to a higher social status or more recognition by others in the community. Although she could not have been a descendant of Robert Fulton, she may have shared an earlier ancestor with him among the Fultons of Ireland.

As a young man Hibbard went by the name of Samuel H. Phillips, but as he grew older he switched the order of the names to become Hibbard S. Phillips. During different periods in his life he would go by the name of Hibbard, or Hibbard S., H.S. or Samuel. Those who did not know him well would sometimes refer to him as Herbert, but he never used the latter name. Samuel seems to have been the preferred name in his youth and in his older years.

Hibbard was a tall, lanky man, whose physical appearance would later be described as resembling Abraham Lincoln. He cared little for physical labor and would much rather lie under a tree and read a book than do any manual labor. He and most other members of the Phillips family had some facility with foreign languages; they picked them up rather easily and could converse with foreign workers brought to Western Pennsylvania to work in the coal mines of that area.

Hibbard must have received some type of formal education as a young man. Most likely he attended the Jefferson Academy in Canonsburg, but he did not graduate from that school according to surviving records. Nevertheless, he was probably in the process of getting an education prior to 1869 because in that year he was hired to be the principal of a school in Smith Township of Washington County and presumably some academic credentials would be necessary for the position.[1] On August 25 of the following year he was hired by the town of Brownsville to teach in their school.[2] Then in 1871 he was awarded an A.M. degree from Washington & Jefferson College, a school that replaced the Jefferson Academy and Washington College. The new school was located in the town of Washington, county seat of the county with the same name.

In 1875 Hibbard married Anne (more commonly referred to as Annie) Miller of Brownsville, who was eight years younger than he was. After their marriage the couple set up housekeeping in the town of Canonsburg to the north of Washington, and by 1880 three of their sons were born. It is likely that Annie had all of her children in Brownsville where her mother could assist her. Later on, Annie appears to have missed Brownsville and probably her mother. It was common for her and the boys to make the

---

[1] Boyd Crumrine (ed.), *History of Washington County*, Philadelphia: L.H. Everts and Co., 1882, p. 925.

[2] Franklin Ellis (ed.), *History of Fayette County, Pennsylvania: with biographical sketches of many of its pioneers and prominent men*, Philadelphia, L. H. Everts and Co., p. 441.

30-mile trip from Canonsburg to Brownsville by buggy to visit her mother for a few days. During the early years of their marriage and the decade that followed, Hibbard served as the principal for schools in Brownsville, Uniontown and Connellsville, all towns in Fayette County of Pennsylvania.[3] In every case it would appear that Annie remained at their home in Canonsburg, or possibly with her mother in Brownsville, and Hibbard would return there on weekends.

Hibbard took a teaching job as early as the late 1870s down the river toward Pittsburgh in what is today Donora. Local histories suggest that he was the first teacher in that community. At the time the school was in Carroll Township of Washington County and it was referred to as the Gilmore School.[4] He probably was a boarder with someone in Donora even then because railroad access was non-existent and stage travel would have taken too long for him to return to Canonsburg each night. It is known that he left the position in a short time.

By the September term of 1879 Hibbard had taken another position, probably leaving one of the other schools in Washington County or Fayette County for the opportunity to become the principal of the Fourth Ward Public Schools in Pittsburgh. He took a room in the home of John L. Ferson, a homeopathic physician in Pittsburgh who lived not far from the school where Phillips was to be principal. Going back and forth from Canonsburg to Pittsburgh was still not possible by train and even if it was, train travel would have been more costly, more time-consuming and as a result less frequent. As before, Annie and their sons remained in Canonsburg. The local newspaper reported later: "Sometime in October H.S. Phillips, Principal of the Fourth Ward, Pittsburg Public Schools came to his home in Canonsburg one evening and took to his bed with typhoid

---

[3] *The Three Towns: A Sketch of Brownsville, Bridgeport and West Brownsville*, published from The Three Towns of September, 1883, Second edition, Brownsville: Brownsville Historical Society, 1976, "H.S. Phillips, Former Principal, Dies at Scranton," *Daily Courier* (Connellsville, PA), November 13, 1929.

[4] Untitled, *Charleroi (Pennsylvania) Mail*, April 24, 1920.

fever."[5] For weeks he was very ill, but then he began to recover. At that time Annie became ill with the same disease.[6]

By March of 1880 Annie had recovered. The family stored most of their household goods in Canonsburg and moved to Brownsville, where they stayed with Annie's mother. It is likely that Annie needed her mother's help in caring for the boys.

On June 3, 1880, the Canonsburg newspaper stated, "H.S. Phillips has resigned his position as Principal of the Fourth Ward, Pittsburgh, Public Schools, on account of continued illness."[7] It is not known if this was the actual reason, or just a good excuse for his departure, but it is known that he soon took a position with Dr. Pershing's Pittsburg Female College, which would later become Chatham College. Hibbard probably viewed the college appointment as better than his public school position.

It can be assumed that his stay at the Pittsburg Female College was also brief because in the fall of 1881 he began a three-year course of study at the Hahnemann Medical College in Philadelphia, Pennsylvania (now affiliated with Drexel University). This was a school specializing in the practice of homeopathic medicine and Hibbard completed the program in 1884 and followed this with some post graduate and specialized courses. The interest in homeopathic medicine may have come from his former landlord, Dr. Ferson. In any event he began practicing medicine in Canonsburg in 1884 and this continued until March of 1889. At that time he moved to Pittsburgh and began a medical practice there in association with Dr. W. D. King. A city directory for Pittsburgh in 1890 has Hibbard listed as a physician and other sources state he was viewed as very successful. Then in 1892 he moved from offices next to Dr. King at 326 Fifth Avenue to 73 Congress Street. [8] Throughout this period

---

[5]   In December of 1891 the United States Board of Geographic Names changed the name of Pittsburgh to Pittsburg. The city kept this name for the next 20 years and in 1911, it was changed back to Pittsburgh. This is the reason why documents written and names of organizations created during this period have a different spelling than is used today.

[6]   Fulton Phillips, "Sickness." *Rural Notes* (Canonsburg, Pennsylvania), December 25, 1879.

[7]   Fulton Phillips, Untitled, *Rural Notes* (Canonsburg, Pennsylvania), June 3, 1880.

[8]   Fulton Phillips, "About H.S. Phillips," *McDonald PA Outlook*, January 23, 1892; *The Homeopathic Physician*, March 1889, p. 168; *The Homeopathic Recorder*, Vol. VII,

Dispatches from the World

he kept in contact with Washington County friends and relatives. In the fall of 1882 he and two other men purchased *Rural Notes*, the local newspaper published in Canonsburg, from his brother, Fulton Phillips, who had decided to move to the West. It soon became apparent that the newspaper business was not something Hibbard enjoyed, or perhaps he was too busy to get involved in the venture. In any event, he sold his interest in the newspaper to one of his partners the following spring.[9] At the time he placed the following rather strange note in the newspaper:

> I have sold my interest in the Rural Notes to D.H. Fee. He is now the sole editor and proprietor. Am I sorry? I don't know. Are you glad? I don't care. I can't say that you will at once see a decided improvement on the paper, for I have not done anything since the first of February. What more need I say? Gab is long, and space in the Rural Notes is 50 cents an inch a month, and I am not going to pay more than $3 to get this printed. That you may live long and happy together is the wish of H.S. Phillips.[10]

Hibbard's marriage to Annie lasted longer than his newspaper career, but on November 27, 1886, he filed for divorce from Annie charging her with desertion.[11] Apparently, Hibbard's movement from one school to another was not to Annie's liking and she refused to move along with him preferring instead to live with her mother in Brownsville. Becoming a physician and practicing in Canonsburg for most of the 1880s did not change this situation; apparently she preferred to stay in Brownsville even then. The following spring, on May 20, 1887, the divorce was granted.

    January 1892.

[9] Joseph F. McFarland, 20th *Century History of the City of Washington and Washington County, Pennsylvania.* Chicago. IL: Richmond Arnold Publishing Company, 1910, p. 405.

[10] H.S. Phillips, "Valedictory," *Rural Notes* (Canonsburg, Pennsylvania), November 4, 1886.

[11] Continuance Dockets, Prothonotary's Office, Washington County Courthouse, Washington, Pennsylvania.

In the midst of all this familial turmoil Hibbard became an exhorter and social preacher in the Methodist Episcopal Church.[12] An exhorter was slightly lower than a lay-preacher in the church hierarchy. He would preach wherever necessary in the community, but did not have a regular congregation as such.

At some point Hibbard met Caroline Cummings of the town of Hickory in Mt. Pleasant Township of Washington County, and he developed some strong feelings for her. On July 13 of 1887, less than two months after his divorce became final, Hibbard and Caroline Cummings applied for a marriage license in Washington County and six days later they were married at the home of Caroline's parents in Hickory.[13] Hibbard was eighteen years older than Caroline's twenty-four years. In spite of this age difference they would remain together until his death.

Something took Hibbard and his new family to Toledo, Ohio, in 1892. Perhaps it was the desire to start a medical practice in a new location. It is known that one of their children, an infant son he had with Caroline, died there on June 18 of 1893, and the family returned to the McDonald area (of Washington County) for the infant's burial six days later. During 1896 Hibbard and his family left the Toledo area and moved to Pittsburgh where he set up a practice on Third Avenue.[14] Coincidentally, Dr. John L. Ferson died in 1896.

By 1900 Hibbard and Caroline had four children: three girls and one boy. They lived in a large house on Forbes Street of Pittsburgh and they took in boarders, eight at that time. Hibbard practiced medicine in Pittsburgh from prior to 1889 until some time around 1905, except for the time in Ohio.[15] Advertisements that he placed in the region's newspapers in 1899 listed his name as Hibbard S. Phillips or H.S. Phillips. In these ads he promised cures for all sorts of ailments including cancer, "without pain or the use of a knife," and

---

[12] *Biographical and Historical Catalogue of Washington and Jefferson College, 1802-1902*, Philadelphia: George H. Buchanon and Company, 1902.

[13] Marriage Records, County Clerk, Washington County Courthouse, Washington, Pennsylvania.

[14] *Medical Century: An International Journal of Homeopathic Medicine and Surgery*, Vol. IV, No. 4, 1896, p, 100.

[15] *Pittsburgh City Directory, 1890*, Pittsburgh, Pa., J.F. Diffenbacher, 1890.

Dispatches from the World

> # IT'S SO.
>
> If you have Health and Strength, and freedom from pain, you can push your business and make money and enjoy life. BUT IF you are tortured with pain, you become irritable and ill-tempered, neglect your business and your health soon goes to wreck and ruin. Are you suffering with Piles, Fissure, Ulcerations, Pruritis Ani, or any other rectal trouble? Have you Stomach Trouble, which is sure to lead to liver, kidney and rectal troubles? And have you taken treatment and been faked? Don't let that discourage you. You must be cured or bad will go on to worse. I wish to say to both sexes who suffer from any of these troubles that I will positively cure them, without use of knife. No old methods. No bad results. No failures. I am not a traveling doctor, but permanently located in Pittsburg, and fear no competition in the field anywhere in the treatment of these diseases.
>
> ## Dr. Hibbard S. Phillips,
> ### 408 Third Ave., oppo. Postoffice, Pittsburg, Pa.

*Advertisement of Dr. Hibbard S. Phillips,
father of Percival Phillips.*

although this latter statement is consistent with the homeopathic tradition, his claims of a cancer cure were obviously overstated.

Hibbard and his family next moved to the Scranton, Pennsylvania, area and settled in a suburb named Dunmore to the east of Scranton at some time after 1905. He worked in the medical field for about five more years, until he was 65. He then retired from practicing medicine; this was about 1910.[16] Why the family moved to the

---

[16] "Dr. Herbert S. Phillips Dies in Home in Dunmore," *Scranton* (PA) *Times*, November 13, 1929.

Scranton area and why Hibbard gave up the practice of medicine are not known. It is known that after retiring he became quite serious about religion and preaching. By 1920 he was reporting to census takers that he was an "evangelist" and that his place of work was a mission. Actually he had become the organizer of the Pentecostal Church at Scranton and the East, and it was an interest that he was to keep for the rest of his life.[17]

It seems quite apparent that Hibbard had a minor role in raising Percival and the other boys. Even before leaving Annie he was rarely at home, having taken positions often too distant to make the trip to Canonsburg each evening. Shortly after Percival's ninth birthday Hibbard filed for divorce from Annie and shortly after his tenth birthday he remarried and started another family.

There is one exception to the above statement and that has to do with geography. Geography at the time was almost exclusively what would be called physical geography today: rivers and streams, mountains and plateaus, coastal areas, bodies of water, and similar physical features. When Hibbard was teaching at the Fourth Ward School in Pittsburgh, he did not use a textbook but taught the course exclusively using "maps of raised surfaces." [18] Many years later Percival would develop his own raised relief maps when covering the Western Front. Coming into the press chateau during the war years one might very well see the correspondents "bending over a relief map cleverly fashioned from cardboard by Percival." [19] As we will see later Hibbard's son loved maps and would use them and study them to the point of having almost perfect knowledge of the terrain he would encounter in his travels and reporting assignments.

Aside from this we should probably credit the Phillips' ancestral line for the height that Percival would attain. He would grow to a height above six feet. The remainder of his physical appearance resembled his mother's family. This is particularly so when he reaches his fifties. A high forehead and the general shape of his head make

---

[17] "Dr. H.S. Phillips, Former Principal, Dies at Scranton," *Daily Courier* (Connellsville, PA) November 13, 1929.

[18] "Geography," *Rural Notes*, March 11, 1850.

[19] *The Windsor Magazine*, Vol. 49, 1918-1919, p. 152

him resemble one of his uncles on his mother's side of the family (Philander Chase Knox). This brings us to Annie Phillips.

Percival's mother, Annie, was the daughter of James Smith and Sarah Knox Miller. She was born in Brownsville on March 19, 1853. Her mother Sarah was the daughter of David S. and Sarah (Francis) Knox. David S. Knox had begun work as a printer, and then as a teacher, before finally ending up as a banker in Brownsville. David's father was the Rev. William Knox, a native of County Tyrone, Ireland, who had emigrated to the U.S. in 1797. Sarah Francis Knox was the daughter of James Francis, a native of Ireland who it is said served in the Revolutionary War as a surgeon.

David S. and Sarah Knox had three children: two daughters and a son. Their first daughter, Sarah, was born in 1830 and educated at the Brownsville Seminary. Later in life she would teach at the Pittsburg Female College. In 1850 she married James Smith Miller, who ran a saw mill in Brownsville with his father. This couple had two children: Annie, who later married Hibbard Phillips, and David Knox Miller, who became an architect in Pittsburgh. James Smith Miller was never particularly healthy and he died in 1854. From the time of his marriage to Sarah until his death he was sickly, suffering with symptoms that resembled tuberculosis, referred to at the time as consumption.[20]

The son born to David and Sarah Knox was William Francis Knox. This son graduated from Allegheny College and attended medical school at the University of Pennsylvania. He began practicing medicine in McKeesport, down the river from Brownsville, in 1855 and continued to practice there until his death in 1915. David and Sarah's third child was a daughter, Isabella, who died in infancy. David's wife Sarah died in the 1830s.

Following the death of his wife, David S. Knox married Rebecca Page of Connellsville, also in Fayette County. This marriage resulted in nine more children: Thomas, Samuel, Richard, Mary, Caroline, Alfred, Narcissa, Philander and Harriette. Of these, Thomas and Samuel would relocate to Santa Barbara, California, and become a druggist and doctor, respectively. Mary married a man named

---

[20] Based on correspondence in the William F. Knox Papers, Darlington Memorial Library, The University of Pittsburgh.

Graff and moved to Omaha, Nebraska. Caroline and Narcissa died of typhoid fever while young. Alfred became a Vice President of the Mellon National Bank in Pittsburgh and Harriette never married and remained in Brownsville for most of her life. The fate of Richard is unknown, but it would appear that he died as a young man.

Without a doubt the youngest son, Philander, would become the most famous member of this generation of the family. Philander Chase Knox was born in Brownsville on May 6, 1853. His grandfather, the Rev. William Knox, had been a minister and the grandson was named for Philander Chase, a well-known evangelist in western Pennsylvania and Ohio, who had died during the year prior to Philander's birth. As a young man Philander had worked in the offices of the *Brownsville Clipper*, one of the local newspapers that endured longer than the others in that community. Knox left Brownsville to attend West Virginia University (Morgantown), but in a short time he transferred to Mount Union College in Alliance, Ohio, from which he received his degree. While at Mount Union College he met William McKinley, the future U.S. President, something that would prove to be an advantage later in life. He studied law while he was at Mount Union and in 1875 he was admitted to the Pennsylvania bar and began working for David Reed, an attorney in Pittsburgh at the time. Two years later David Reed died and Philander along with James Hay Reed, nephew of the deceased Reed, started the law firm of Knox & Reed. Today these men would be viewed as very well-connected. In addition to McKinley, Knox had known Henry Clay Frick, the coke-making millionaire of southwestern Pennsylvania, since he was a boy. James Reed went to college with Andrew Mellon, a very wealthy banker and industrialist of Pittsburgh, who would later serve as Secretary of the Treasury under Presidents Harding, Coolidge and Hoover. The firm of Knox & Reed was very successful with fees in 1889 of $110,000; this was at a time when the average wage for the nation was $500.

There is no need to dwell on Philander Knox's public service career, but it is worth noting that he served nine years as a U.S. Senator from Pennsylvania (1904-1909 and 1917-1921), was Attorney General of the U.S. under Presidents William McKinley and Theodore Roosevelt (1901-1904), and served as Secretary of State under

President William Howard Taft (1909-1913). He died in Washington, D.C. on October 21, 1921, during his second Senate term. It is difficult to say how much contact Annie's boys had with their great-uncle, but they had to be aware of his accomplishments even early on in their lives since he would appear at family gatherings in Brownsville for birthdays, funerals and reunions.

It should be apparent that the Knox family was collectively and individually very ambitious. Each of the children had a drive to succeed and they became merchants, doctors, lawyers, and teachers. This had to have an influence on their male children who also tended to seek professional careers.

The three sons of Hibbard and Annie were followed by a fourth son who was born before the couple separated. Of these sons, the first was William and he died in infancy, perhaps during the typhoid fever episode of his parents in Canonsburg during the winter of 1879-80. The next son was Leslie Percival, who was born in 1877. Robert Fulton was the third son and he was born in 1879; as previously noted the family said it was descended from Robert Fulton and as unlikely as this seems, it is undoubtedly the source of his name. The last son was James Smith Miller Phillips and he was born on March 16, 1882, and was named for James Smith Miller, his maternal grandfather.

As young boys, Percival and his surviving brothers lived with their mother Annie and her mother Sarah Knox Miller, a teacher. Annie was also a teacher. She offered music lessons to a relatively large class of students in her home in Brownsville. She would then have public recitals for the class a couple of times a year. For one of these occasions the social column of the local newspaper noted "Mrs. Annie Phillips' music class composed of misses of the three towns, [21] went with their teacher to Bellevernon by the steamer "Mason" last Friday afternoon and gave a musicale at the residence of Mr. Winfield Shunk in the evening."[22] The class was made up of the daughters of some of the wealthier members of Brownsville society: the Coulters, Springers, Kisingers, Chalfants, and others.

---

[21] The three towns were Brownsville, Bridgeport, a town located near the bridge that spanned the Monongahela, and West Brownsville, which was located across the river.

[22] "Mrs. Phillips' Class Gives a Musicale," *Brownsville Clipper*, June 28, 1894.

Percival and James accompanied them on the trip down river and returned with them at the end of the evening.

The three boys that lived beyond infancy played in the neighborhood of their home at 417 Church Street. This was next to the high school, which was located on the corner of Church Street and New Street (later Fifth Avenue) in Brownsville. Just down the block from their house and toward the river was the Christ Episcopal Church, a huge stone structure that had been built in the 1850s and was continually in a state of being repaired. The church had a large turret similar to what one would see on a castle in England. It was said that some of the design ideas for the church, as well as substantial funds for the structure, had been contributed by the Bowman family. That family had built a castle-like structure with a similar turret several blocks away on a large tract of land cleared in the 1700s by an ancestor named Jacob Bowman. One can imagine the games boys would play in the presence of such castle-like structures.

One should not get the impression that Brownsville was an idyllic place. The town was located in the middle of the southwestern Pennsylvania coal mining region. Fresh, clean coal miners, as many as two hundred on a shift, would walk down the hill to the bituminous coal mines along the river with their metal hats and carrying their meals, sometimes wrapped only in an old newspaper. At the end of the shift they would walk up the hill, unrecognizable even to their families; their bodies and clothing covered in coal dust.

In the cool and cold weather all of the homes in the area were heated with coal-burning fireplaces. No one thought about pollution in those days; it was an accepted part of life. In the winter the dust in the air would be so thick that visibility was limited. Breathing would be labored and the air would taste slightly acidic. Snow when it fell in winter seemed to come down gray, but this was probably due to the continuous deposition of coal ash and particles. Summer would have been better except for the coke ovens in the area that were used to concentrate the carbon in the coal for the steel mills in Pittsburgh.

Those living along the creeks and the river were subjected to floods on an average of one in three years. Basements would fill with silt carried by the flood waters, and when the waters receded

Dispatches from the World

the inhabitants would shovel it out into the street as though this was just a natural part of life, in Brownsville it was. So in spite of the castle-like structures, this was no Camelot.

The boys attended the local schools in Brownsville, and although Percival would claim in later years that these schools were his only alma mater, this was not quite true. There is nothing remarkable about the Brownsville school years. The boys attended school on a regular basis and were recognized for their attendance. They frequently made the honor roll; this and perfect attendance were regularly published in the local newspaper. During these years James, the youngest of the boys, went by the name of Smith Phillips and Percival was Percy. Robert chose to be called Robert and not Bob.

Percival had some additional education following the Brownsville schools. "In the spring of 1890 at about the age of thirteen years, he went to Pittsburgh and that fall entered the Forbes Street School and the next summer passed the examination for high school. However, in the fall of 1891 he entered the law offices of Knox & Reed as an office boy, where he learned stenography and typewriting." [23] The firm that hired him was the law firm of his great-uncle, Philander Chase Knox.

At the time Knox, who was a specialist in corporate law, was the attorney for such men as Henry Clay Frick and Andrew Carnegie of Pittsburgh. Frick controlled a great deal of the coal and coke operations in southwestern Pennsylvania, and Carnegie, more or less, created the steel industry in the United States. They were also strongly opposed to the formation of unions in their yards, mines and mills. Philander had some role in preventing the unionization movement in the area during the summer of 1892 and he would later draw up the papers creating what would eventually become the U.S. Steel Corporation.

During the strikes in the coal mines and mills in 1892 Percival was working in the law offices of Knox & Reed. It is difficult to know what Percival's views were regarding his great uncle's activities. It is known that he left Knox & Reed and accepted a position as a

---

[23] J. Percy Hart, *Hart's History and Directory of the Three Towns: Brownsville, Bridgeport and West Brownsville*, Cadwaller, PA: J. Percy Hart, 1904.

stenographer and typewriter, as typists were called at the time, with a firm on the South Side of Pittsburgh. Shortly after entering his new position Percival became ill and had to return to Brownsville. This would have been during the winter of 1893-94.

It was during the winter of 1894 that Percival began working in the offices of George W. Lenhart. Lenhart had an insurance company in Brownsville, with offices in the downtown area above the local post office. In addition to insurance he was involved in numerous other pursuits. Percival's shorthand and typing skills would have been quite useful to Lenhart in part because of the need to keep records, but also because Lenhart had lost an arm in a piece of machinery in 1875.

Quite unexpectedly in the summer of 1895, Percival's younger brother Robert became ill. He was sent to a hospital in Pittsburgh where doctors diagnosed his illness as spinal meningitis. The condition of the sixteen-year-old boy did not improve during the following weeks and Robert died a month after the onset of the ailment on October 28.[24] This left Percival and his brother Smith as the only surviving sons.

The boys were raised in a home without men. Their grandfather Miller had died decades earlier, prior to their births, and the departure of Hibbard, for what were undoubtedly perceived by him as better opportunities, left the boys without a male influence in their household. Growing up without a father around would have been difficult for Percival as it would be for any boy. There would have been none of the little things that a father teaches a son, as well as no hunting, no fishing, and no sports of any kind. Later on in his career as a correspondent there would be no mention of any of these activities in his columns. He had no reference point or knowledge of these pursuits. The only exception to this statement would be his coverage of various events at the Olympics, but these are not quite the activities of young boys. Instead he was exposed to the activities that were of interest to his mother and grandmother: music and the arts.

There would have also been visits to the house on Church Street by brothers, uncles, and cousins of Annie and Sara, and the appearance

---

[24] Death Records of Fayette County, The Courthouse, Uniontown, PA

Dispatches from the World

of such men at the house would likely prompt the question from other boys: "Is that your father?" Percy and Smith were different from the other boys in this regard. Earlier the Civil War had left many boys without fathers, but that was nearly two decades earlier. Now there was no war and the boys without fathers were the exception.

There was a strong male in the family, if not in the home, in the form of Sarah Knox Miller's brother, Philander, a very successful attorney by any standard at the time and later believed to be a millionaire. He did show up for family reunions and the like, but it is hard to imagine that he had an active role in the lives of the boys although it was his law firm, Knox & Reed, that gave Percival his first job, a job he held for two years.

It is possible for one person to have an influence on another without even realizing this. This may have very well been the case with Philander Knox's influence on Percival. Knox could and did argue either side of a question depending on whom he was representing during a trial. He was often referred to as a corporate lawyer prior to his government service. But once he became attorney general under Theodore Roosevelt he went after major corporations.

In this way Percival was similar to Philander Knox. When he worked for a newspaper, he adopted their editorial outlook on the world, but if he moved to another newspaper his view would change to match the policy of the new newspaper, even though this was often the opposite of his former employer. In addition, he could easily cover either side of a war or conflict, and represent that side convincingly, he was that detached. In some cases Percival shared the same view of a situation that Knox did. Knox would later object to the U.S. joining the League of Nations, and Percival shared this view and opposed the creation of the League. Even Percival's dress seemed to imitate that of his uncle Phil.

In spite of this it is reasonable to assume that the boys' mother, Annie, was the leading influence in their lives. Whether she was domineering is unknown, but there can be little doubt that she expected the boys to do well. She had to do very little exaggerating later in life to relay Percival's accomplishments, but for Smith she would elevate him from a bank clerk to bank president without a thought.

Although Annie was an independent woman in many ways prior to her divorce from Hibbard, she became even more independent after it. At the same time it is difficult to imagine the stigma attached to divorce that existed in the late 1800s. Most women would do anything to avoid divorce, and although Annie was not like most women of that era, she would have a hard time admitting to anyone that her husband had divorced her. She would have preferred to think of Hibbard as dead and this is what she did. She stated on several occasions that she was a widow and that Hibbard had died in 1889. At the time it was not uncommon for women in Pennsylvania, whose husbands had left them, to state their husbands died in 1889. Their children would often say the same thing, believing what they had been told. The women if pressed on the question could easily say he had been killed in the Johnstown flood of that year. [25] Many of those lost in the flood were carried downstream, buried in the silt of the flood waters and never found. However in Annie's case she had to know Hibbard was alive. If for some strange, obscure reason she did think he had died, then she had to be quite surprised when news of his death appeared in the Fayette County newspapers forty years later.[26] He actually died in Scranton, Pennsylvania, on November 12, 1929, at the age of 84.

Regardless of what Annie believed or pretended, Percival was aware that his father was alive and that he was living in Scranton, Pennsylvania, as early as 1915 based on his passport application of that year. It is likely that he knew this much earlier, but there are no records to confirm this since whether one's father was living or dead, and if living, where he was living were not questions asked on passport applications before 1915. Nevertheless, in the mid 1890s Percival had to know Fulton Phillips, a newspaper man in the Monongahela Valley and Hibbard's brother, and he would have set the record straight.

---

[25] Annie Phillips would have been very familiar with the Johnstown flood since her uncle, Philander C. Knox, was a charter member of the South Fork Fishing and Hunting Club. It was this club that erected a dam to create its own private lake retreat. When the dam failed on May 31, 1889, the flood was the result (see David McCullough, *The Johnstown Flood*, New York: Simon and Schuster, 1968).

[26] "Dr. H.S. Phillips, Former Principal, Dies at Scranton," *Daily Courier*, Connellsville, November 13, 1929.

CHAPTER 2

"four miners shot"

Perhaps Percival's job with the George W. Lenhart Insurance Agency was not very stimulating, or perhaps the young man simply liked to write. In any event he began writing for any newspaper that would take what he had to offer. He soon became the "Home Happenings" writer for the *Brownsville Clipper*, the local newspaper and the one his great-uncle, Philander Knox, had worked for as a boy. Percival would write about the illnesses and accidents, the births and deaths, and the gatherings of residents in and around the Brownsville community. These were not the most exciting things to write about, but in the small town of Brownsville they constituted the daily events that made up people's lives. Writers were not identified in by-lines or even listed by name in the *Clipper*. This was typical for newspapers of the day. A newspaper's reporters were to be anonymous. The lack of recognition and the subject matter of his newspaper writing would not satisfy a young man who had what Dickens would have called "great expectations," dreams that were much greater than anonymously written local events.

Alfred Claybaugh, who was the editor of the *Brownsville Clipper* from May 10, 1894 until March 7, 1895, was to recall in later years:

> Percival Phillips haunted my newspaper office in old Brownsville back in the nineties. He was a handsome, eager-eyed youngster, with the urge to write. I gave him a try at local happenings; he developed; it was in him; he was a born reporter. He had the sanguine temperament which a renowned Boston preacher

said every newspaper reporter has. He let himself out when there was a boat launching over at Axton's yard or anything like that; I doctored his 'copy.'

Meanwhile Percy was reporting at home the kind of newspaper man I was—his fertile imagination helping out. Finally his mother came to see me. When the waiter at the Adams House came and told me Mrs. Phillips was in the parlor and wanted to see me, I thought I knew what it was about; she was worried about Percy. She wanted him to go back into high school; so did I; Percy was holding back hard. He didn't love school; what live boy does? He has had a taste of newspaper life—he had sent some stuff to the Pittsburgh newspapers.

I went in and met that quiet, wonderful mother. We discussed Percy that evening; we discussed the future of the boy—always a momentous question. She wanted him back in high school, oh, so much! Percy was rebellious; but he was a mother's boy, too; he would go back—against his will. Wise Mrs. Phillips herself the daughter of a locally celebrated teacher, did not want to make any mistake; it might mean the marring of a life. To me the question, 'What do you think?'

I had considered the matter before; I knew Percy; he had the writing bug, and he had the temperament. He would do his best when his heart was in a thing—he would break his neck; he would not do much good at school—not Percy Phillips with a temperament. I thought these things. I said to Mrs. Phillips, 'I wouldn't drive him.' There was a long pause. 'Well,' she said, 'will he make a newspaper man?' I could answer this question enthusiastically, 'He certainly will, Mrs. Phillips.' [27]

---

[27] Alfred M. Claybaugh, "Current Comment," *Daily New Standard* (Uniontown, PA), April 9, 1925, p. 1.

Percival did not return to school.

It is difficult to say with certainty if Percival was concerned about family finances and whether this played a role in his decision not to return to school. He had started working for his uncle at the age of fourteen and he had to know that money was scarce. Annie and the boys lived in the home of Annie's mother, Sarah Knox Miller, who was in her sixties, retired and a widow. It is unlikely that Sarah was wealthy. Annie's music lessons would probably bring in very little income. There would be no money from Hibbard.

Although Sarah's father David Knox had helped out all of his children when it came to schooling, he had died a decade earlier. It is unlikely that any of Sarah's siblings would do this for a nephew. As a result it is also unlikely that Annie and her mother had the resources to cover Percival's high school expenses beyond what they had already done. So the decision not to return to school may have been based, in part, on a shortage of funds and it was probably a great relief to Annie when Percival opted to become a reporter. It would be up to Percival to make his own way in the world.

Percival was up to the challenge. He was an impressive and striking young man, good-looking by most standards of the day. He was on his way to a height of slightly more than six feet, which is not impressive by current standards, but was very impressive in comparison to the average height of men at the time (five and a half feet). His hair was light brown, some say it was golden, and his eyes were blue. He would be considered handsome to most in Britain and America.

In the spring of 1894 Percival submitted his first application for a passport to the U.S. Department of State. He stated that he was 17 years and eight months of age. Actually he was 16 years and eight months of age, but it does not appear that he knew the year of his birth until about 1913. His application noted that he was a stenographer. John B. Smith, another clerk at the Lenhart Insurance Agency, swore to the facts in the application. There are no indications that Percival had any particular destination in mind for which he would need a passport, but he could dream and apparently he wanted to be ready if his dream to go abroad should ever come true. It was also in the spring of 1894 that Percival wrote articles for the *Clipper* on the coal strikes that were taking place in the Monongahela River Valley at that time, and he sent these to the Pittsburgh newspapers. It was said that the articles he submitted "showed such unmistakable signs of reportorial ability that his services were soon sought by other newspapers." [28] This sounds as something a mother might say, and it is possible that Annie was the source of the statement given to the writer of a local history volume for Fayette County.

Percival is also credited with having reported on what was called at the time the Stickle Hollow riots. These were protests against working conditions in the coal mines of Fayette County and the surrounding area of southwestern Pennsylvania. In the most severe one of these strikes, five miners were killed. This event occurred in late May of 1894, and Percival wrote the following which appeared under the headline "Four Miners Shot:"

> A riot occurred near Connellsville, Pa., at Washington Run mines of the Washington Coal and Coke Company at daybreak Friday morning. Four men were instantly killed, and a dozen or more were wounded. The killed are: Barney McAndrews, single, of Woods Run; Joseph Golitho, a Slav, from the Van Meter mines of Osborne, Saeger & Co.; Omisky, of Stockdale, near Fayette City; [and] an unknown German from Jacobs Creek. Those seriously wounded and who will likely die are John Troy, a coker, from Fayette City; an unknown Italian from Bellevernon, and a Hungarian from the Ellsworth mines at Taylorstown, near Suterville.
>
> The first shot was fired by a deputy, who, in the excitement which attended the rush of the strikers, discharged his rifle in the air and fled. In an instant the conflict was on and before the shooting ended four strikers were lying in the road dead, and 12 to 18 others were wounded. Among the wounded were four deputies. The strikers assembled near

---

[28] Hart, J. Percy (1904), *Hart's History and Directory of the Three Towns: Brownsville, Bridgeport, West Brownsville*, Cadwallader, Pa.: J. Percy Hart.

Dispatches from the World

Percival Phillips Passport Application of 1894 (National Archives, Washington, D.C.)

the works about midnight. Nine hundred of them were from the works along the Monongahela River, in the vicinity of Fayette City, the others were from Banning, Whitselt, Smithton and other mines along the Yough River. The two delegations met near the works and bivouacked in the road, ready to intercept the men as they went to work. The united force numbered 2,000 men. Many of them armed with Winchesters, shotguns, revolvers and clubs. During the early morning hours squads of strikers marched up and down the road, to the music of brass bands and fifes and drums, shouting and cursing the deputies and workmen, and firing occasional volleys in the air.

Committees were sent to the men and the deputies, warning them that any attempt to start the mines would precipitate a deadly riot. The last notice sent the deputies a short time before the men went to work, stated:

> We are fully prepared to resist every effort to start these mines. We know the workmen here would join the strike if they were not intimidated by armed mercenaries. We are heavily armed, and will return bullet for bullet if the deputies fire on us. We are American citizens and demand the protection that is afforded the company.

> All the demonstrations were closely watched by the officials of the company. They had been notified early in the evening of the contemplated attack, and massed all their deputies from their other plants at the Washington mines. At midnight 50 men were on guard, and at 5 o'clock, the hour of the attack, 75 men were on guard. These men were placed in charge of Capt. Anderson, of Pittsburg.

Dispatches from the World

> The coroner held an inquest Saturday afternoon on the four men killed. The verdict was that these men came to their deaths from gunshot wounds inflicted by deputy sheriffs of Fayette County, while said men had assembled with guns and other weapons for the purpose of citing a riot, and that said deputies had acted only in line of their lawful duty.

The piece does not have Percival's name or anyone else's name as its author, but editor Claybaugh basically suggests that Percy had written this and other pieces related to the riots, and that the editor had 'doctored' what was written,' as editors tend to do. As a result this is probably the earliest piece that can be attributed to Percival. He was 16 years of age at the time.

As for the incident and Percival's writing about it, he does this in a very neutral tone, not taking sides regarding the incident or the outcome of the coroner's inquest. The same could not be said for his great-uncle, Philander Knox. He was the attorney for some of the coal interests affected by the riot and he may have been advising the owners what to do regarding the situation as it evolved.

During the summer that followed there was a disagreement between editor Claybaugh and the editor of another local newspaper, the *Union Monitor*. Claybaugh wrote in his newspaper, "We spoke of our error to a young man with literary aspirations, who begs the privilege of contributing to this paper. After careful editing, his articles are allowed to appear in the *Clipper*, not so much for their intrinsic value, certainly not for their literary attractiveness, but simply because of our disposition to please everybody." [29] Although these comments were trivial, the young Percival would probably have been offended by Claybaugh's statement.

Later that month Colonel Chill Hazzard, editor of *Monongahela Daily Republican* in a town that was named after the river, sent for Percival and "induced him to take charge of his paper during the following fall and winter of that year." [30] This may be true, but

---

[29] Alfred Claybaugh, "The 'Literary' Monitor," *Brownsville Clipper*, August 9, 1894.
[30] Hart, J. Percy, op. cit.

Percival may have had more than his ability going for him. Fulton Phillips, a brother of Hibbard who had gone to the West, had now returned and was employed as an editor by both the *Daily Republican* and the *Canonsburg Notes*, and he most likely had some influence with Hazzard in his decision to hire Percival.

On September 6, 1894, editor Claybaugh inserted the following in his *Clipper*:

> L.P. Phillips, who has been doing very creditable newspaper work from this point for the *Pittsburg Times, Press* and other Pittsburg papers, has taken the position of local editor of the *Monongahela Daily Republican*, and during Editor Hazzard's absence he will have entire charge. The *Daily's* local department is already showing the marks of his practiced hand. [31]

This last short piece by Claybaugh appears to be an attempt to soften the impact of the earlier one, but it may very well be that Percival, who was described by others as sensitive, left the *Clipper* because of the earlier article.

Even if there was some influence from the Phillips' family in getting Hazzard to hire Percival, it is important to bear in mind that this was a young man who had turned seventeen only a month earlier. Percival accepted the position, but at its conclusion in March of 1895 he left the *Republican* and joined the staff of the *Pittsburg Times*.

There are only a few additional examples of what are believed to be Percival's early writing. It is difficult to be sure given the prevailing attitude that those writing the news should be anonymous. Exceptions to this, in the form of by-lines, were granted to those with established reputations as writers or to those who were otherwise well known, but Percival was not in either group yet. We can obviously attribute the Stickle Hollow riot pieces to him and these are considered to be relatively good.[32]

---

[31] Untitled, *Brownsville Clipper*, September 6, 1894.

[32] There were two follow-up pieces to the previously cited piece on the Stickle Hollow riots. They are: "The Coal Miners' Strike," June 7, 1894, and "Acquitted of Stickle Hollow Riot," June 21, 1894. Both of these first appeared in the *Clipper*.

While he was working for the newspapers of the Monongahela Valley and Pittsburgh he would write other pieces and send them around the country to newspapers that he thought might have an interest in the subject. These were not news stories as much as they were what would be called "human interest" stories today. Percival's first published article that appears with his name on it was on Stephen Foster and his music. It was received as a letter from Pittsburgh and published by *The Washington* (DC) *Post, The Fort Wayne* (Indiana) *Gazette, The Daily* (New Orleans) *Picayune,* and probably numerous other newspapers. It closes with the by line of Percival Phillips.[33] In the article the writer suggests that there is a need for a monument to Foster, who contrary to popular opinion was not from the South, but was born, lived, died and was buried in Pittsburgh. The article was published as early as June of 1896, when its author was eighteen.

Thomas J. Keenan, editor of the *Pittsburg Press* newspaper at the time, also became quite interested in the possibility of such a monument to Foster. He initiated a fund-raising effort for its creation in the late 1890s. The Foster statue, in bronze, was created by Giuseppe Moretti. It was unveiled near the entrance of Highland Park in Pittsburgh on September 12, 1900. It remained there until 1944 when it was moved to the Oakland area of Pittsburgh, near the University of Pittsburgh campus.

---

[33] Percival Phillips, "Songs a Nation Loves," *Washington Post*, June 28, 1896. P. 20; "Songs That We Love," *The Fort Wayne* (Indiana) *Daily Gazette*, July 26, 1896; and "S.C. Foster, the Composer," *The Daily* (New Orleans, La.) *Picayune*, June 28, 1896, p. 22.

CHAPTER 3

first wars

While Percival was clearly interested in writing and being a newspaper reporter, his true desire was to be a war correspondent. He would write several years later:

> . . . for more than a generation a near-Eastern conflagration has been the dream of nearly every newspaperman who wanted to write about a war. When I was a cub in Pittsburgh the dizzy pinnacle of fame presented itself as the opportunity of riding a tired horse through the Balkans after a smashing big battle and staggering into an obscure telegraph office with the scoop of the century. MacGahan and Forbes, the Russo-Turkish war correspondents, were my heroes; anyone could be president of the United States as far as I was concerned. [34]

The first of these correspondents was Januarius MacGahan (1844-1878), who was born in Ohio and became well known as an American foreign correspondent with his coverage of the Franco-Prussian War and the Russo-Turkish War in the 1870s, before dying at the young age of 34.[35] The other correspondent was Archibald Forbes (1838-1900), who was British and also covered the

---

[34] Percival Phillips, "Out in the Cold: The tragedy of the war correspondent," *The Saturday Evening Post*, February 1, 1913, p. 14.

[35] Dale L. Walker, *Januarius MacGahan: The Life and Campaigns of an American War Correspondent*, Athens, Ohio: Ohio University Press, 1989.

Franco-Prussian War of 1870, the Russo-Turkish War of 1877, as well as numerous other conflicts in the late 1800s.[36] These were Percival's heroes and the men he yearned to emulate.

Percival was to realize his dream of covering a war in the spring of 1897 when revolutionaries on the island of Crete attempted to overthrow the ruling Turkish government there. Greece supported the revolution and declared war on Turkey starting what was later referred to as the Greco-Turkish War. According to the *New York Times*, Percival started off for the Greek war against the Turks in 1897 with $76 he had saved. "He had made no arrangements for any newspaper to take his dispatches, but on the train to New York he chanced to meet H.H. Kohlsaat, publisher of *The Chicago Inter-Ocean*. The boy's sales-talk impressed the publisher, who agreed to buy his stories."[37] This would not have been an easy matter since Kohlsaat had a reputation as a genial and shrewd businessman. He had started his career as a caterer and later owned or was involved with several Chicago newspapers.[38] These newspapers included the *Chicago Times Herald* and the *Chicago Record Herald*, both of which he owned and the *Chicago Inter-Ocean* of which he was a part owner and later editor.

Other sources state that Percival was sent to cover the war by the *Pittsburg Press* and other newspapers. Given that this war occurred in 1897, a year after Percival's Stephen Foster piece, it is quite possible that Keenan, who supported the ideas of the Foster article, and the *Press* would fund his involvement. It was common for reporters of the day to have several newspaper sponsors. His reports from the war were very impressive, but probably to his dismay the conflict was over in five weeks.

The *Clipper* which tended to follow the exploits of Brownsville's favorite son would later write: "Mr. Phillips represented several American newspapers during the Greco-Turkish war of a year ago, and was with the staff of the Crown Prince during the campaign from Laressa to Molos. He witnessed three of the most important battles."[39]

---

[36] Archibald Forbes, *Memories and Studies of War and Peace*, 1895.
[37] "Percival Phillips, Journalist, Dead," *The New York Times*, January 30, 1937, p. 17.
[38] *Time*, October 27, 1924.
[39] Untitled, *Brownsville Clipper*, April 28, 1898.

Dispatches from the World

Seven years later Phillips was stuck for a period of time at the Imperial Hotel in Tokyo, Japan, awaiting permission from the Japanese government to observe the Russo-Japanese War. During this time he was asked to write a short piece on an interesting experience for a collection of articles being prepared by two of his fellow correspondents, George Lynch and Frederick Palmer. He chose to write about his experience in the Greco-Turkish war.

> A small condensed war was fought in the southeastern corner of Europe seven years ago. It was fought and finished in less time than the Campaign of the Imperial Hotel has occupied. This was annoying, especially to correspondents who missed steamer connections and to one of the military attaches, whose uniform was not finished before the treaty of peace was signed.
>
> The principal annoyance, however, was the regularity of the retreats indulged in by the lesser combatant. Its army was never too fatigued to fall back. A penchant for night retirements, coupled with cheerful disregard for tired correspondents who joined these inglorious processions, made the plains of Thessaly anything but a pleasure resort for the chroniclers of events. [40]

Phillips then proceeds to explain that he deserved a medal in walking from Domokos to Molos because he clearly beat everyone else.

> I did walk rapidly. I passed regiments of infantry attempting to maintain a semblance of marching order—and left them in the rear. I came up on some fragments of cavalry and dodged around them and

---

[40] Percival Phillips, "The War and the Walker," in George Lynch and Frederick Palmer (eds.) *In Many Wars by Many War Correspondents*, Tokyo: Tokyo Printing Company, 1904, pp. 149-153

left them in the rear ... I continued through the night without hunger or fatigue, walking steadily. At seven in the morning we reached Molos, where the village schoolmaster played the Good Samaritan. I slept for a day and a night in the military telegraph office and when I woke up the war was over.

The entire piece is obviously done with tongue in cheek and it is one of the most humorous pieces that he ever wrote. At the same time there is a grain of truth running through the piece in the sense that he was trying very hard to get away from the approaching Turkish forces.

Richard Harding Davis, an established war correspondent at the time, was in Europe for most of the Greco-Turkish conflict. According to Davis, "Scovel and Phillips of *The World* arrived just as it was over." [41] He is referring to Sylvester Scovel and Percival. Scovel would become much better known during the Spanish-American War, but would die in Havana in 1905 at the age of 36 following an operation for a medical problem.

Years later it was noted that Percival had gone to the war as a steerage passenger. While at the front during that conflict, he worked for the famous English war correspondents of that day. He was a messenger and a runner. He did these things for the opportunity to be at the front and to eat with other correspondents at their mess.

At the close of hostilities in the Mediterranean region Percival began his trip home. He came through Paris, remaining there for three days. At this point he had only fifty cents left to eat on and to get back to the States. It is said that he came across someone that he knew from Pittsburgh and that individual staked him to $50, which he used to get back to the U.S. [42] He sailed from Boulogne on the S.S. *Maasdam* on June 19, 1897; his full name, Leslie Percival Phillips,

---

[41] Charles Belmont Davis, *Adventures and Letters of Richard Harding Davis*, New York: Charles Schribner's Sons, 1917, p. 210.

[42] "Phillips, War Correspondent, A Pittsburgher," *Pittsburgh Dispatch*, August 17, 1914, p. 6.

appeared on the passenger list and he stated he was a reporter. The *Maasdam* arrived in New York ten days later and Percival proceeded to Pittsburgh. Upon his arrival there he took a position on the *Pittsburg Post* newspaper.

While he was with the *Post* another conflict developed; this one was in Cuba. Spaniards on the island were getting a reputation for their brutal treatment of the local population. It is difficult to say if this was true or not given the yellow-press of the day. There was also a growing desire for independence from Spain among the Cuban population. American sympathies were clearly with the Cuban people and when the U.S. battleship *Maine* exploded and sank in the harbor at Havana in February of 1898 the U.S. was ready to do battle. In April Congress declared war on Spain even though it was never quite clear that Spain was behind the explosion or whether it was an accident.

The Spanish American War extended beyond Cuba with other Spanish possessions involved; these were Puerto Rico and the Philippine Islands, but the former was not very significant and the latter conflict was primarily a naval operation. The most significant land action was in Cuba during June and July of 1898, based on news coverage of the day.

In May Percival was sent to be with the Pennsylvania troops that were to take part in the ground assault in Cuba. They were training at Chickamaugua, on the Georgia/Tennessee border. This was the site of one of the major battles of the Civil War; it had since been designated as a national park. There were numerous delays in getting the troops to Cuba due to a lack of equipment, an outbreak of measles, and what appears to have been indecision on the part of the military. In the end none of the Pennsylvania troops were sent to Cuba.

Percival spent a considerable amount of time with the troops at their training site. As it became evident that the troops would not be sent to Cuba, he made his own way to the island to cover the conflict.

Percival Phillips (right) with George S. Reinoehl, a fellow correspondent, in Cuba during the Spanish American War, 1898 (The Telephone News)

It is generally acknowledged that Percival covered the Spanish American War for the *New York World* newspaper, which was owned by Joseph Pulitzer at the time.[43] There are other sources that state

---

[43] Mitchell P. Roth, *Historical Dictionary of War Journalism*, Westport, CT: Greenwood Press, 1997, p. 236.

Dispatches from the World

he was sent by the *Pittsburg Post,* but there were no news stories from Cuba in the *Post* that carried his by-line.[44] At the same time he was still relatively new and probably had not yet earned this type of recognition. There were numerous stories that had a *New York World* and *Post* heading regarding the Pennsylvania troops at Chickamauga with the credit being given to "a staff correspondent." When some of these troops finally left the training camp, they went to Puerto Rico or the Philippines, but Percival was in Cuba. Without a by-line it has not been possible to identify exactly what Percival wrote about the war in Cuba. Even if this were possible it is unlikely that we would read what he actually believed about the U.S. effort in that case. He revealed this fifteen years later in a piece that he wrote for London's *Daily Express.*

> When Spain was kicked out of Cuba, the whole country turned upside down in an effort to construct the army that no one had thought of in time of peace. The martial spirit became a mania. Entire cities suspended business to see its volunteer regiments march away to mobilisation camps, where overworked officers of the regular establishment spent many weary days in examining and sifting them and swearing in the residue as Federal troops.
>
> Then came the disillusioning delay when tired staff officers (recalled from far western posts, where they had wasted the best years of their lives as lieutenants or captains and suddenly promoted to brigadiers in the hope that they could work miracles), tried to hammer this unpromising field material into efficiency.
>
> Do what they might, the citizen army could not be made competent in a few weeks after war was declared. Blunders were made, even by the most patriotic. The first stage of the war fever passed and

---

[44] *Brownsville Clipper,* April 28, 1898.

there came a reaction. Public criticism succeeded indiscriminate praise.

Men died in fever camps. Bad beef killed many others. There were scandals about the commissariat, the medical service, a thousand and one other shortcomings due to inexperience and incompetence. Public money was wasted. Contractors profited by the official frenzy and pocketed fortunes.

Politics tainted the campaign. Old officers, equipped with the arduous training of West Point, found themselves outranked by civilians who knew a Senator at Washington and bought gold lace accordingly. Volunteer regiments with a "pull" were drafted into the expeditionary force, and died of fever in Cuba, while less fortunate regiments wrote violently to the newspapers and died in the mobilisation camps at home.

Even with such weak opposition as was offered by the half-starved soldiers of Spain, the campaign was one of heavy losses. More men were killed by disease than by Spanish bullets. It was a campaign of wild patriotism, and in some respects of ill-directed, undisciplined effort, of unnecessary hardships.

Some men sought death on San Juan Hill, when they should have lived and become good soldiers. Others perished miserably in the jungle because an inefficient commissariat could not feed them. Spain left Cuba, but the cost was great. [45]

So this is what Percival actually felt about the war he had covered in Cuba and the U.S. involvement in the conflict. As noted previously

---

[45] Percival Phillips, "The Luxury of Chaos. What War with Mexico has in Store for America." *Daily Express*, November 5, 1913.

he would have never written that at the time, and if he had, no American editor would have published it!

The war in Cuba was a difficult war to cover because at the outbreak of hostilities the telegraph cables were cut. This was done by the U.S. in order to keep Spanish forces from contacting their command structure in Spain. The cut cables necessitated news being taken to Florida, usually Key West, and having it relayed to newspapers in the U.S. by telegraph. This was not as easy as it sounds because there were only two cables out of Key West, and one of these was used almost exclusively by the government. As a result one would have to wait their turn to make sure their news got out. [46]

There is no record of Percival re-entering the country after the conflict, but he could have very easily come back into the U.S. through Florida, or arrived back with the troops, and not been recorded. In addition, ship records of arrivals at U.S. ports are very poor for this time period.

Percival left his employment with the *Pittsburg Post* after about a year and a half to join the staff of the *Pittsburg Dispatch*, where he would become more visible to readers through the presence of his by-line. The *Dispatch* offices occupied a relatively new building at the time on the corner of Smithfield and Diamond Streets in Pittsburgh. The building was constructed in 1891 and had a large arched entrance that opened into the newspaper's business office. Percival and the other reporters had rooms with "marble wainscoted walls, electric lights, and oak desks" on the second floor. [47] Composition took place on the third floor and the presses and electric motors to run them occupied the basement of the structure.

It is known that Percival was back in Pittsburgh from his Cuban war coverage by late February of 1899 and he began some investigative reporting for the *Dispatch* at that time. He was first sent to the small town of Scio in Ohio. It is located about 100 miles due west of Pittsburgh. Oil had been discovered there and all types of criminals were being attracted to the town. As Percival wrote:

---

[46] Ray Stannard Baker, "How the News of the War is Recorded," *McClure's Magazine*, September 1898, Vol. XI, No. 5, pp. 491-495.

[47] "A Newspaper's New Home. The Pittsbug Dispatch Fitted out with Fresh Equipment," *The New York Times*, June 7, 1891.

> Sudden wealth has burdened Scio with all the vices of a frontier town. No mining camp ever held more wickedness or possessed less law . . . It is simply overrun with criminals of every class. Gentlemanly gamblers with interstate reputations, and other gamblers not so gentlemanly, are reaping a phenomenal harvest. Pickpockets, short card men . . . and cheap beggars fairly outclass the oil operators.[48]

He went on to itemize the crimes taking place based on his three-day stay in the town. This was followed by his description of law enforcement in the town.

> There are three policemen in Scio. They are unique characters, wearing high boots, caps, an enormous badge and double brass-buttoned uniforms resembling those of street car conductors. They stand on corners, chew tobacco and occasionally prevent two men from beating each other to death. They are harmless individuals and have not been known to offend anyone. [49]

Percival's article was nearly three columns in length and it infuriated local oil interests in Scio according to *The Evening Democrat* of Warren, Pennsylvania, for March 11, 1899.[50] The Warren newspaper quoted some material from a publication called *The Oil Exchange* that was written in response to Percival's *Dispatch* article. It referred to him as "one of the biggest liars with a pencil we have ever read." The Warren newspaper also quoted some Scio individuals who stated: "We advise Percival not to attempt another visit to Scio anyways soon, as there are some fellows laying for him." The Warren newspaper of the same day also noted that the Scio town council had passed an ordinance prohibiting gambling and had hired

---

[48] Percival Phillips, "Scio Harbors Many Gambling Dens and Crooks," *Pittsburg Dispatch*, March 5, 1899, p. 1.
[49] Ibid., p. 2.
[50] "Not Little Scio," *The* (Warren, PA) *Evening Democrat*, March 11, 1899.

additional policemen. Both actions were obviously in response to Percival's article.

The content of Percival's work with the *Dispatch* was quite variable. He was known to review art and dramatic performances, but he would also be assigned heavier topics. These would include the Scio incident noted above, but also murders and trials for major criminal cases of that nature. Three such cases were covered by him shortly after the Scio case.

His first crime/investigative report was of a murder case in New Castle, Pennsylvania, to the north of Pittsburgh. On January 7 of 1899 the City Treasurer, one John Blevins, was murdered in his office in the center of the city, which was across the street from police headquarters and very near the mayor's office. By March no one had been arrested and Percival began looking into the case. He talked to all of the investigators and city officials, he interviewed others and it became apparent to him that much time had been wasted in trying to find someone with a criminal record. He also talked with those who had been looking at the city's finances and it also became apparent to him that funds were missing according to the record books. Percival concluded that an audit that was to be made public two days after Blevin's death would have revealed the shortage of funds. He also concluded that Blevins had lent the money to a local citizen and the treasurer's insistence that the funds be returned led the borrower to murder him. It is not known if anyone was ever arrested for the crime, but Percival's article concluded there were only two suspects in the case, and although he did not name them, it is likely their identities were known to local authorities.[51]

The second case involved the murder of a Benedictine monk from St. Vincent's Monastery in Westmoreland County, Pennsylvania. Brother Herman Strattman was on his way back to the monastery from Latrobe where he had sold a number of animal hides. He was met on the way by two highwaymen who took his money and killed him with a swift blow to the back of his head. Percival wrote a rather

---

[51] Percival Phillips, "Blevins Murder Narrowed Down to Two Persons," *Pittsburg Dispatch*, March 19, 1899, p. 1-2.

lengthy article on the case and Brother Strattman's funeral.[52] It is not apparent that anyone was ever arrested for the crime.

The third assignment involved a murder trial. This was the George Saxton case with a trial in Canton, Ohio, in which one Annie George, an ex-lover of Saxton was tried for his murder. The case would seem like just another murder case, except for the fact that George Saxton was the brother-in-law of President William McKinley. The case initially seemed overwhelmingly against the defendant. However, Annie George's attorney was able to demonstrate that she had no motive to kill Saxton and that she had a convincing alibi for the time of the crime. As a result Annie George was acquitted much to the joy of Canton residents, however Pittsburgh residents thought an injustice had been done based on the reaction of that city's press. [53]

In the fall of 1900 a position opened up with the *Dispatch* in their New York City office. Other reporters were under consideration for the position, which would also be a promotion, but Percival was the one selected. The night he was to leave for New York City his colleagues gathered in the news room to give him a send-off. He had brought his overcoat and suitcase to the office that night and he went around saying good-byes to his fellow newsmen. As he was doing this one of his friends pasted a label on his suitcase that stated he was with the *Xenia Torchlight and Examiner*, a small rural Ohio newspaper. Percival's response when he saw this was to say, "I'm country looking enough without being labeled."[54]

Percival left Pittsburgh that evening and the next day he took over the New York office of the *Pittsburg Dispatch* in the World Building. This would not be a completely new environment for Percival since he had previously done some reporting for the New York *World*, which was located in the same building. He also knew some of the reporters that worked for the *World* from the wars

---

[52] Percival Phillips, "Benedictine was Murdered for His Money," Pittsburg Dispatch, April 7, 1899, p. 1; Percival Phillips, "Monks Burial at St. Vincent's Deeply Solemn," *Pittsburg Dispatch*, April 7, 1899, p. 1.

[53] Untitled, *Brownsville Clipper*, April 23, 1899.

[54] Untitled, *Charleroi Mail*, October 28, 1911, p. 2.

that he had covered. While he held the New York position, he was a member of the Correspondent's Press Club of New York. [55]

There is little to indicate his presence in New York. On April 11, 1901, Annie Phillips boarded a train and went to New York to visit her son.[56] This would have been near the end of his term in that city. He showed her the various sights of the day, which would have included the Brooklyn Bridge, the Statue of Liberty and Grand Central Station. Annie returned to Western Pennsylvania on April 26. His assignment continued until July or August of that year, at which time he also returned to Western Pennsylvania. He was returning to Pittsburgh to take the position of city editor for the Pittsburgh *Dispatch*.[57] He would have been twenty-four at the time and the youngest city editor in the newspaper's history.

---

[55] Correspondent's Club of New York, "How Can the Influence of the Press be Increased? A Symposium, February 14, 1901. This pamphlet shows Percival Phillips as a member of the group.

[56] Untitled, *Brownsville Clipper*, April 11, 1901.

[57] J. Percy Hart, Ibid., p. 248.

CHAPTER 4

the move to london

Being the city editor of the *Dispatch* was not one of Percival's goals in life and in a very short time he was able to get out of the position. Another position as London correspondent for his Pittsburgh newspaper had become available and this was much more to his liking. It also enabled him to return to Europe. One writer has suggested he went to London for his health. It is difficult to believe that anyone would go to London for their health in the early 1900s. The city had six and a half million people and coal was the primary residential fuel. The word "smog" which tends to be associated with Los Angeles today, had its origin in London and was formed by combining the words smoke and fog. So it is unlikely that anyone would go there for their health. If there was some underlying rationale for the move, beyond his ambition, it was probably his desire to be closer to the location of probable future conflicts and wars, although this can hardly be viewed as independent of his ambition.

Percival left the U.S. on October 12, 1901. He sailed on the *Westernland* of the American Line, and arrived at Liverpool on the 23nd of the month. Upon his arrival he began a tour that took him to, among other places, Edinburgh. He very much enjoyed that city and said it was so rich in historical associations "that I could have spent a month there with pleasure and profit." [58] He left Edinburgh for London on the 31st of October and on the way he stopped to see the cathedral at York, which was one of the finest in Europe. He had

---

[58] Letter: Percival Phillips to Annie C.M. Phillips, November 5, 1901 (published in the *Brownsville Clipper*, November 28, 1901).

hoped to also stop in Lincoln and Ely and see the cathedrals in each of these towns, but he was also anxious to get to London.

The primary reason for rushing to London was the expected return of the Duke and Duchess of Cornwall to that city after a tour of Canada. King Edward VII and Queen Alexandra had gone to Portsmouth earlier to accompany them back to London on Saturday, November 2. The King had only held the office for less than a year following the death of his mother, Queen Victoria. All that one could imagine for such an event in the sense of pomp and celebration was realized by Phillips that day. There were six carriages, each drawn by six horses in gold harness. The band played "God Save the King" and the artillery fired off a salute in St. James Park, the old bell in St. James palace was ringing, and the crowd was cheering. Phillips found it all very exciting and picturesque. At the same time he found the hero worship offered the King by the crowd disturbing, although he thought this might be because he was an American.

Phillips had taken up residence at The Waverly, a hotel in Southampton Row in the Bloomsbury section of the city, when he arrived on Friday. On Sunday he spent most of the day in Hyde Park; it was a bright day with plenty of sunshine. In the evening at seven he entered Westminster Abbey for the evening service. When he came out at 8:30, the fog was so dense that he was unable to see a street light directly above his head. Visibility was about five feet and nothing could be seen at ten feet. These 'black fogs' as they were called at the time happened periodically and were due in part to the use of coal for heating the many homes of London. Phillips noted that he was covered with grime and soot after being out in it.

He also found the black fog unpleasant physically. He described the fact that the eyes and nostrils would smart for a time and breathing was hard work until you got used to it. Pittsburgh, a city often criticized for its smoke at the time, "was a marvel of cleanliness in comparison," according to Phillips.

At least initially Phillips was not sure that he cared for London; he liked New York much more, but he felt he had to give the city a chance. "One must spend some time over here in order to thoroughly appreciate this country." He played the tourist for several more days in November visiting St. Paul's cathedral, the Houses of Parliament, the British Museum, and the Tower of London. He also said that he had a new reason every day since his arrival, to thank Heaven he was an American.

Although it was pleasant being a tourist, he soon had to begin working for the *Pittsburg Dispatch* in their London bureau. These offices were located in Effingham House on Arundel Street off the Strand and Fleet Street. It was not far from Chancery Lane where he would move shortly. The *Dispatch* shared the Effingham House with several other provincial newspapers and clients of The United Associated Presses. The facilities were very good, but the articles that Phillips sent were not very thrilling.

One of his more interesting early pieces involved a February 1902 interview with Guglielmo Marconi that was done over wireless.[59] This was an exceptional piece, but most of what he was writing resembled his work for the Brownsville newspaper nearly a decade earlier. Phillips was not writing "home happenings" for the *Clipper* any longer, but he had to recall this part of his career as he wrote now from London. His articles focused almost exclusively on which Americans, and more specifically which Pennsylvanians and residents of Pittsburgh, were visiting London at the time. In order to get information for his articles he would visit most of the hotels where Americans would tend to stay—the Savoy, the Cecil, the Carlton, and so forth—and see who had registered. Then he would go around to the U.S. Embassy and check for anyone he might have missed. Often the visitors would come by the *Dispatch* offices, probably to make sure that their names appeared in the newspaper back in Pittsburgh. It was very much like "home happenings" in the Brownsville newspaper.

Phillips' columns appeared in the Sunday *Pittsburg Dispatch* and often included the travel plans of Pittsburg visitors above, but they might also include little stories that would be of interest to American readers. In May, June and July of 1902 the following were representative of the content in what the *Dispatch* called "Phillips' London Letter": Andrew Carnegie's visit to London and English hopes for a major library gift from him; the completion of a

---

[59] Percival Phillips, "World's News in Mid-Atlantic Marconi's Feat," *Pittsburg Dispatch*, October 11, 1903. This was reproduced as an advertisement for the Marconi Wireless Telegraph Co. in the *Atlanta Constitution* of November 29, 1903. The event is first mentioned in the *Brownsville Clipper* on February 20, 1902.

Westinghouse plant in Manchester; the forthcoming coronation of Edward VII; high prices in London; how to get by on little money in London; the cancellation of the coronation due to the King being ill; the out of date firefighting equipment in London; and, the major British contracts being captured by Pittsburgh companies. These were hardly the exciting topics that had brought Phillips to London.

In the early 1900s London was seven or eight days by ship and rail travel from Western Pennsylvania. One wonders what impact Percival's moving to England would have on members of his family and his relationship with each of them. It is clear that the young Percival never had much to do with his father, but it is obvious that he was very concerned about his mother Annie and he seems to have had a very good relationship with his brother, Smith. These were the two that mattered most to him and in each case the ties became stronger.

Percival for all practical purposes had a formal education that stopped prior to high school. At the same time he had an exceptional ability to write for one so young. He also knew the arts and from all indications was able to impress people with his charm and intellect. He was able to speak foreign languages, not just of Europe, but also of Asia, well enough to get by in these areas. The adeptness with languages was one thing he had in common with his father's family; it was said that members of the Phillips family were quite good with foreign languages. Nevertheless, someone had to teach him the languages, the arts, and the writing and the schools of the day were not quite up to the task. This role must have fallen primarily on his mother and possibly his grandmother, Sarah Knox Miller.

So while Percival felt concern for his mother during most of her life, she also had concerns for him and how he was doing. By September of 1902 Annie Phillips felt the need to visit her son in London. According to a November issue of the *Clipper*:

> Mrs. Phillips has been abroad since September 1st, and since then has spent two weeks in visiting the cathedral towns of England and Scotland, as well as a week in Paris and the rest of the time in London.

>She witnessed the King's procession on October 25th from one of the government stands in Whitehall. [60]

On November 19 she sailed from Liverpool to Philadelphia on the American Line's S. S. *Haverford*. Ship records indicate that Annie was accompanied by her cousin, Jennie Knox, the daughter of her uncle Dr. William Knox of McKeesport, Pennsylvania, although the notes she placed in the *Clipper* made no mention of this, an unlikely oversight by Annie.

Percival would often telephone his mother in later years during his trips to the U.S. and add a few days to these trips so that he could visit her in Brownsville. Gifts were also common and brief little notices of these visits and the gifts would appear in the Brownsville newspaper's social columns, without a doubt submitted by Annie. The following is typical of these:

>Mrs. Annie C. Phillips is the owner of a valuable set of Shakespeare, ten volumes in all. They are clearly printed and substantially bound, but their value is in their age, being over one hundred years old having been purchased by her son Percival while in London. Originally they belonged to a royal family. [61]

Aside from the musicales that Annie and her students would put on, she was active in the community as well. There were the various social functions tied to the First Methodist Episcopal Church, which was located about three blocks from her house. The Knox family was large and there were frequently marriages and little reunions when any member of the family came back to Brownsville. Smith Phillips was living in Pittsburgh during the early 1900s. Nevertheless, he was a frequent visitor of his mother and grandmother and he never missed a holiday dinner. He came down with typhoid fever during the summer of 1901 and at that time he returned to Brownsville for care and managed to survive the illness. Annie visited Percival in New York as well as London and toured these areas with him as well.

---

[60] Untitled, *Brownsville Clipper*, November 20, 1902.
[61] Untitled, *Brownsville Clipper*, Thursday, March 24, 1904.

On another occasion she hired the steamboat *Admiral Dewey* and took a number of other women on a cruise down the Monongahela River to Charleroi where the ladies spent some time walking around the town. Lunch was served on the steamboat. She would also take a train to Pittsburgh and attend concerts at Carnegie Hall by herself. Then there were still the numerous packages, letters and telegrams that Percival would send to her. On Christmas day of 1903 she received a telegram early in the morning from Percival wishing her a Merry Christmas.

Probably one of the major events in the Knox and Phillips families was the appointment of Philander Chase Knox as Attorney General by President McKinley in 1901. Then his reappointment by Theodore Roosevelt in 1903 was just as pleasant for the extended Knox family. A reunion of sorts was held by Harriette Knox, Philander Knox's sister, at her home on Front Street in Brownsville in July of 1903 while P.C. Knox was Attorney General. He and his son attended the reunion, but Mrs. Knox was at home, exhausted from the recent Washington, D.C. social season. P.C. Knox's brothers, Dr. Samuel Knox of Santa Barbara and Dr. William Knox of McKeesport, Pennsylvania, were there with their wives. Two other brothers, Alfred Knox of Pittsburgh and Thomas Knox of California, were also there. A sister Mrs. Mary O. Graff of Omaha, Nebraska, was there. Sara Miller and her daughter Annie Phillips also attended. There were also numerous children and grandchildren present at this and similar events.

Annie continued living with her mother Sarah Miller on Church Street until the mother died in 1918. At that time she inherited the house and continued living there alone until her health began to fail a decade later.

Aside from his mother and grandmother, Percival's only other close relative was his brother, Smith. Smith held several jobs with banks in Pittsburgh beginning as early as 1900, when he was barely out of his teens. Percival would keep in touch with his brother over the coming years.

At the time when Percival moved to London, he was 23 years old. He was a good-looking young man, tall and thin. He had blue eyes and his hair was blond. He was described by his colleagues as a very charming individual and by the women he met as a very attractive man. His colleagues also saw him as someone who was always

Dispatches from the World

well-dressed, not showy, but very well-groomed in a conservative manner.

He nearly always looked and was serious. He was modest. Some of his colleagues saw him as reticent and sensitive. He was viewed as a friend by individuals who hardly knew him. He was once described as helpful to everyone he knew.

Today Percival would be referred to as an Anglophile. He had not always felt that way, and when he arrived in England he was uneasy about all the ceremony and adoration involving the royal family, but this was to change. He had an air of sophistication that many of his English colleagues found unusual. They were used to the loud, demanding Americans they would meet at the Savoy Hotel, and Percival did not fit that mold at all. He was thought to be an Englishman by those who did not know him, which would suggest that he might have adopted an English accent.

In 1901 and even later he undoubtedly felt a little insecure around some of his newspaper colleagues. Most of them had college degrees, but he had never finished high school. As a result he was often shy, and would blush quite easily around strangers. During group conversations he was often quiet, rarely speaking. When he did add a comment, it was usually snappy or dry. Many thought he was more of a good listener than a talker. In addition, when he did talk, he tended to have a nervous cough as well as a nervous laugh. Of course over the years he gained far more confidence and these mannerisms disappeared.

Percival's dream was to be the best journalist that he could be. He had no desire to do or be anything else. His writing style was not "flowery", but straight to the point. He was concerned with reporting what he saw as accurately as he could without embellishment and exaggeration, but he also had an acute sense of the dramatic. He studied everything that he wrote about so that he knew the terrain, the problem, and the participants in every piece that he sent to his editors. He had an encyclopedic memory for the details that he saw and he organized these details precisely, leaving nothing out. He made no mistakes. Another journalist described Percival's battle pieces as having "the accuracy of camera plates and the brilliancy of lightning flashes." He would study maps until he knew the battlefield better than the generals fighting there. Later during the World War it was said that the French and British general staffs would read his columns since they were always accurate in their details. Percival's fascination with maps would continue throughout his life and he rarely went anywhere without detailed maps of the areas where he would be based and from which he would report.

His training as a stenographer and typist back in Pittsburgh in the early 1890s came in very handy when he became a journalist. Percival brought his typewriter with him from America. They were not that common in England and they were missing from newsrooms. It is said that he introduced typewriters to the London newspaper scene in 1901. Fifteen years later many London newspaper reporters were still writing their stories in longhand. However, Percival not only typed his articles, he typed them incredibly fast. He would also take the typewriter onto the battlefield in a bullet proof case that he had secured.

Writing as he did about wars, revolutions, crimes and conflicts, there was little room for humor. There are very few examples of humor in any of his writing. Even the photographs that exist of Percival do not show him smiling very often. He was a serious individual and he wanted to be seen in that way. [62]

It is possible to add a few more observations about his personal attributes. Before he reached forty he used a walking stick, though not a cane. This seems to be something that he began doing during the World War. He seemed to prefer to wear a hat when out of doors. He smoked a pipe. Without a doubt he enjoyed alcoholic beverages of all types.

In 1934 he wrote,

> A physician whose middle name should be Gloom declared with cold detachment of a neutral observer that the next fifteen years would see an increase in the number of hostages to Harley-street (or

---

[62] Most of the above is based on articles written by three of Percival's friends: Philip Gibbs, Sidney Dark, and Haydn Church, The articles are: Philip Gibbs, *The Pageant of the Years: An Autobiography*, London and Toronto: William Heinemann Ltd., 1946, p. 163; Sidney Dark, "Little Portraits. Four Journalists. Sir Percival Phillips," *John O'London's Weekly*, February 17, 1923, p. 699; and, Haydn Church, "First American Made a Knight," *The Los Angeles Times*, July 18, 1920.

Dispatches from the World

> words to that effect), particularly of women, due to over-indulgence in pre-dinner drinks and their effect on the liver. This is sad news; but I doubt if it will affect the consumption of cocktails. Their popularity has been diminished here and there by the higher cost of drinking, but, given a fair chance, the allies of gin and cracked ice will continue their world-wide operations for the creation of synthetic cheer. [63]

In the same article he gives his reader a tour of the world and the drinks and clubs that may be encountered from France to Japan.

Writing in the 1980s about events in Ethiopia during the 1930s, one reporter wrote that Percival was "rarely found more than a few feet from the coolest bar in Addis Ababa." [64] This statement is somewhat inconsistent with the facts that the average temperature in Addis Ababa is 59 degrees F (one of the cooler places on the African continent), and Percival spent little time there because the elevation of nearly 9,000 feet bothered his breathing due to a heart condition, and he moved to the coast. On the other hand it is quite likely that he enjoyed having drinks with his colleagues whether he was in London at the Savoy or in a club elsewhere in the world.

Percival had an avid interest in wireless radio dating from his interview with Signor Marconi in February of 1902. That interview was actually the first wireless interview. It was carried out from the Lizard wireless station in Cornwall, England, to a steamer on which Marconi was a passenger, one hundred fifty miles from shore.[65] Apparently that experience had a significant impact on Phillips because he became very interested in experimental wireless as a hobby. When radios became available commercially he purchased dozens of these. Then in 1931 he made the first wireless telephone call from India to England. The telephone call was made from the Red

---

[63] Sir Percival Phillips, "With Cocktails Round the World," *Daily Mail*, August 7, 1934.
[64] John Fraser Gam, "Truth About 'Scoop' is More Bizarre than the Book," *The Globe and Mail* (Canada), April 29, 1987.
[65] Lizard, sometimes called The Lizard, was actually Lizard Point in Cornwall, the most southerly point in Great Britain. It was near this location that Marconi sent his first transatlantic wireless radio message to Newfoundland in December of 1901.

Star liner *Belgenland*, which was in Bombay Harbor at the time, to the *Daily Mail* offices in London.[66] It is not clear how long his interest in wireless was to continue, but it was noted as a hobby of his in a news article thirty-five years after the cited interview with Marconi.[67] More than likely Phillips saw this as a way of sending stories back to his editors, but it is not evident that he ever used anything but the mails, cables and telegrams for this purpose, with the exception of the India call noted here.

A little more than a year after his interview with Marconi, Phillips wrote a piece for the *Express* with the title, "No Peace for the Weary, Mr. Marconi Destroys the Mid-Atlantic Rest Cure." The gist of the piece is that it is no longer possible to get away from civilization. The piece begins:

> It is time to suppress Mr. William Marconi. Wireless telegraphy threatens to become a bore instead of a benefit, and it is already encroaching upon the personal liberties of inoffensive travellers.
>
> I refer particularly to the Transatlantic voyage. Heretofore it has been a blessed period of seclusion for the weary. A man had to be quiet whether he wanted to or not. It was a better rest-cure than a holiday in the Sahara, and far more convenient.[68]

The article continues noting all of the possible negative aspects of being continuously available to your boss, your relatives, your friends and others. Does one really need to know the closing stock quotations, or the latest divorce proceedings? The article is an excellent piece on the impacts of new technology on individuals and the way in which that technology changes the way one lives, not necessarily for the better.

---

[66] "First 'Phone Call from India," *Daily Mail*, March 19, 1931.
[67] "Sir Percival Phillips," *Daily Mail*, January 30, 1937, and Untitled, *Daily Express*, January, 30, 1937.
[68] Percival Phillips, "No Peace for the Weary," *Daily Express*, May 2, 1903.

In later years Percival was a member of numerous clubs in London. Some of these have slipped into history, but his various, brief biographical entries in *Who's Who* note his memberships in the Garrick, Royal Societies, Savage, Thatched House, and the Press Club, all in London. Abroad he was a member of the Royal Bombay Yacht Club, and the Shanghai Club. He was a Fellow of the Royal Geographical Society. The Garrick Club was primarily for those interested in supporting drama in London. He had a long term interest in drama and the arts and he often wrote reviews of these performances for the newspapers in Pittsburgh before moving to England. The Savage and Thatched House Clubs were gentlemen's clubs in London. The Royal Bombay Yacht Club and Shanghai Club were in Bombay (now Mumbai, India), and Shanghai, China, respectively. He was a member of the Royal Automobile Society and although he often drove vehicles while on assignment, he did not own one in London. Last, he was a member of the Royal Aero Society, and seems to have been fascinated with aviation.

As early as 1910 Percival had an interest in flight. On one occasion he attended a centenary celebration in Bournemouth, a large town on the south coast of England between Southampton and Plymouth. An air show of sorts was one of the events on this particular occasion, and the pilot of one of the planes had some difficulty resulting in his plane crashing. Percival wrote the following after watching the event:

> How can I describe the feelings of those who stared at the diving aeroplane and the doomed man poised above them? What must have been the thoughts in the brain of the man himself in the last second of life? He was not 200 feet beyond me. I could not see him, for the plane hid him. He must have looked back instinctively when the spars were splintered. He must have tried instantly to jam his elevators up, just as a drowning man grasps naturally at a stray piece of wreckage, even though he knows that it will not save his life.

Too late! All balancing power was gone. The aeroplane dropped like a thunderbolt. There was not time to shut off the engine. Not that the shutting off would have mattered much. It dropped in a straight line, turning nose downward, rushing the man at the tiller end so quickly to his death that he must have passed into merciful oblivion after that one sharp pang of realization that he was beyond aid.

There was a muffled crash as the wreck hit the earth—an irregular pile of wreckage that bore no resemblance to an aeroplane.

Another second had passed.

I think the utter silence that followed was one of the grimmest things about this lightening tragedy. There was the wreckage, tumbled together near the wooden fence that skirts the course not 200 feet beyond me, a mere patch to the mechanics and friends, who gazed with dry lips from the victim's shed on the other side of the field.

For a moment no one dare approach that heap of canvas. A man beside me was saying, in a curiously quiet voice, 'Why doesn't he crawl out?'

It seemed that all the people on that broad plain were saying to themselves, 'Why doesn't he crawl out?' Yet in their hearts they knew, every one of them, that Charles Rolls was dead.

The faces of the first five men who came haltingly toward the wreckage reflected their despair. The pile of canvas and fragments of support, so like a tent blown down in a gale, hid the tragedy from our eyes. The first man lifted what had been the lower main plane.

> There he lay, huddled up beside the battered engine, a web of twisted wires and the ends of splintered supports around him. His face was the color of gray wax, and there was a cut on his forehead. Two ambulance men arrived, and some police, and then a hundred other people who were induced to form a deep ring with linked hands, and thus keep a space clear.
>
> A gray-haired physician who had been applauding the flight a moment before shook his head as they lifted the limp body clear of the debris and laid it on the grass. There was a faint quiver of life, but so faint, indeed that only the physician who bent over him could detect it.
>
> There were useless injections of strychnine. A lady pressed forward with her smelling salts. They bent over him for several minutes long after the physician saw the last flicker of life vanish.
>
> His neck had been broken in that headlong plunge. [69]

This incident occurred only seven years after the Wright brothers' flight at Kitty Hawk, North Carolina. It is apparent that Percival knew something about flying and airplanes at that early date.

Two years later he was writing about biplanes in the Balkans being used for reconnaissance with the suggestion that he knew what the pilot could see, and what it would look like, which could only come from one who had already flown. [70] He would not be able to say this at the time because the correspondents covering that war were not permitted to go near the front during the conflict and to suggest that he had flown over the area would have resulted in

---

[69] "Comedy and Tragedy at the Bournemouth Centenary," *The New York Times*, July 24, 1910, p. C2.

[70] "Aeroplanes Great Aid in War," *Chicago Daily Tribune*, November 14, 1912, p. 1.

his being sent back to England immediately. On another occasion during the World War, he was able to write: "If you care to experience really cold weather go aloft with a British flying man over the frozen battlefield of the Somme, or stand for hours wedged in the narrow basket of an observation balloon, swinging in an Arctic gale, and try to read the secrets of the enemy as they are unexpectedly revealed by the snow." [71] Whether he had flown or not, it is clear that he had a sincere interest in flight that would continue for the rest of his life and he would use commercial aviation in the early 1930s, when it was also a relatively new innovation.

As noted earlier Percival was a handsome man who dressed well and was attractive to women. He was serious and confident, yet sensitive or perhaps shy. Philip Gibbs, another war correspondent whom Percival would work with later, notes in one of his volumes a visit to a restaurant in Constantinople with his son Tony and Percival:

> Tony and I used to go with Percival Phillips to one of these Russian restaurants. The cook had once been the admiral of the Czar's yacht. The waitresses were little Russian princesses, very dainty and charming. Cossack officers, in their long black coats and astrakhan caps, and cartridge belts across their chests, came in for food and kissed the hands of these little ladies before taking their place at table.
>
> Phillips liked this place. It appealed to his sense of romance. Also his little shy smile and his blue eyes found favour with one of the pretty princesses and he was having a pleasant flirtation with her when she could spare a few moments from other tables. Phillips was like that. His shyness, his little nervous cough, his blue eyes and his smile were very attractive to women and he had love affairs, of a mild kind mostly, in many cities of the world where he sipped golden

---

[71] Percival Phillips, "Battles in the Arctic Air," *The Strait Times* (Singapore), March 20, 1917, p. 2.

>liquids of infinite variety while he watched the world
>and recorded its drama . . . [72]

Above all Phillips was viewed as an excellent journalist and his writings during the Great War were viewed as "models of expert war correspondence." He was capable of absorbing all that he saw and then writing it down in such a clear manner that his readers felt they were there. The Bournemouth piece illustrates this very well, but it also reveals his interest and knowledge of aviation at an early date.

There is no doubt that Percival was ambitious, but he seems to have only wanted to be a journalist. His fellow correspondent, Philip Gibbs would go on to write major histories of the war, as well as novels, while another friend, Sidney Dark, who was also a newspaperman, would go on to write plays and novels. Although Percival would have five books published over his lifetime, four of these were compilations of his previously published newspaper articles and the fifth was a report of the Far East tour of the Prince of Wales, who Percival accompanied. Percival was content to report the news of the world.

It is worth reemphasizing the fact that Percival was a sensitive individual. This is mentioned by both Sydney Dark and Hayden Church in brief comments on him. It is also noted elsewhere that he had a serious disagreement with Philip Gibbs during the war that almost ruined their friendship. He also appears to have had a serious disagreement with Claybaugh, the editor of the Brownsville newspaper, years earlier. Later it will become apparent that he left some positions in part because of disagreements with editors or owners of newspapers. All of this is suggestive of the fact that he didn't quite know how to get along well with some men. This may go back to the lack of a male influence in his life. He was always friendly with men, mostly fellow reporters, but only up to a point.

Although the absence of a father figure undoubtedly had an impact on Percival, his mother's claim that the father had died may have had more of an impact. His brothers, William and Robert, were dead before he reached his eighteenth birthday. If in his early years

---

[72] Philip Gibbs, *The Pageant of the Years: An Autobiography*, London: William Heinemann, Ltd., 1946, pp. 294-295.

he believed his father had also died he may have very well had a fatalistic view of life. It was a view that allowed him to take chances that others would have avoided. Mingling with angry coal miners during the Stickle Hollow riots when he was sixteen and going off to cover a war at nineteen were dangerous feats and he had to know this. But if he believed that death could come at any time, why not take the chance?

CHAPTER 5

the *daily express* and another war

London's *Daily Express* began publication in April of 1900. Its owner and editor-in-chief was C. Arthur Pearson, an entrepreneur who was involved with several other newspapers during his lifetime. He soon found it difficult to serve as editor of the *Express* with his various other activities and as a result he hired S.J. Pryor in November of 1900 as editor, but Pearson retained the title of editor-in-chief. Pryor left the *Express* the following year. [73]

In 1901 Pearson hired Bertram Fletcher Robinson as editor. Fletcher Robinson, as he was known, gained some fame as a journalist covering the Boer War in South Africa for the *Express*. It was also during that war that he met and became friends with Arthur Conan Doyle, author of the Sherlock Holmes stories. Both Robinson and Doyle were active writers of short stories. Following the publication of The Hound of the Baskervilles, viewed by some as the best of the Sherlock Holmes stories, there were questions regarding Robinson's role in the writing of this story, with some writers suggesting the book was written by Doyle and Robinson instead of just Doyle. These questions were never resolved since Robinson died in 1909 under mysterious circumstances.[74]

---

[73] D. Griffiths (1992), *The Encyclopedia of the British Press 1422-1992*, New York: St. Martin's Press.

[74] B.W. Pugh and P. R. Spiring,(2008), *Bertram Fletcher Robinson: A Footnote to the Hound of the Baskervilles*, London: MX Publishing.

Fletcher Robinson was the editor of the *Daily Express* when Phillips joined the newspaper in the fall of 1901. The newspaper was viewed as one of the liveliest papers in Europe at the time, and Phillips becoming a reporter and correspondent for such a newspaper at the age of twenty-four was notable.[75]

It is hard to say how well Phillips got along with Robinson. The latter seem to have spent a considerable amount of time writing poetry and short stories during his term as editor with the *Express*. With so many secondary interests it is unlikely that Robinson would pay much attention to his correspondents or their columns. By 1902 Pearson hired Ralph D. Blumenfeld, another American, as foreign editor and later as news editor. Two years later Blumenfeld was appointed overall editor of the newspaper and he would retain that position for 28 years. Phillips worked with Blumenfeld more than any other editor at the *Express*.

Some sources state that Percival kept his position with the *Pittsburg Dispatch* until October 1, 1902, but that newspaper was still claiming him as late as the middle of July 1903. Why he retained both positions is unclear. Perhaps he wanted to be able to return to the Pittsburgh newspaper if things did not work out in London. One cannot be sure of his motives, but that would make some sense for a young man who was not that sure of himself.

It is misleading to talk about any reporter at that time working for a single newspaper. The articles that were written would appear all over the civilized world in newspapers that sometimes had financial relationships with the reporter's home newspaper, but often did not. This was common for smaller newspapers of the day. Even Percival's first newspaper back in Brownsville more or less admitted to this practice by naming itself the *Brownsville Clipper*. It would get most of its non-local articles by clipping them out of other newspapers. Some other newspapers would give credit to a reporter and his newspaper by burying the credits in the body of an article.

There is little to indicate Phillips presence in the *Express* newspapers of the day. Perhaps he was covering only matters of local interest. There was still the belief that reporters should be somewhat anonymous, and perhaps one could add unless their name in a by-line

---

[75] Hayden Church, "First American Made a Knight," *The Los Angeles Times*, July 18, 1920.

Dispatches from the World

would sell more newspapers. As an illustration of the latter point, the by-lines of Jack London and Stephen Crane in America, and Arthur Conan Doyle and Winston Churchill in Britain were often seen, but they were also very well known writers or personalities at the time.

On July 18, 1903, the *Pittsburg Dispatch* announced that their correspondent in London would accompany King Edward VII on a forthcoming tour of Ireland. This was seen as a very important assignment in view of potential nationalistic demonstrations that could take place.[76] The King and Queen left London on the 20th of July arriving in Dublin on the 21st. They also visited Belfast, Londonderry, Cork and Galway, among other places, before returning to England two weeks later. The royal couple was well-received and there was a general outpouring of affection shown toward them. There were no major demonstrations, even though the death of Pope Leo XIII occurred during the visit, and this caused some concern given the predominantly Catholic faith of Ireland.

On the other side of the world Japan had been negotiating with Russia during the latter months of 1903 for that country to remove its troops from the Korean Peninsula. Japan believed that it had certain rights over the Korean Peninsula, as well as Manchuria. Russia was not convinced of this. Observers around the world realized a major conflict was coming.

On Saturday, December 19 of 1903 Phillips received orders from London's *Daily Express* to go to Japan. In order for him to make it to Liverpool in time, a special train was ordered. Later that day he boarded the *Etruria*, an ocean liner of the Cunard Line and sailed to New York. He arrived there on the 27th having spent Christmas at sea.[77]

During the trip he was asked to edit the ship's newspaper. He later told a reporter in western Pennsylvania about the experience and the reporter wrote the following: "'Percy,' as he is familiarly known, while on his way across the ocean, enjoyed for a single hour, ecstatic joy and supreme pleasure of editing a newspaper in

---

[76] Untitled, *Monessen Daily Independent*, July 18, 1903.

[77] "War Correspondent Hurrying to Japan," *The Philadelphia Inquirer*, December 28, 1903, p. 5.

mid-ocean." He was referring to the "Cunard Bulletin," which was given to the full extent of the passenger list, and included items of personal interest to each passenger. 'Editor' Phillips wrote:

> Chance is a curious juggler. He has picked us up from the four quarters of the earth and assembled us in mid-Atlantic, that we know each other for a few hours before being scattered over the globe. It is a small world, but I doubt if we ever meet again. Beyond doubt, chance is a curious juggler, but his combinations are never quite the same. Therefore let us be merry while we may. Tomorrow we go our appointed ways—some to Cuba, some to the busy mills of New England, some to Hong Kong, one to Japan and Manchuria, another to Australia. We are indeed a boat load of globe trotters. In our tales of travel may our story of the Christmas ship be given the place it deserves. [78]

Obviously, Phillips was the one headed for Japan and Manchuria, although it is not clear that he ever sent dispatches from Manchuria. Arriving in New York eight days later he took a train to western Pennsylvania and had a short visit with his mother in Brownsville.

After a few days in Brownsville Phillips took a train to Washington, D.C., probably in an attempt to get some background information on exactly what was happening in the Far East, as well as to try and get some insight into the American position on the conflict. It is not clear that he learned anything of value, but he was able to write a rather lengthy human interest piece on how accessible members of the U.S. cabinet were at the time. He contrasted this with his memories of Pall Mall and Whitehall in London.[79] It is not evident that the access led to any additional insight on the Russo-Japanese conflict or the U.S. position on that conflict.

The piece that he wrote serves as an illustration of Phillips reporting less than the entire story. There is no doubt that Phillips encountered

---

[78] "The Ship's Paper: Edited in Mid-Ocean by a Well Known Monongahela Boy," *Brownsville Clipper*, January 7, 1904, p. 1.

[79] Percival Phillips, "Walk in Everybody," *The Washington Post*, February 15, 1904.

many open doors in Washington, but this is not necessarily what most British or American correspondents would have experienced. He should have noted that one of President Roosevelt's cabinet members was Philander Chase Knox, who was Attorney General of the United States, and Phillips' great-uncle. Knox could probably get Phillips into anyone's office given his position and the fact that there were already discussions of Knox being a future presidential candidate. Perhaps Phillips' relationship with Knox should have been mentioned in the article, but there was not a hint of it.

*Percival Phillips
at the time of the Russo-Japanese War, 1904*

Leaving Washington he took a train to the West Coast and San Francisco. It was there that he encountered several other newsmen on their way to cover the eventual war in Asia. Most notable among these was Jack London, the novelist and part time correspondent, who was going to cover the conflict for the *San Francisco Examiner*. Also in the group were John H. Hare, the photographer, Robert L. Dunn, and Frederick Palmer, all three representing *Colliers'* magazine, O.K. Davis of the *New York Herald*, and Captain Lionel James, of *The Times* of London. James had left Liverpool on December 23, 1903, arriving in New York on the 31st. So perhaps Phillips's special train was necessary for other reasons, i.e., the trips to Brownsville and Washington, D.C.

On January 7 the group sailed for Japan aboard the Pacific Mail's S.S. *Siberia*. The correspondents seem to have had a reasonably enjoyable time during their crossing of the Pacific. They arrived in Honolulu on January 13 and some of them went ashore there. On the 14th they left Hawaii. Dinners were at the captain's table as they were on the first leg of the trip, but there were fewer people on board for the second leg of the trip, a number of newly married couples had stayed on in Hawaii.

One day out of Honolulu, London jumped three feet and landed on a piece of wood resembling a broomstick. This strained one side of his left foot and sprained the other side. He had to lay flat on his back for sixty-five hours. After that Phillips, the youngest of the correspondents, but also five inches taller than London, would carry him on deck so he could get some sun. [80] The games and amusements continued among the others. Jack London wondered if he would be able to get around once they reached Japan. On January 25 the S.S. *Siberia* reached Yokohama, Japan. London had recovered by that time. The correspondents separated there with some going to different cities in Japan or China, and still others going to Manchuria. [81]

Several days later on February 8, 1904, Japanese forces attacked the Chinese coastal city of Port Arthur (now Lüshan) where most of the Russian fleet was anchored in the harbor, and this began the Russo-Japanese War.

---

[80] Russ Kingman, *Pictorial Life of Jack London*, New York: Crown Publishers, 1979, pp. 126-127.

[81] Charmian London, *The Book of Jack London*, New York: The Century Company, 1921.

Dispatches from the World

Phillips went to Tokyo and checked into the Imperial Hotel. Like the other correspondents, he was unable to do much to cover the war. He wrote: "The censorship here is very strict. A spirit of elation is noticeable everywhere over Japan's successes at Port Arthur. A vigorous denial is made by the government officials that Japan's troops lack provisions and are poorly horsed. A high government official said to me: 'We are not burning our bridges behind us. On the contrary, wherever our troops have gone, a way has been left safe for supplies to follow. We are prepared for all emergencies.'" [82] This appears to be a reporter's way of getting a response when there is no news: "Is it true your supply lines are too thin?" This may be the case, but the military has to deny it, stating that all is well. Suddenly there is a story about the military denying the story. This is probably indicative of Phillips' frustration with the level of censorship he encountered in Tokyo.

At some point while he was in the States, Phillips may have stopped by the offices of the *Inquirer* in Philadelphia. Or, it is possible that the London *Daily Express* reached some agreement with that newspaper about using what would be Phillips' Japan dispatches. In any event he did begin sending dispatches to the *Philadelphia Inquirer* and they were published under his by-line.

It is not known what he sent to London. Articles appeared in the *Daily Express* noting they were from a staff correspondent in Kobe, Tokyo, or another city in that country. It is not clear which articles were from Phillips. One thing that is clear, Phillips sent back some photographs. Several of these were considered good enough to be included as five panels of pictures of the Russo-Japanese War in the Kodak exhibition of 1904-1905.[83]

One of the earliest dispatches sent by Phillips to the *Inquirer* was sent on the 9th of February. It stated that the Russians had already crossed the Yalu River and were pouring into Korea. The Japanese felt they had to try and stop this Russian move.[84] Newsmen had requested permission to accompany the troops northward, but this

---

[82] "Brief News Items from the World," *Los Angeles Times*, March 3, 1904, p. 3.
[83] Douglas Collins, *The Story of Kodak*, New York: H.N. Abrams, 1990, p. 103.
[84] Percival Phillips, "Korea Fast Filling with Armed Forces," *The Philadelphia Inquirer*, February 10, 1904.

was denied. This may have reflected the desire on the part of the Japanese to avoid injuries or fatalities to the correspondents. But more than likely the Japanese wanted to control the flow of news, or censor what went out.

The concern over censorship was a theme that Phillips would return to numerous times in the years that followed. It was especially bad in this case. The Japanese were particularly leery of Western reporters; they thought many of them were spies interested in supporting Russia. In reality, most of the Western press and their national governments were pro-Japanese, although this may not have been true of Westerners generally.

The Emperor of Japan appears to have been directing the campaign against the Russians. The three major goals of the Japanese campaign, as they were given to Phillips, were as follows: to clear the seas in the region of Russian vessels; to make sure that they controlled Korea (i.e., they would force out the Russians that were there); and, to make it impossible for the Russians to maintain a presence in Manchuria. [85]

Phillips' dispatch of February 19 noted:

> Most of the European and American correspondents sent to join the Japanese force are still at Tokyo awaiting permission to go to the front. Only personal permits, signed by the War Minister, are to be given. This far none have been issued. There is much grumbling in consequence. The censorship is more rigid than ever. [86]

The war was primarily fought in Manchuria and at sea. Being unable to observe most of the conflict many of the reporters returned home.[87] This in itself was not an easy task. Louis Hinrichs, who would later join *The Times* of London, was also trying to cover the war, but

---

[85] Percival Phillips, "Mikado's War Policy is of Wide Scope," *The Philadelphia Inquirer*, February 11, 1904.

[86] Percival Phillips, "Russians Moving on the Way to Seoul," *The Philadelphia Inquirer*, February 20, 1904, p. 1.

[87] Mitchell P. Roth, *Historical Dictionary of War Journalism*, Westport, CT: Greenwood Press, 1997, p. 268.

as a free lance correspondent. It was difficult to cover the war as a correspondent with an established newspaper, trying to do it as a free lance correspondent proved to be impossible. Finding neither the Russians nor the Japanese willing to provide him with journalistic facilities, he came in contact with Phillips, who was about to return to England. They came back together by way of Shanghai, Hong Kong, Singapore, and Saigon. [88] It is known that Phillips was back in London prior to April 24 because he sent a cable to the *Pittsburg Dispatch* on that date.[89] In the end the Japanese were successful and the war ended in May of 1905; the victory helped to secure Japan's position as a major power, as well as a formidable naval power, in the new century.

The role of censorship had increased over the years since the wars in Europe in the late 1800s. Part of the problem was the telegraph and its ability to instantly relay news of a battle. The Japanese were early to realize the potential problems this could create at the time that battles were being fought. They would not be the last.

---

[88] Obituary, "Mr. Louis Hinrichs: Half-a-century of reporting on the American Scene," *The Times*, September 5, 1967, p. 10.

[89] "Fitzgerald Divorce," *The* (Connellsville) *Daily Courier*, April 25, 1905.

CHAPTER 6

a very short engagement

Following the return of Phillips from the Far East in 2005 there is a quiet period in which little is known of his activities. It was common for Phillips to take a break from his reporting after being away for an extended period of time. In this case he had left for Japan in late December and returned in April. In part he was able to take such breaks because all of his expenses were covered by the *Daily Express* while he was on assignment. In this case he would still have most of his salary for the four months he was gone.

While in London, he would attend plays, operas, and concerts. He would dine at his Chancery Lane apartment or at one of the gentlemen's clubs where he was a member. Sometimes he would leave town and go off to Paris, or travel to see cathedral towns in Britain or on the Continent. He always took his camera with him. However, shortly before Christmas of 1905 a few lines appeared in the *Brownsville Clipper* that clarified at least some of his activities. The article stated:

> Percival Phillips, whose mother, Mrs. Annie C. Phillips, resides on Church Street, Brownsville, will before long be married to a young lady of London, England, where he has been prominently identified as a writer on a London daily newspaper. It is not unlikely that he will extend his wedding tour

across the ocean and bring his bride to his former Brownsville home. [90]

So Phillips had probably been courting for the better part of the fall and there were already plans for a wedding followed by an American honeymoon, or possibly this was Annie's wishful thinking. The newspaper a month later gave more details:

> The engagement is announced of Mr. Percival Phillips, of the editorial staff of the London Daily Express, to Miss Frances G. Huxham, of Dalkeith Villa, Gillingham, Kent, England. Mr. Phillips is the son of Mrs. Annie C. Phillips of Church Street. He was engaged in newspaper work in Pittsburg prior to joining the Daily Express staff four years ago, and did his first work on the Clipper. Miss Huxham's father is one of the officials at the Royal Naval dockyard, Chatham, and her eldest brother is Lieutenant Percy J.B. Huxham, Royal Navy, who was attached for two years to the battleship Prince of Wales, flagship of the British Mediterranean fleet, as an engineer officer. [91]

Frances Huxham was born in Scotland in 1883 to English parents and she was six years younger that Phillips. Exactly how the two met is unknown. Phillips had colleagues who covered activities of the navy. As a general rule, he did not. He may have covered a story in the area of Gillingham, which lies to the southeast of London, or she may have had friends in London who were known to him and he met her at a social function.

There were other articles that followed in the Brownsville newspaper stating that Annie Phillips and several of her friends had made a phonograph recording, which they were sending to Miss Frances Huxham in London. A month later:

---

[90] "Social Notes," Brownsville (PA) *Clipper*, December 21, 1905
[91] "Social Notes," Brownsville (PA) *Clipper*, January 25, 1906

Dispatches from the World

> The phonograph record made by the ladies of the Round Table for the intended of Percy Phillips arrived at her London home safely and she will make one to be sent to the ladies here. [92]

The June 21, 1906, issue of the *Brownsville Clipper* noted that Phillips' uncle, Philander C. Knox, along with his wife and his son were leaving for a vacation in Europe, and it is easy to believe that they may have been going to England for Percival's wedding. The Knox family was to return in September. Then there is nothing through the end of the year in the Brownsville newspaper regarding the engagement, letters exchanged, or phonograph records. In January of 1907 Percival left London to cover a conference in Jamaica.

Annie Phillips, whose name regularly appeared in the social columns of Brownsville's newspaper, is strangely silent for most of the remainder of 1906. It seems apparent that something had gone wrong with Percival's engagement and she was embarrassed, so much so that she was maintaining a very low level of social interaction. She continued meeting those lady friends who were members of her church's Round Table group, conducting her music classes and being involved with other church functions, but otherwise there was little being reported. She was not sending any stories to the *Clipper*.

It probably came as a great relief when her son Smith announced his engagement to Miss Lucille Warner. [93] Lucille was the daughter of Rev. W.G. Warner of Cleveland, Ohio. She was also a niece of W. Scott Bowman of Uniontown, Pennsylvania, and he was related to the Bowman family of Brownsville. The Warner family had recently moved to Cleveland from Oxford, Ohio. While the family was in Oxford, Lucille's father William had been the editor of the local newspaper.

Smith married Lucille Warner in 1908 and they began their lives together in Bellevue of Allegheny County, outside of Pittsburgh. They had two sons, Wilbur Warner and James.Knox. In 1918 Smith was working for the Thomas Spacing Machine Company in Glenshaw

---

[92] "Social Notes," *Brownsville* (PA) *Clipper*, March 22, 1906
[93] "Social News," *The Clipper Monitor* (Brownsville), December 13, 1907.

near Pittsburgh. This company made machinery for punching and shearing, among other things. By 1920 he had moved to the Pittsburgh suburb of Library and he was working as cashier at the Library National Bank. A Fayette County history states that he was "president of Merchant's Bank of Pittsburgh, which he organized."[94] This seems unlikely. It does seem like the kind of boast that his mother might have made when interviewed for a local county history book in the early 1900s. On the other hand he did work for several different banks during his career.

Returning to Percival, there is no record of him ever marrying in England and it is reasonable to assume that he and Frances ended their engagement. Married life would have been somewhat inconsistent with the life of a war correspondent, and only a few such correspondents were able to manage this. Even something as minor as crossing the Atlantic to America and returning would take two weeks at a minimum and this would be without any time spent collecting information for a story. Percival had to recognize that a prolonged war would mean a prolonged absence. Therefore, as long as his primary goal in life was to be a war correspondent he would have to delay thoughts of a marriage and he did.

As for Frances Grace Huxham, there is a record of her marrying a gentleman named Francis Charlton Lanaway during the spring prior to the beginning of the Great War. When the war began, he enlisted. Second Lieutenant F.C. Lanaway of the Royal Sussex Regiment was 'killed in action or died of his wounds in an advance on or about August 21st of 1918,' just a few months before the end of hostilities.[95] The ambiguity in the statement is a reflection of the use of artillery in the Great War that left many bodies unidentifiable.

Frances Lanaway never remarried following the death of her husband on a battlefield somewhere in Europe. She received her husband's medals and ribbons, but these were probably far less useful than the pension she also received. In the decade that followed her mother died. This was in 1929 and her mother, aware of the pension, left her entire estate to her husband John and a daughter, Kate, who

---

[94] John Jordan (ed.), *Genealogical and Personal History of Fayette County, Pennsylvania, Vol. I*, New York: Lewis Historical Publishing Company, 1912.

[95] "Killed in Action. Francis Charlton Lanaway," *The Times*, November 8, 1918.

never married. Also left out of the will was Frances' brother, Percy J. B. Huxham, who had decided to remain with the navy. He would also never marry, dying in 1953.

Frances traveled to Australia in the latter months of 1933 following the death of her father earlier that year. This was also the time when Phillips was in Australia, but there is no indication that they ever saw each other after 1906. When she returned from her trip, it was to the family home in Rochester, Kent. In the years that followed Frances and her sister Kate moved to Bournemouth, Dorset, on the south coast of England. Frances again traveled to Australia in 1953, but upon her return to England she never traveled outside the country again. Her sister Kate died in 1966 at the age of 88 and five years later Frances died, also at the age of 88.

As for Phillips he would have many female friends over the years to come, but there is no indication that these relationships ever became serious enough to lead toward marriage. He would flirt with women and many of them were attracted to him. They would send him letters from time to time or perhaps the occasional book, but that was about as far as these relationships went.

Editors over the years were always complaining about their single, male reporters getting into difficulties with women, which the newspaper would have to try and straighten out. But they praised Phillips, as one of the few who avoided such situations. As a result they had no concerns regarding his behavior when they sent him to various parts of the world.

CHAPTER 7

between the wars

Phillips was later lauded by some of his fellow correspondents, and perhaps envied by others, for his uncanny ability to be "in the right place at the right time." The conference that he attended in Jamaica was such a situation and it resulted in his being present when a major earthquake occurred.

Phillips was assigned to cover the Conference of Cotton Growers and Spinners to be held in Kingston, Jamaica, in early January of 1907. It might have seemed like a relatively unimportant event, but cotton was a major import of Britain, and its mills in the north of England needed a continuous supply of this raw material. The *Clipper* stated that "[Phillips] will remain until the 30th of January inspecting the advantages and improvements in the island." [96]

Phillips steamer, the *Port Kingston*, had no sooner arrived in Jamaica when the earthquake occurred. The initial shock was said to have lasted seven or eight minutes with several aftershocks. Sir James Ferguson, a former governor of New Zealand, was killed at the British army base on the island, while forty soldiers in the base hospital were crushed when that building collapsed. The earthquake brought comparisons with the San Francisco earthquake of the previous spring and the Valparaiso (Chile) earthquake of the previous August.[97] Initial reports focused on the British casualties on the island and it was estimated that only about thirty Jamaicans were

---

[96] Untitled, *Brownsville Clipper*, January 3, 1907.
[97] "Quake Wrecks Kingston," *The Washington Post*, January 15, 1907.

killed. This turned out to be a gross underestimate as the total death toll was in the neighborhood of twelve hundred.[98]

Phillips found that Kingston had lost its telegraph services due to the earthquake, so after he had most of the immediately available news on the damage, he took a steamer to Holland Bay on the northeast coast of Jamaica. His report was late arriving in London for that day's edition of the *Express*, but it appeared in another newspaper that evening because of its pressing news content. The next day the *Daily Express* reminded readers that this report was from the Percival Phillips "whose graphic dispatches from the Far East during the Russo-Japanese war will be remembered by our readers."[99] Since the *Daily Express* didn't give him a by-line at the time of the Russo-Japanese War, this statement would have meant very little to the newspaper's readers.

Phillips' story on the Jamaica situation as sent from Holland Bay began with:

> I arrived here by the coasting steamer *Arno*, which left Kingston at 11 o'clock this morning. I left Kingston destroyed by fire and earthquake, a scene of pitiful desolation.
>
> The shocks occurred yesterday afternoon. There were three in succession within a period of three minutes, the direction being from west to east. The first was the severest and did the greatest damage.
>
> The entire city seemed to shrivel up. The buildings crashed together, and fell in a crushed mass like egg shells.[100]

He went on to discuss the deaths, destruction and panic of the inhabitants. He returned to Kingston and remained there for

---

[98] Vaughan Cornish, "The Jamaica Earthquake (1907)," *The Geographical Journal*, Vol. 31, No. 3 (1908), pp. 245-271.
[99] Percival Phillips, "Scene of Desolation," *Daily Express*, January 18, 1907, p. 1.
[100] Ibid.

several days reporting what he had seen using the repaired cabling facilities.

He told a different story to writer Eleanor Early of New England several years later. In that case he said he walked across the island living off of bananas on the way until he found a working cable station.[101] Of course it would have been impossible for him to walk that distance and this is probably an example of his feeling quite comfortable around women, joking with them and generally having an enjoyable time.

Having three wars that he had covered by 1908, Phillips was gaining a reputation as a war correspondent. However, if that becomes your specialization you are naturally always waiting for the next war. It is fortunate that there is not a continuous series of wars, although sometimes it does appear to be that way. In Phillips' case he was being paid a salary and in order to collect this he had to report on something. He had picked up the cotton and spinners meeting in Jamaica for this reason and stumbled upon an earthquake, but that was an unusual outcome. Most of the stories were not nearly so dramatic.

In February he was sent to Berlin to cover the visit of England's King Edward and Queen Alexandra to Kaiser Wilhelm in Germany.[102] The visit was more one of courtesy than anything else and apparently nothing of strategic importance was discussed. The German reception was pleasant though subdued. The King and Queen returned to London on the 12th of February.

Another such story that he covered was the return of the British fleet to England in July of 1909.[103] This may sound like a minor event but it involved forty-two of Britain's finest battleships and cruisers, which anchored off of Southend, and the positioning of numerous additional small craft between Gravesend and Westminster Bridge on the Thames. The shoreline held an estimated 60,000 who had come to see the return of the fleet. The British fleet was the protector of

---

[101] Eleanor Early, *Ports of the Sun: A Guide to the Caribbean, Bermuda, Nassau, Havana and Panama*, Boston: Houghton Mifflin Company, 1937, p. 188.

[102] "Social News," *Clipper Monitor* (Brownsville, PA), March 12, 1909.

[103] Percival Phillips, "Armada in the Thames. How the Great Fleet Came to the Gate of London. One Vast Machine. Ships on a Sea of Silver." *Daily Express*, July 19, 1909, p. 1.

the British Empire's island home. The Empire did not maintain a large standing army. It recognized that any attack on Britain would have to come by sea and it was up to the British fleet to "rule the sea," which it did at the time. Phillips' coverage of the fleet story filled half of the front page on that occasion.

On July 26 a group of republicans attempted to begin a revolution in an area of northwestern Spain known as Catalonia. The revolution was aided by anarchists who were also interested in overthrowing the government simply on principle. On July 27 there were 36 religious establishments, including churches and convents that were burned or damaged. The uprising was suppressed by August 1. Phillips found it impossible to get to Barcelona (the largest city in the region known as Catalonia) from Madrid until August 4.

> I arrived here this morning from Madrid by the first train leaving the capital for Barcelona since the revolt, and among my fellow passengers were a number of anxious relatives of the rioters, who hurried to the Parelelo quarter only to find the person they sought had been taken to Montjuich [a fortress that had dungeons in its lower levels]. [104]

Phillips walked through the areas of the city that had seen the most damage by rebels and government forces.

> An absolute reign of terror prevails among the cowed inhabitants of the Parelelo quarter since the final victory of the authorities. This quarter is notoriously the Anarchist headquarters of Europe, and herein have been hatched most of the Terrorist conspiracies which of late years have troubled London and other cities as well as Barcelona. [105]

---

[104] Percival Phillips, "Iron Hand in Spain. Terrible Punishment Meted Out to the Rebels. Doomed Women." *Daily Express*, August 6, 1909, p. 1.
[105] Ibid.

Reliable sources told Phillips that 160 of the revolutionaries had been executed since the end of July and others were being executed at the rate of 30 a day. Phillips seemed concerned that a number of the revolutionaries were women, but he found that they had also been heavily involved in the burning of convents and injuries to nuns. Phillips added, "There is little likelihood that in consequence that those women in prison will escape death."

Ralph David Blumenfeld took over as editor of the *Daily Express* in 1904 and Phillips was to work for and with him for the next seventeen years. [106] Blumenfeld was originally from Wisconsin and he had been living in London for more than a decade at that time. Phillips got along very well with RDB, as he preferred to be called. Blumenfeld would compliment Phillips on some of his articles, but at the same time needle him about his writing. He once wrote to Phillips, "You are still splitting your infinitives." RDB did not confine his criticism to Phillips. He started a manual of newspaper grammar and style for the *Express* commonly referred to as the 'Do's and Don'ts.' [107] At the same time he could offer praise to Phillips for the well-written article, "Everyone is talking about your last piece." The correspondent would respond that he was going to need to order a larger hat. It was Blumenfeld who decided where and what Phillips would cover next.

On April 2, 1910, Phillips was in Naples. Blumenfeld had sent him there to meet and cover the travels of the former U.S. president, Theodore Roosevelt, on his tour of Europe. The former President visited nearly every major city in Europe during this tour. In addition to the regular tourist sites and events, Roosevelt gave a speech and several lectures. The speech was accepting the Nobel Peace Prize in Stockholm on May 5. The prize was awarded for his work in ending the Russo-Japanese War. The lectures were given at the Sorbonne in Paris, the University of Berlin, and the University of Oxford. He also represented the United States at the funeral of King Edward VII in London. Phillips accompanied Roosevelt for part of his travels,

---

[106] Dennis Griffiths (ed.), (1992). *The Encyclopedia of the British Press 1422-1992*, New York: St. Martin's Press, p. 117.

[107] Arthur Christiansen (1961). *Headlines All My Life*, New York: Harper and Brothers, p. 46.

but there are no indications that he ever talked to him about his uncle, Philander Chase Knox, who had served in Roosevelt's cabinet. Phillips had also been in Cuba when Roosevelt and his Rough Riders were becoming famous during the Spanish American War and he may have known him from that occasion. All that is known for certain is that he did write several articles about the former President's visit while he was traveling in Europe. [108]

By April 18, Phillips had gone to Biarritz, a small French town on the Bay of Biscay of the Atlantic Ocean, apparently leaving Roosevelt to finish his trip without *Express* coverage. The King of England was there on a holiday and Phillips was there to informally record the occasion for *Daily Express* readers back in England.[109]

Less than ten days later Phillips was reporting on an air race between an Englishman, Graham White, and a Frenchman named Louis Paulhan. The race was in response to a prize offered by the *Daily Mail* for the first flight from London to Manchester. This is such a short distance that it seems almost humorous to us today, but this was a deadly serious race in 1910. At the time the pilot of such aircraft sat on a seat exposed to the wind, the cold, and the rain. Phillips covered the flight for the *Daily Express*; the flight was won by the Frenchman, who received a prize of $50,000. [110] The race was of some importance to aviation development at the time, and it was interesting enough to Phillips that he rewrote the episode for a magazine. [111] Writing for magazines was something he rarely did.

---

[108] Percival Phillips, "Same Old Teddy Ten Years Younger," *Daily Express*, April 4, 1910; "Mr. Roosevelt and the Pope. Episode Which Has Stirred Two Continents. American Feeling." *Daily Express*, April 5, 1910; "Save Me from My Friends. Mr. Roosevelt Between Two Fires." *Daily Express*, April 6, 1910; "A Sentimental Journey. Mr. Roosevelt Visits the Scene of His Honeymoon," *Daily Express*, April 7, 1910; "The Man with the Smile. Mr. Roosevelt, the Etna of Energy," *Daily Express*, April 11, 1910.

[109] Percival Phillips, "With the King in Biarritz. The Town of Sunshine and Content." *Daily Express*, April 19, 1910.

[110] Percival Phillips, "Race in the Air. Thrilling Contest Between White and Paulhan. Perfect Flights. Interrupted only by Cold and Darkness. Frenchman Leads," *Daily Express*, April 28, 1910; Percival Phillips, "The Race of Centuries. How Paulhan Won the Contest from White. "The Better Man." Amazing Spurt in the Dark," *Daily Express*, April 29, 1910.

[111] Percival Phillips, "A Race in the Air," *Outlook*, May 28, 1910, pp. 145-148.

Dispatches from the World

On May 6, 1910, King Edward VII, who had been in Biarritz three weeks earlier, died. He was to be replaced by his son who would become King George V. Phillips was back in England to cover the ceremonial aspects of this transition.

This was the manner in which Phillips worked. Even after the above he was still on the move with a funeral for the King of Denmark in the latter half of May, followed by a return to England on June 7. Next he was on his way to the 1910 Olympic Games in Stockholm where he would report on the same for the *Express*. [112]

The years that followed saw Phillips covering riots, civil wars, and revolutions, but these add little to our knowledge of Percival Phillips, the man. The greatest insight comes from his coverage of the ceremonial aspects of King George V replacing his father, King Edward VII, upon the death of the latter. This was not the coronation. That was to come a year later on June 22, 1911, at Westminster Abbey. As Phillips wrote on May 9, 1910:

> George V stood at an upper window of Marlborough House this morning looking down on a scene which will live in his memory as one of the greatest episodes of his life.
>
> His heart must have been very full as he gazed across at the gray quadrangle of the ancient Palace of St. James, where a glittering assemblage, symbolizing the greatness and splendor of the empire had gathered to proclaim the beginning of his reign.
>
> Heralds, pursuivants and great officers of state were clustered on a little balcony around a man in gorgeous medieval dress who held an open

---

[112] The articles that appeared in the *Daily Express* under Phillips' by-line were: "Olympic Tug of War, London Police Defeated by Swedes," July 9, 1910; "British Victory, British Team Wins the Olympic Relay Race," July 10, 1910; "Camera as Racing Judge, World Record Broken by an Englishman, Olympic Victory," July 11, 1910; "Olympic Medals Split, American Victory at Stockholm," July 12, 1910; "Olympic Games. South African Wins the Marathon," July 15, 1910; "Four Olympic Giants. America's Fund for the Next Great Contest. £ 1 Buttons," July 22, 1910.

parchment, and, as he read, some of the phrases came faintly across the sea of upturned faces to the listening monarch behind the curtain at the half open window.

'Beseeching God, by whom kings and queens do reign, to bless the royal Prince George the Fifth with long and happy years to reign over us. God save the King.'

Phillips wrote of the ceremonial aspects of this event at length, covering most of the front page of the *Express* and other newspapers that picked up the story of that day. He concludes the article with:

The Earl Marshall called for three cheers for his Majesty, but his voice was drowned in the volume of sound from the people below. The band crashed out the national anthem. It gripped all hearts with new fervor and affection. Still cheering, the crowd turned involuntarily to Marlborough House. They saw the little princes standing at salute and the royal standard flying mast high. The guns in St. James Park were booming out their message to the world. It was well worth the dreary waiting in the bitter wind. It was a picture to be treasured by one's eye for a lifetime. [113]

The full text of the article reveals that at some point Percival Phillips had come to love England. Gone is the criticism of the manner in which the citizenry pay homage to their king that Phillips had written about a decade earlier. Is the ceremony described the beginning of Phillips becoming an Englishman? It would appear so and his later actions only reinforce this interpretation.

On July 27 of 1910 Phillips boarded the ship *Kaiser Wilhelm Der Grosse* out of Bremen, Cherbourg and Southampton, at the latter port

---

[113] Percival Phillips, "George The Fifth Is Proclaimed King Under Sullen Skies," *The Post-Standard*, Syracuse, New York, Tuesday Morning, May 10, 1910, p. 1 and 11.

and sailed for New York. He was following the trail of a man named H.H. Crippen, an American medical doctor, who was wanted for the murder of his wife. Crippen had done a fairly good job of hiding the fact of the murder, if there was a murder. In a panic he had fled to Antwerp and then to Canada with his mistress, who was disguised as a young boy, on an earlier vessel, the *S.S. Montrose*. Representatives of Scotland Yard pursued the two fugitives by taking a faster ship and they arrested the couple on July 31, 1910.

Also on board the *Kaiser Wilhelm* with Phillips was Bernard Grant, a photographer with the *Daily Mirror*, assigned to get pictures of the fugitive and his mistress. Grant wrote many years later, "On board I found my old friend Percival Phillips (now Sir Percival), then the special correspondent of the *Daily Express*, also bound for Canada on the Crippen story, and I was indeed happy to have as a companion one who is ever ready to help those less experienced than himself." [114]

Arriving in New York on August 3, the newsmen did a quick tour of the city and then Grant headed for Quebec. Phillips knew the two captured fugitives would be held in Quebec for a while pending extradition to England so he remained in New York.

Earlier Phillips had sent a cable to his mother Annie, urging her to come to New York City along with his brother Smith and his new wife, Lucille. He wasn't sure how long he would have in the U.S. Annie and the others were in New York on his arrival. They had a short visit with Phillips and then returned to Brownsville. He promised to come to Brownsville as soon as he could. Things seemed to be moving slowly so he made a quick trip to Brownsville and spent a few days there with relatives before going to Quebec. [115]

Arriving in Quebec Phillips organized the reporters so that they would be aware of any attempt to move the captured pair. The police were less than cooperative. There followed numerous attempts to find out how and when the prisoners would return to England. When the ship finally left, it was from Montreal. Phillips was able to get his story and Grant was able to get his photographs before the ship finally steamed into the River Mersey, arriving at Liverpool

---

[114] Bernard Grant, *To the Four Corners: The Memoirs of a News Photographer*, London: Hutchinson and Company, Ltd., 1933, p. 37.

[115] "Percival Phillips, Famous London Correspondent Visits His Native Town," *Clipper Monitor*, August 19, 1910, p. 1.

on Saturday morning August 29. In the trial that followed, the jury deliberated for 27 minutes before finding Crippen guilty of murder. He was sentenced to be hung; his mistress was found not guilty.

At the time the signing of execution warrants rested with the Minister of the Home Office in England. Winston Churchill was in his first year in that position and generally disliked the signing of such warrants. He had no trouble with the warrant in the case of Crippen and when the execution took place on October 18 of 1910, Churchill celebrated with a champagne breakfast. [116] As much as the celebration may have appeared appropriate at the time, recent DNA evidence makes it very unlikely that Crippen killed his wife. The remains found by the police were not those of his wife and there is a suggestion that police may have framed Crippen due to their poor performance in the "Jack the Ripper" case twenty years earlier. [117] So rather than an illustration of the efficiency and competence of the criminal justice system in Britain at the time, it stands as a very good argument against capital punishment.

Phillips also covered the sentencing of Stinie Morrison for the murder of one Leon Beron on New Year's day of 1911. The verdict and the sentence were delivered on March 16, 1911. Phillips wrote:

> It was like a scene from a play. The scarlet-robed judge, under the black and gold sword, gravely referring to his notes; curious spectators banked together on the right side of the dock, their eyes on the prisoner, a compact group of barristers in the centre; the jury box on the left, filled with 12 men in various attitudes of fatigue. Behind the dock—although he could not see them—more spectators, craning their necks for a glimpse of the central figure through the glass panels of his cage [118]

---

[116] William Manchester, *The Last Lion: Winston Spenser Churchill; Visions of Glory, 1874-1932*, Boston: Little, Brown & Company, 1983, pp. 414-415.

[117] Roger Graef, "Desperate police framed Crippen for wife's murder," *The* (London) *Sunday Times*, June 29, 2008, p. 13.

[118] Percival Phillips, "Morrison Sentenced to Death," *Daily Express*, March 16, 1911, as cited in Francis Hereward Maitland, *One Hundred Years of Headlines, 1837-1937*. London: Wright & Brown, Ltd., 1938, pp. 138-139.

The man was found guilty of the murder and the judge sentenced him to death. However, in this case a petition for leniency was circulated and after receiving 70,000 signatures, his sentence was commuted to life in prison.

These cases probably led Phillips to recall the murder cases that he had covered a decade earlier in Pittsburgh. These were unusual events for him to cover in England and he may have asked to do the Crippen story as a way of visiting the States.

CHAPTER 8

a revolution, a riot and a little war

Portugal was ruled from May of 1886 by King Carlos and Queen Amelia. Growing pressure to end the monarchy and create a republic resulted in republicans assassinating the king in 1908. Also killed at the time was the royal couple's oldest son. The younger son was wounded, but survived. This younger son became King Manuel and he ruled the country along with his mother who became Queen Mother Amelia until the fall of 1910.

On October 5 of 1910 the republicans in Portugal began a revolution. Their rebellion began with two regiments of the military—one infantry and the other artillery—and they along with as many as 8,000 to 10,000 armed insurgents proclaimed a republic. Republican flags were raised and a provisional government was established. Warships that had gone over to the republican side shelled the city of Lisbon resulting in about one hundred fatalities, but beyond these deaths the revolution was relatively nonviolent. The royal family sought sanctuary in Gibraltar and the new government took over in Lisbon. Phillips covered the story, but it was over very quickly.

Following the fall of the ruling family, the soldiers and sailors who joined the revolutionary party demonstrated an obvious lack of control. Phillips wrote of the revolutionary infantry seeking out the Jesuit priests, the convents, and the churches. He saw one Jesuit killed and two others wounded.

The so-called Champagne riots in the north of France in 1911 were the result of a series of problems faced by grape growers in the region: four years of crop losses, an infestation of a louse that destroyed considerable acreage of vineyards, low income and what was believed to be unfair competition from wine merchants who were using cheaper grapes from Germany and Spain. Also related to the riots was the creation of a Champagne district in France, which among other things would create certain economic advantages for that region. As a result of these factors, grape growers lost control, destroying vineyards, shops, warehouses, and houses. The French government sent in 20,000 troops to restore order.

Phillips was there to cover the events and was impressed with the use of airplanes by the military to follow what was happening on the ground.[119] Calm was restored but the estimates of damage were significant.

Percival's travels resulted in him very quickly filling up the pages of his U.S. passport. He held several of these over the years. On April 25 of 1911 he applied for one of these from the U.S. Embassy in London. This was common; he would often apply for a passport from the London American embassy, or in another instance the American embassy in Paris. The thing that makes the 1911 London application notable is that instead of a local newspaper colleague verifying the details of his passport application, he had his great-uncle, Philander Chase Knox, write a letter swearing that the information in the application was true. Knox was Secretary of State in President Howard Taft's administration at the time.

In 1911 Tripoli (Libya today) was the only part of Mediterranean Africa that was not controlled by a European power. Both Turkey and Italy had an interest in taking over the area although for ten years prior to that the Italians had told Turkey they had no interest in the region. Turkey did have loose political control over the area, but even boundaries were nebulous when it came to the region. Italy

---

[119] Percival Phillips, "Champagne Warfare. Towns and Villages Filled with Troops," *Daily Express*, Friday April 14, 1911, p. 1; Percival Phillips, "Aeroplanes in Wine War. Aerial Scouts Keep Watch on Rioters," *Daily Express*, Saturday, April 15, 1911, p. 1

Dispatches from the World

began to see Turkey's control over Tripoli as the last part of a wall that would have them completely surrounded. On September 29, 1911, Italy declared war against Turkey. Troops were sent by Italy to Tripoli.

Phillips covered the land events which were insignificant in the total conflict in comparison to naval activity. His first reports came from the French colony of Tunis, located next to Tripoli, on October 4. He reported on Turkish refugees arriving in Tunis.[120] This was followed by an article on health concerns in the form of a possible cholera epidemic,[121] and one on the arrival of the Italian marines.[122]

In a letter sent to his brother Smith about this time Phillips wrote:

> I am off by a coastwise steamer this afternoon down the coast to Djerba, and we are trying to pass the blockade into Tripoli, 180 miles southward. No detailed news has come out yet, and I am most anxious to be among the first to enter. The French Consul General of Tripoli, who was turned back last week, goes by the same boat. I left Paris last Sunday night for Marseilles, thence on a mail steamer to Tunis, arriving Tuesday morning, thence 250 miles by rail to Sfax.
>
> This is a beautiful town—the European quarter is clean and healthy and the walled Arab city one of the most beautiful sights I have ever seen. In color, variety of costume and type it excels China and Japan. The white buildings, the veiled women, the camels in the narrow streets, the Mosques and the dazzling tints of costumes fairly took my breath away, although I have seen a good many strange places.

---

[120] Percival Phillips, "Turkish Refugees in Tunis. French Task of Neutrality," *The Daily Express*, October 5, 1911, p. 1

[121] Percival Phillips, "Epidemic Danger at Tripoli," *The Daily Express*, October 10, 1911, p. 1

[122] Percival Phillips, "Vigil of the Vanguard," *The Daily Express*, October 12, 1911, p. 1

> The moonlight is wonderful. Weather excessively hot and humid; nothing can be done in the middle of the day. I am feeling splendidly fit; wear the usual cholera belt and sun helmet.[123] It is a great comfort to get into khaki and putties once more. One can keep quite well even in the cholera district by eating only cooked food and evading local water and wearing flannel across the abdomen.[124]

On October 11, 1911, a major naval battle was fought between the two nations at Prebesa. Italy was the victor, destroying three Turkish vessels. By the 13th the Italians had twenty thousand troops in Tripoli, along with artillery.[125] Although there was additional combat in Tripoli, the conflict there was more or less under Italian control by early November.

Phillips also described the situation of the Italian soldiers in Tripoli:

> At daybreak they began entrenching themselves in an irregular, snakelike line along the first sand dunes. Here I found them digging laboriously, still wearing heavy cloth tunics over woolen jerseys, unprotected from a blazing sun such as Londoners have no conception of, and tormented with flies.
>
> They constantly refilled absurdly small water bottles from tins brought from the white-washed

---

[123] A cholera belt was a piece of cloth, usually flannel, which was worn by British soldiers who served in India where cholera was common. American naval officers serving in the tropics also used the belt. It was worn night and day, the year around, as a waste band to keep the abdomen from becoming cold and damp and to protect the abdomen from sudden changes in temperature. It was believed that a chilled abdomen would lead to cholera and various other gastrointestinal disorders. Although researchers soon learned that cholera was due to a fecal bacteria in drinking water, the use of the belt continued in several cases through the mid 1940s.

[124] Untitled, *The Charleroi Mail*, October 27, 1911.

[125] Percival Phillips, "Soldier Life in the Desert, Trials of Italian Troops in Tripoli," *The Daily Express*, October 17, 1911, p 1.

wells by patient bullocks which toiled up the slope to lower the buckets for water to quench the ragging thirst of this regiment from Florence. One could not help wondering what the death-rate would be if the troops were exposed a few weeks to such a climate under such conditions.

I have seen officers drinking water from the public fountain amid an Arab throng, and soldiers, unwarned by the sanitary staff, eating raw fruit and gulping down iced beer when they first came ashore. Their splendid discipline and marching efficiency, which won universal admiration as the 84th took up their position on Wednesday, are no protection against disease germs, which thrive on this unhealthy coast. [126]

With regard to this latter point, Francis McCullagh of the New York *World* in his memoir of the war in Tripoli noted: "My friend Mr. Percival Phillips was scoffed at because he prophesied that, owing to the way in which the Italian soldiers were allowed to drink water from the public fountains and to eat unripe fruit, cholera would soon make its appearance in the Italian camp—as it did." [127] The extent to which the troops fell ill to the disease is not known.

While in Tripoli, Phillips, McCullagh and Thomas E. Grant (of the *Daily Mirror*) went out one night to check Italian defenses and a group of well-armed Italian civilians mistook them for Turkish soldiers. "Some special Providence (or perhaps it was the sight of Mr. Phillips' typical American outfit) saved all three of us from being shot as we suddenly emerged out of the shadow into the moonlight and confronted the terror-stricken gang." [128] Phillips would have most likely been wearing his khaki, putties and a pith (or sun) helmet and it would be hard to mistake him for a Turk of that era.

---

[126] Ibid., p. 1.

[127] Francis McCullagh, *Italy's War for a Desert: Being Some Experiences of a War-Correspondent with the Italians in Tripoli,* Chicago: F.G. Browne & Co., 1913, p. xxix.

[128] Ibid, p. 101.

McCullagh took numerous photographs of different incidents during the time that he was covering this war. One such incident is referred to as the Oasis Repression. The publisher of McCullagh's volume on the conflict noted: "Some photographs of the Oasis Repression taken by Mr. McCullagh, and submitted to us, have been found unsuitable for publication in a work intended for general circulation, and have not, therefore, been reproduced in the present volume."[129] Given the photographs that were published this is hard to believe. So while this may have been a brief war as these things go, it was no less brutal.

Following the battles in Tripoli, the conflict shifted to the Aegean Sea area and fighting continued there until the following November when the Turkish forces were defeated. Phillips rarely covered naval events so in the latter months of 1911 he was sent to India.

---

[129] Ibid., p. vi.

CHAPTER 9

coronation durbar in new delhi and the balkans

The Durbar Coronation of 1911 was held in December of that year in New Delhi following the coronation of King George V in England. The celebration was for the coronation of King George and Queen Mary as Emperor and Empress of India. Nearly all of the royalty of India was in attendance at the event. The Emperor and Empress (in this case) appeared before nearly a half million Indians who were present to wish them well. The Emperor wore the Imperial Crown of India.

One aspect of the Durbar involved the King (Emperor) riding five miles on horseback to the Durbar camp. Phillips writes about this as follows:

> The King rode quite alone, a figure of real kingly dignity, eyeing steadfastly the multitudes to the right and left, who, peering from mosques and housetops, watched the scarlet figure sitting impassively on the magnificent black charger, with wide-eyed interest, till it was lost in the dust and haze of the distance.
>
> No king ever bore himself better under the piercing scrutiny of a people who saw their ruler from the faraway island over the seas for the first time

> It was a strange and curious array, natives of every caste and condition filling the bazaar from end to end. The king was the loneliest figure in all that multitude as he reined his horse to a slower pace in order the better to see and respond to the tumultuous welcome accorded to him.
>
> Thus he rode mile after mile out through the Mori gate, until he ascended the famous Ridge. Silver trumpets heralded him along the road stained with the blood of men who held India for his Empire in the dark days of the Mutiny. Every foot was historic ground telling not only of the glories, triumphs, and trials of the British occupation, but of the romantic story of the great native empires that have long since faded into the past. [130]

In spite of his being very impressed by the King, the Durbar tour did not go as well for Phillips as some of the previous events or subsequent tours due to his failure to cover a story and an illness that he developed.

Phillips was able to write in great detail dispatches that had to be cabled back to England at no small expense. The unreported story concerned the Gaekwar of Baroda, a provincial nobleman, who had violated protocol when he met the King. At the time he turned his back on the King as he left the pavilion of the Durbar, he may not have worn all of his jewelry, and he may have swung his walking stick as he left.[131] Although some of the reporters took these actions as a slight, Phillips did not see it that way and he did not file a story on the incident.

Back in London, Blumenfeld, Phillips' editor at the *Express*, would read over the newspapers of his competitors to see what they were reporting on the Durbar. On December 18 an article appeared in the *Times* of London offering a public apology for the behavior of the

---

[130] Percival Phillips, "Pageant of the Durbar. The King-Emperor Welcomed to Delhi," *Daily Express*, December 8, 1911, p. 1.

[131] Charles W. Nuckolls, "The Durbar Incident," *Modern Asian Studies*, Vol. 24, No. 3, July 1990, pp. 529-559.

Gaekwar of Baroda for his failure to observe the proper etiquette during the Durbar ceremony. He attributed this failure to nervous confusion in the presence of their Majesties. He also noted that he was unable to note all the steps that the Nizam of Hyderabad, who preceded him, had taken. He added that he was second in line so there was no one else to observe.[132]

That should have been the end of it, but another item appeared on the same page inferring that an affront had taken place. It took issue with the behavior of the Gaekwar. It also noted that the Gaekwar tended to disregard his duties. It further suggested that he was involved in sedition, i.e., rebellious conduct.[133] It was suggested that seditious literature was being circulated in India and the printing of this was taking place in Baroda. There were also statements made to the effect that extremists were employed by the Gaekwar. This was sufficient to prompt a cable to The Times by the Gaekwar.[134] The Times continued to run stories and letters regarding the Durbar incident. It is hard to say based on the various exchanges whether the incident was a genuine affront or simply the actions of a nervous individual.

Later on the same day, The Times published the cable from the Gaekwar. Blumenfeld sent a cablegram to Phillips asking why he had not submitted the story. Phillips replied to Blumenfeld that he had deliberately avoided sending the Gaekwar story for two reasons. First, he had received a telegram from Blumenfeld that instructed him not to send any further dispatches from the Durbar unless it was on a very serious matter. Phillips said he interpreted this to mean a truly grave event such as a threat on the King's life or something comparable. He assumed that the readers of the Express had their fill of George and the Durbar. He expressed his regret to Blumenfeld for this error in judgement on his part, adding that the failure to send the story was not due to another reporter beating him to the story.

---

[132] "The Gaekwar's Homage," The (London) Times, December 18, 1911, p. 8.
[133] "The Gaekwar and the Indian Sedition," The (London) Times, December 18, 1911, p. 8.
[134] "The Gaekwar and Indian Sedition: A Reply to the Times," The (London) Times, December 22, 1911, p. 6.

Phillips second reason for not sending the story was that he didn't really think it was a story. He had seen the Gaekwar incident and he was of the belief that the Indian nobleman had a touch of stage fright, not insolence or any disrespect for the King. Phillips noted that others had also made mistakes or forgotten their instructions. When the Gaekwar made some mistakes, Phillips noted it to other reporters in attendance. Some thought the errors were intentional, but others thought he was simply nervous. Phillips discussed the situation with others in attendance after the ceremony was over and the same differences in opinion were expressed. In the end he concluded that there really wasn't a story to be written. Nevertheless, he again expressed his regrets to Blumenfeld. [135]

By the end of the year motion pictures of the ceremony had arrived in London. The motion pictures were shown at the Palace and Empire theaters on New Year's Day. What appeared on the screen was written up the following day in *The Times*:

> There could hardly be a more striking contrast than between the ceremonial salutation of the Nizam of Hyderabad, full of sincerity and solemn significance, and the apparently indifferent attitude of the Gaekwar of Baroda. Dressed in white and carrying a cane, the latter approaches the Royal Throne after the Nizam has bowed three times. The Gaekwar bows once only in a perfunctory manner, retreats a pace or two, then turns his back on the King and walks slowly away. [136]

The Times description of the motion picture does not seem as bad as some of the earlier news articles. There can be little doubt that from some perspectives the incident was an affront to the King, but it is quite likely that Phillips did not see it in quite that way. He could be impressed by the pageantry of the various events he witnessed, but the American in him could not quite accept the adulation that the English people expected from others for their king.

---

[135] Letter, Percival Phillips to Ralph David Blumenfeld, December 26, 1911. The United Kingdom Parliamentary Archives, London, BLU/1/17/PHI. 1-2.

[136] "The Gaekwar of Baroda, The Durbar in Pictures," *The* (London) *Times*, January 2, 1912, p. 6.

Dispatches from the World

After New Delhi, Phillips followed Queen Mary to Agra. As the queen was preparing to go to Jaipur, the Durbar planners asked the members of the press to more or less 'fade away' until later when the events planned for Calcutta were to take place.

Phillips decided to go to Lucknow, one of the sites involved in the Mutiny of 1857 when native sepoys or soldiers mutinied, killing their British officers. The sepoys then killed nearly all of the women and children there. Phillips wrote to Blumenfeld that he found Lucknow to be a very sad place with its ruined Residency and the small English cemetery with its sad inscriptions on the stones. Phillips went on to Cawnpore (now called Kanpur), with a half dozen British officers, two of them were in tears during the visit. Women and children had been butchered at Cawnpore as well.[137] Phillips returned to Lucknow with Ivor Castle, a friend and correspondent with the *Daily Mirror*.

Upon his return Phillips became very ill with influenza-like symptoms that were shared by at least twenty other attendees of the Durbar, including Castle. These symptoms were severe aches in the joints, rheumatism and a high fever of more than 103 degrees in Phillips' case. He was treated by the local Civil Surgeon, Lieutenant Colonel William Vost, and a Moslem doctor, Mohammed Ramasen. The doctors brought in a Hindu gentleman who proceeded to wrap all of Phillips joints with bandages soaked in a hot liquid. These were changed hourly.

Nevertheless, Phillips began hallucinating. In a letter that he wrote to Blumenfeld later he admitted that he had produced a play at His Majesty's Theatre, addressed the Parliaments of the World, talked with Kings, and various other activities that require one to have a temperature of 103 degrees.[138] By Christmas day he had recovered and the following day he moved to Wutzler's Royal Hotel in Lucknow.

Returning to England Phillips took it easy for most of 1912, but troubles were beginning in the Balkans by the fall. The goal of Bulgaria (and several other nations) in the Balkan Campaign was to remove Turkish influence from the Balkans and ensure Slavic control

---

[137] Letter, Percival Phillips to Ralph David Blumenfeld, December 26, 1911. The United Kingdom Parliamentary Archives, London, BLU/1/17/PHI, 1-2.

[138] Ibid.

over the region. The conflict began in October of 1912. Phillips was assigned to the Bulgarian General Staff. As he was to describe later in one of his articles, this sounds much better than it actually was. The Bulgarians were concerned that some of the correspondents could be injured if they got too close to the battle front. Or, even worse, the correspondents might want to report what was actually happening in the war. The government was anxious to keep both of these outcomes from occurring so they managed to keep the correspondents away from the combat, and censorship was a significant part of filing any story. Phillips wrote up most of his experiences in covering this conflict and published it in two parts in the *Saturday Evening Post* in 1913. [139]

More than seventy individuals had arrived in Sofia, Bulgaria, to cover the war. Phillips thought only about thirty of these were actually recognized correspondents with the rest being there primarily for "the experience." The Bulgarians refused to allow any of the correspondents to leave the Mustafa Pasha (now Svilengrad) area to cover any of the battles of the war. Those that did leave the area were summarily arrested and sent home. When they requested permission to visit sites of the various past battles, the response would always be something like, "Maybe tomorrow." When they wrote up their articles for the cablegrams back to their respective news outlets, the cable operator would spindle them and later send them to Sofia. Phillips thought it took eight days to two weeks to get a cable back to London. The major sources of most of the news the correspondents did receive were the official government news releases, and these would often arrive several days after their release in Sofia. In effect, censorship prevented any reporting of the actual conflict as it took place.

Related to the censorship situation was an incident that occurred in Bulgaria during that war. Phillips, Henry Nevinson, the correspondent for *The Daily Chronicle* in London, and a German correspondent named Gottberg were stuck together in a house trying to get news for their respective outlets. Both Phillips and Nevinson were suddenly recalled by their newspapers because the *Daily Mail*

---

[139] Percival Phillips, "Out in the Cold: the tragedy of the war correspondent," *Saturday Evening Post*, February 1, 1913.

was printing much better copy than they seemed able to obtain. The *Mail* was getting their news from the *Reichspost*, an Austrian newspaper out of Vienna. Its correspondent was one Lieutenant Wagner, who Phillips and Nevinson later found was staying at the Hotel Bulgarie in Sofia and "more or less" fabricating most of what he was reporting. [140]

Phillips was back in London by January 29 of 1913. When asked about the Balkan conflict, he admitted that he saw very little of the war.[141]

The year 1913 had its rebellions, coups, and revolutions, but most were over before a correspondent could reach them. As a result we find Phillips in London writing human interest pieces and book reviews. The human interest articles were about the "House of a Million Good Wishes," otherwise known as London's Mount Pleasant Post Office, and Christie's auction house, where families sell off the belongings of their ancestors.[142] Book reviews were an unusual thing for Phillips to tackle but he did one on the memoirs of Lady Craven, who lived during the Georgian era, and another on the autobiography of Theodore Roosevelt.[143] These may suggest that Phillips had few assignments at the time, but also that he did not care for contemporary fiction.

---

[140] Angela V. John, *War, Journalism and the Shaping of the Twentieth Century: The Life and Times of Henry Nevinson*, London and New York: I.B. Tauris, 2006, pp. 130-131.

[141] "Percy Phillips Back in London from Balkans," *The Charleroi Mail*, Wednesday, January 29, 1913, p. 3.

[142] Percival Phillips, "Gifts That May Never Arrive," *Daily Express*, December 24, 1913; and, Percival Phillips, "Fate's Clearing House," *Daily Express*, December 9, 1913.

[143] Percival Phillips, "The Beautiful Lady Craven," *Daily Express*, November 4, 1913; and, Percival Phillips, "Apostle of the Furious Life," *Daily Express*, December 12, 1913.

CHAPTER 10

war is declared with germany

Belgium has a history of neutrality and when it was apparent that a war was to be fought in 1914, they again took this position. Germany on the other hand wanted to go through Belgium to attack France soon after the Great War began on July 28, 1914. They issued an ultimatum demanding freedom to pass through Belgium. However, the Belgians would not allow this and as a result Germany declared war on Belgium and vice versa. On August 3 Germany invaded Belgium. This dimension of the eventual conflict would be brief in comparison to the war that evolved.

In early August Phillips began to prepare for his move to Belgium to cover the war. He purchased a Jaeger sleeping bag, waterproof boots, three khaki shirts, and a waterproof tunic and breeches. A field mattress was acquired along with a rubber bath for the time he would be in the field. A mess kit, water bottle and drinking cup completed his living necessities. To get around and to better understand where he was at any given time, he purchased maps of both Belgium and France, making sure that the maps were on linen and therefore very durable. He then left for Belgium. [144]

Phillips sent his first dispatch from Brussels on Monday, August 3.

---

[144] Sir Percival Phillips Album, ID Number: 99/54/1, 9066, Imperial War Museum Collections, London.

> Since landing from England at daybreak this morning I have travelled through the country from Ostend to the Namur fortifications by train, and seen the quiet, systematic efforts everywhere. The great frontier defenses at Liege and Namur are fully manned awaiting the onslaught of the Germans when fully mobilized. [145]

Phillips went on to describe the enthusiasm and patriotic zeal of the Belgians, the mobilization of the Boy Scouts with bicycles to act as dispatch carriers, the beginning of monetary distrust, and attacks on German merchants in Belgium.

Britain demanded that Germany respect Belgium's neutrality. Germany ignored this demand and as a result Britain declared war with Germany on August 4.

One of the interesting little points about Phillips' dispatches from Belgium is that right below his by-line in parentheses is the statement "Copyright in the U.S.A." Obviously the *Daily Express* was a London newspaper and this phrase is confusing. There are several possible reasons for the phrase. The first is that Phillips was an American and as such he was from a neutral country, at least early on in the conflict. What that could mean was that he would not be viewed as the enemy by German forces until the U.S. got into the war later. Or, it could be simply protecting the newspaper material from automatic duplication in U.S. newspapers. Or, it could be related to the attitude of British military command toward reporters.

When the war started there were several correspondents anxious to cover the hostilities on the British side of the conflict. Lord Kitchner, who was in charge of the British forces, would not allow this. He went so far as to declare any reporters on the battlefield "outlaws," having those he caught sent back to England. This is exactly what happened to Philip Gibbs of the *Daily Chronicle.* He was arrested, held for two weeks and then sent back to London.[146] Kitchner believed that the populace back in Britain would not support the war effort if

---

[145] Percival Phillips, "Waiting for the Great Onslaught. Belgium's Great Forts Fully Manned," *Daily Express*, August 4, 1914.

[146] Philip Gibbs, *The Pageant of the Years: An Autobiography*, London: William Heinemann, Ltd., 1946, pp. 160-162

they knew what was happening. Perhaps he was right. It is possible that Phillips as an American could not be treated in such a cavalier manner by the British general staff.

Phillips continued sending his dispatches. The town of Liege was occupied by the Germans on Friday, August 7. Writing on the following Sunday, he stated:

> Yesterday the town presented a picture in which war and peace were strangely blended. Cavalry remounts were tethered in circles in some of the squares.
>
> The Place Lambert was filled with camp kitchens, and army cooks were stirring boiling soup for the famished soldiers, while the children of the town looked on in wonderment.
>
> The pigeons, which fled in terror from their haunts around the old palace of the archbishop, returned yesterday, and were induced to accept bits of bread from the Prussian troopers.
>
> Piles of bodies still awaiting identification lie under shrouds in the Place Marche. One body is that of a child of twelve, another is an old man in civilian clothes.
>
> Soldiers of the opposing armies mingle freely in the streets. [147]

One thing seems obvious from the above description. Phillips was in Liege in order to see these things. Apparently, he was allowed to enter the town by the Germans.

---

[147] Percival Phillips, "Liege Town Occupied. Germans Enter but None of the Forts Taken. Hungry Soldiers. Starving Uhlans Surrender. Enemy Checked at All Points," *Daily Express*, August 10, 1914, p. 1.

Phillips was familiar with international law as it affected correspondents. Will Irwin, an American reporter who went to Europe to cover the war in 1914 benefitted from his knowledge on this topic. He noted in his memoir:

> . . . the systematic Percival Phillips had looked up the laws of war as regarded correspondents and imparted them to me. A war correspondent captured by the enemy ranked as an officer-prisoner. But if he found himself in enemy terrain and did not at once unfold himself, he was in the status of a spy. [148]

Phillips already had a very good reputation as a correspondent. So when hostilities broke out other newspapers wanted to print his dispatches. By August 17, 1914, his editor, R. D. Blumenfeld, had reached agreements with the *New York Herald* and Phillips former U.S. newspaper, the *Pittsburg Dispatch,* to allow them to print his material on the war and its progress.

By August 19 Phillips was sending dispatches from "a British camp in France." The war in Belgium would continue and Antwerp would fall in October. Nevertheless, the actions that took place there were sufficient to slow down the Germans and allow France and Britain to become better organized for the war that would last for four more years.

Phillips did not remain in France or Belgium for long; he was back in London when the correspondent, Will Irwin, arrived from the States. Irwin notes:

> At the Savoy Bar—on its way to become the news center for Western Europe—I met Percival Phillips, fringed with weary British correspondents. They had been in Belgium, dodging round the edges of battle. Suddenly the War Office had ordered them home. [149]

---

[148] Will Irwin, *The Making of a Reporter*, New York: G.P. Putnam's Sons, 1942, p. 215.
[149] Ibid., p. 207.

Dispatches from the World

Shortly after this Blumenfeld informed Phillips that he had been issued License No. 4 to be an accredited war correspondent for the *Daily Express* and that he would be billeted with the British Expeditionary Forces in France. This was on August 27, 1914, only a couple weeks after he was ordered back to England. On the very same day the War Office informed Phillips that he would have to bring his own horse as they could not supply him with one. This should have been an indication of what was going to occur over the coming weeks, but it probably wasn't.

In early September, Phillips received a letter from Major A.G. Stuart, the Press Officer, requesting that he should stop by the War Office for a discussion of messing arrangements. During that discussion Stuart must have informed him that his total baggage was limited to 65 pounds and that a typewriter would require that he cut down on food or personal baggage. This was resolved by September 9 and then there was nothing. A few days later Phillips wrote to Stuart asking him when he would be going over to the Continent.

Stuart responded on September 16.[150] He thanked Phillips for his letter and suggested that he felt as upset as Phillips about the delay in his moving to the front. He suggested that he had put Phillips case to those capable of making such decisions on different occasions, but had received no response. He empathized with Phillips and acknowledged that he was getting sick of the situation as much as Phillips. He also asked Phillips to stop by in two or three days, if he didn't have good news from him before that time.[151]

There are no clear indications that Stuart was able to move the War Office to send the accredited correspondents to France. As a result most of them took matters into their own hands, crossed the Channel, and found destinations in France, Belgium or Holland. In Phillips' case it would appear that be waited less than a week after Stuart's letter before going to Belgium. Undoubtedly, from his point of view, there were few occasions to cover wars and he was not going to pass up this opportunity.

---

[150] Sir Percival Phillips Album, ID Number: 99/54/1, 9066, Imperial War Museum Collections, London.

[151] Letter, A.G. Stuart to Percival Phillips, September 16, 1914. Sir Percival Phillips Album, ID Number 99/54/1, 9066, Imperial War Museum Collections, London.

Phillips began sending stories back, which were being published in the *Daily Express*. These had to be passed by the press bureau, which was actually the censor, and they did not care for some of his material. They apparently passed their objections along to Blumenfeld, who in turn telegraphed their messages to Phillips.

The first of these was sent on the 24th of September and stated that the press bureau would not approve any dispatches or articles that described activities or operations that had occurred within twenty miles of the front. Realizing that it might be natural for a correspondent to suggest what the allies might do next, the telegram also prohibited any speculation on possible responses of the allies. This effectively would prevent any activity near the front from being described and would leave nothing to report. [152]

The following day Blumenfeld sent along a second telegram. In this one the censors modified the previous directive and allowed reporting of operations observed within twenty miles of the front, but not until five days after the events described had occurred. It would take at least another day, or possibly two, before this news would appear in London's newspapers. As a result the correspondents would go out and cover the various offensives and write up their dispatches, but if the dispatches described operations on that day, they would be held until the required five days had passed. So the war's news was reported, but not until nearly a week after it occurred. [153]

Sometimes the copy was late getting to the censors or the correspondent was not around to make the required revisions. Early in the conflict in Belgium, Phillips wrote a piece on "Heroism in Belgium," where he ignored most of the directives of the censors. The article was published in the *Daily Express* for October 8, 1914, but the censors had removed all the questionable parts and replaced them with "Passage deleted by Censor." That particular article had twelve such deletions which could have been replacing anything from a sentence to an entire paragraph. There is no way to know.

---

[152] Telegram, Ralph David Blumenfeld to Percival Phillips, September 24, 1914. Sir Percival Phillips Album, ID Number 99/54/1, 9066, Imperial War Museum Collections, London.

[153] Telegram, Sutcliffe to Percival Phillips, September 25, 1914. Sir Percival Phillips Album, ID Number 99/54/1, 9066, Imperial War Museum Collections, London.

Dispatches from the World

Phillips remained in Belgium until the Germans got a little too close before moving over to Rotterdam in neutral Holland, where he set up operations in the Hotel Weimar. He continued sending almost daily columns to the *Express*. Lord Kitchner was still opposed to having any reporters in France or Belgium and he arrested several and had them sent back to England. Blumenfeld liked the news that Phillips was sending to London and allowed him to use as many as five other correspondents to gather the material for his columns. At the end of November he cabled Phillips: "They have cleared out all the correspondents from Northern France, including Stead and Fox, so I am depending very largely on you." Phillips continued sending columns until the end of the year when there was a significant slowdown in military activity.

Press Camp during the Great War 1916 (front row is Percival Phillips, Colonel Hatton Wilson, Deuch Thomas, Captain A.G. Stuart, back row Basil Clarke, Perry Robinson, Percival Gibbons)

The new year found the *Daily Express* in receivership and about to be reorganized. Blumenfeld, the editor, was named the receiver, and suddenly money became a major issue with him. On January 20 he sent a letter to Phillips complaining about his costs, another letter followed on each of the following dates, January 22, February 8, and March 18. His letter of February 8 pointed out that Phillips had five correspondents helping him collect the news. [154] He argued that Phillips' costs could be cut by two-thirds since much of the material being sent was usable only on page 4. [155]

Blumenfeld's concerns with expenses were understandable given the financial straits of the *Daily Express*. Certainly Phillips expenses were not exactly overwhelming. His expense account for his first month on the Continent included:

```
Travel fares to get to Brussels ................................ £ 5.40
Telegrams /cables .................................................. £ 26.17
Maps ..................................................................... £ 1.10
Car Rental ............................................................. £ 18.14
Hotels and Miscellaneous ..................................... £ 16.50
```

This amounted to a little more than £ 68 or about $320 given the exchange rate in 1914. This was not exactly an overwhelming sum for the time. [156]

Of far more significance than Phillips' cost would be the cost of the reporters that were assisting him in collecting the news. From his arrival in Belgium until his return to England in 1915 he was using as many as five other reporters to gather information. Two of these reporters are known. They were Rene H. Feibelman, a Frenchman, and Louis Pierard, a Belgian national. Both were already established writers and they would continue to cover the

---

[154] Letter, Ralph David Blumenfeld to Percival Phillips, February 8, 1915. Sir Percival Phillips Album, ID Number 99/54/1, 9066, Imperial War Museum Collections, London.

[155] The implication is that the news was not important. Today the common phrase would be "page 7 below the fold." Due to paper shortages during the war the newspaper often had only five or six pages.

[156] Sir Percival Phillips Album, ID Number 99/54/1, 9066, Imperial War Museum Collections, London.

Dispatches from the World

World War as individual correspondents until its end. Following the war Pierard would become recognized as a biographer of Vincent van Gogh and later as a Belgian politician. Feibelman's life following the war is unknown. Certainly Phillips having this many assistants, with some well known at the time, would drive up the costs and as Blumenfeld wrote to him in early 1915, "so long as there is no forward move, but routine stuff to record, it is certainly not worth the expenditure." [157]

Probably as part of the financial problems of the *Daily Express*, Blumenfeld entered into an agreement with another London newspaper regarding Phillips' columns. He wrote to Phillips in February, "I have made a deal with the *Morning Post* to exchange stories."[158] It is not clear what material Blumenfeld received from the *Post* initially, but the *Post* did receive columns written by Phillips although they appeared under the by-line of "staff correspondent." H.A. Gwynne, the editor of the *Morning Post* at the time, paid a small amount for the columns, which probably helped the *Express's* financial problems very little.

During the spring of 1915 the British Government began to realize that Lord Kitchner's position regarding war correspondents was not consistent with the views of a free society and therefore they decided to allow the accredited correspondents identified the previous August to join the British Expeditionary Force and report developments in the war. One should not assume that anyone reading the newspapers back in England would know what was actually happening with this new approach; there would still be heavy censorship, but this would be as good as it gets for the remainder of the war, or at least until the Allies' success seemed certain. Major Neville Lytton, who had been one of the commandants of the Press Chateaux on the Continent during the war, confirmed this when he later wrote in the *Daily Express*:

---

[157] Letter: Ralph David Blumenfeld to Percival Phillips, February 8, 1915. Sir Percival Phillips Album, ID Number: 99/54/1, 9066, Imperial War Museum Collections, London.

[158] Letter: Ralph David Blumenfeld to Percival Phillips, February 17, 1915. Sir Percival Phillips Album, ID Number: 99/54/1, 9066, Imperial War Museum Collections, London.

> Only at the beginning in 1914 when a disorganised handful of free lances sent home fragments of facts relating to that dramatic retreat, and at the end in 1918 when a well-organised band of accredited correspondents, working in perfect harmony with every branch of the Army, described in detail the greatest series of victories in the history of our race, was there any sport to the business.[159]

The implication is that everything in between these two points in time was heavily censored, as it probably was.

---

[159] Major Neville Lytton, "A Great War Witness. Sir Percival Phillips' Work at the Front," *Daily Express*, March 31, 1920.

CHAPTER 11

covering the western front

Initially, there were to be six "accredited correspondents" covering the British forces in the war on the Western Front for the newspapers of England. The actual individuals changed over time, but two of them were present at the beginning of the program in May 1915 and continued throughout the war. The two were Percival Phillips for the *Daily Express* and later the *Morning Post* and Philip Gibbs for the *Daily Chronicle* and the *Daily Telegraph*. The others who were present at the beginning of the program were John Buchan for the London *Times*, Valentine Williams for the *Daily Mail* and the *Standard*, and the latter's brother, Douglas Williams, for Reuters News Service. In time Buchan was replaced by H. Perry Robinson, Valentine Williams by W. Beach Thomas, and Douglas Williams by Herbert Russell. Phillips, Gibbs and these three replacements were to be the five accredited correspondents until the end of the war.

However, there were others who would come and go for brief periods of time as the accredited correspondents were on leave or ill or to fill the sixth position that was authorized. One of these was Frederick Palmer, another American from Pennsylvania like Phillips. Palmer and Phillips met earlier during their coverage of the Russo-Japanese War in 1905. There was also Henry Nevinson, who knew Phillips from the time they were in Bulgaria during the Balkan War of 1912. Two others were Basil Clarke and Percival Gibbons.

It is worth emphasizing that these correspondents were covering the British forces on the Western Front. There were other groups of correspondents covering the French portions of the front and the various other fronts in the war.

Philip Gibbs was the same age as Phillips having been born in 1877. He was the shortest of the five. Some of his colleagues viewed him as an idealist and a poet. More sensitive than the others, his later writings would reveal a certain anguish over what he had observed in the war. The son of a senior civil servant with the Board of Education, he was privately educated. One of his earliest positions was with Cassel, a publishing firm. His newspaper background consisted of a brief spell with the *Daily Mail* followed by a similar brief appointment with the *Daily Express*. His next position was with the *Daily Chronicle* and he kept this position for a number of years. This newspaper and the *Daily Telegraph* were the papers he represented as an accredited correspondent.

John Buchan joined the British Propaganda Bureau at the outbreak of the war in 1914. He was already an established writer at the time. He next joined the accredited correspondents as the representative of *The Times*. At about the same time he was working on a spy novel or novella entitled *The Thirty-Nine Steps*. The work was published in 1915 and it remains in print today. Buchan enlisted in the British Army and served as an officer in the Intelligence Corps in 1916. By 1917 he was named Director of Information. More than forty books, fiction and non-fiction, were authored by Buchan in his lifetime, but none of these achieved the success of *The Thirty-Nine Steps*. Buchan was later named Lord Tweedsmuir, Governor-General of Canada.

Valentine Williams was educated in Germany and joined Reuters as an editor in 1902. In 1909 he joined the *Daily Mail* and covered the Balkan Wars among other events. Named as an accredited correspondent in 1915, he went off to France. He found the level of censorship completely unacceptable and he resigned his appointment. He joined the Irish Guards and saw action in the Somme sector where he was wounded in 1916. At Buchan's suggestion he began writing spy novels. The most successful of these early books was *The Man with the Clubfoot*, which he published in 1918. He went on to write nearly thirty additional novels as well as non-fiction works.

Douglas Williams also left the accredited correspondents and received an officer's commission. He was wounded during combat on the Messines Ridge. Shortly after the war he represented Reuters in New York. He returned to London as Chief Editor for Reuters. This was actually a position that his father had held years earlier, but Douglas preferred gathering the news rather than working as an editor so he returned to his position in the U.S. and later accepted the position of chief correspondent for London's *Daily Telegraph* there.

Henry Perry Robinson, an Englishman, was almost twenty years older than Gibbs and Phillips. In his late 50s he had a head of grey, nearly white, hair with a close-cropped beard to match, which made him resemble a general rather than a correspondent. His writings were described by a colleague as being composed of short, well-weighed sentences. He smoked a briar pipe. The son of a minister, he attended Oxford University. He began his journalism career after moving to New York, where he worked on newspapers. Additional experience came from working for Chicago newspapers. While in Chicago he became interested in railroads and this led to his founding and editing *Railway Age*. He continued as editor of that publication until 1900; *Railway Age* is still published today and it is also the leading American trade publication of the railroad industry. As an accredited correspondent he represented *The Times* of London and *The Daily News*.

W. Beach Thomas, tall and physically fit, was also the son of a minister in England. Like Robinson he attended Oxford. After Oxford he was a teacher and an admirer of the countryside and the outdoors, but he was also a lover of the classics. He wrote occasionally for *The Globe* and then the *Outlook*, periodicals in Britain, primarily about the outdoors at the time. He was hired by Lord Northcliffe to be a writer on the countryside for the *Daily Mail* in 1907. He covered the fall of Antwerp in 1914 prior to joining the accredited correspondents in 1915.

The last of the five who would continue with the group throughout the remainder of the war was Herbert Russell. Born in 1862 he was closer to Robinson in age than the other correspondents. He was from the north of England, the son of a novelist. His schooling was at the Royal Grammar School at Newcastle-upon-Tyne. His career in journalism began with the *Newcastle Chronicle*, a newspaper. From there he moved to London and joined the newly formed *Daily Express*. This was followed by appointments with several other newspapers. Shortly after the war began in 1914, he was the Reuters News Service correspondent who covered the Gallipoli campaign and he continued to represent Reuters as a member of the team of accredited correspondents.

As noted above there were several others who joined the accredited correspondents as some members of the original group would drop out and others would be on leave. With the possible exception of Nevinson, it is unlikely that anyone at the time had a war correspondent's background that could match Percival Phillips, and none of these could surpass him. Phillips was viewed by colleagues as a scholar of war and combat. He had sought out as many conflicts as he could find prior to ending up in Belgium at the time war was declared in 1914.

When the first group of five, Phillips, Gibbs, Buchan and the Williams brothers arrived at the French village of St. Omer in May of 1915, they found that no one on the General Staff wanted them there. The Chief Press Officer was a well-meaning, but non influential major of the Indian Army, who had as a primary concern holding his job according to Valentine Williams. [160] This officer was none other than Major A.G. Stuart, the officer who back in England had wondered if Phillips really needed to take a typewriter to the front. According to Williams there were four Press Officers, all of whom had ties to the Indian Army, and they "were all alike in their abysmal ignorance of everything appertaining to newspapers."

In his biography Valentine Williams describes the treatment of the correspondents regarding the Battle of Loos.

> That a big attack was fixed for the latter end of September was an open secret at the Press Chateau. Permission was curtly refused to our request that we might be conducted to a previously designated spot and witness the opening of the battle, although we were given a preliminary survey of the ground, without, however, being told that it was to be the scene of the attack. The morning of the battle, we were pitilessly confined to our quarters. However, as

---

[160] Williams, p. 273.

Dispatches from the World

soon as it became apparent that the first advance was successful, we were given plenty of news and we were able to forward long and comparatively uncensored messages home. When at length we were given leave, on the third day of the battle, to go up to the front to witness the attack of the Guards Division, we were so far back that we saw no more than a line of smoke on the horizon and, though we collected abundant material from different sources, without warning the censorship came down like an ax and chopped our dispatches to meaningless 'pie.' This did not prevent the English newspapers from publishing detailed stories of the fighting gleaned from the wounded as they arrived from France including accounts of the first use of gas by the British, which we had been expressly forbidden to mention.[161]

These conditions continued for much of the first year of the conflict and did not change until the Somme offensive in July of 1916.

Aside from being prevented from reporting the news of the war, the correspondents were treated reasonably well. They were given officers' uniforms, which displayed no rank or insignia, but they had the honorary rank of captain. They were given lodging, usually in a chateau about halfway between the front and the general headquarters in the rear. W. Beach Thomas recalls that they stayed at a chateau just outside of St. Omer in 1915. In the summer of 1916 they were near Montrevil. During the Passchendaele and Ypres campaigns they were near Cassel and during the Somme campaign they were at a chateau near Amiens.[162] There is general agreement that during July of 1918 they were at Chateau Rollancourt near Hesdin. This last chateau, as was true of nearly all of these chateaus, was built in the eighteenth century. The Rollancourt chateau had a large green avenue at its front, a broad classic center and two wings of grey stone. The interior had changed little since the earlier century of its construction.

---

[161] Ibid., p. 276-277.
[162] W. Beach Thomas, *A Traveller in News*, London: Chapman and Hall, 1925.

The accredited correspondents were fed, provided with transportation (in the form of Vauxhall automobiles), and given access to cable facilities to get their news out. Nevinson described the situation. "Copious food was provided three times a day, not to speak of afternoon tea! I had a real bedroom all to myself, and servants to make the bed, wash up, and cook."[163] This was quite a bit different from Bulgaria, where he had served with Phillips a few years earlier. However, one thing had not changed: they still had to submit all of their material to the censors before it left for newspapers in England.

In spite of the more than adequate treatment of the accredited correspondents, one of the young Indian officers attached to the press unit confided to Gibbs that they were told to 'waste the time of the correspondents.' The officer told Gibbs he had no intention of doing that. Nevertheless, this also reflects the continuing hostile attitude of the British General Staff to the idea of having correspondents anywhere near the actual combat. Following the Somme offensive of 1916 the correspondents were allowed to cover events more thoroughly, but there was no let-up in the level of censorship.

It was impossible for any one of the correspondents to cover all of the activities in their area. Philip Gibbs described the manner in which the correspondents handled this situation:

> On mornings of a big battle we divided up the line of front and drew lots for the particular section which each man would cover. Then before dawn, or in the murk of winter mornings, or the first glimmer of a summer day, our cars would pull out and we would go off separately to the part of the line allotted to us by the number drawn, to see the preliminary bombardment, to walk over newly captured ground, to get into the backwash of prisoners and walking wounded, amid batteries firing a new barrage, guns moving forward on days of good advance, artillery

---

[163] Henry W. Nevinson, *Last Changes, Last Chances*, London: Nisbet & Co. Ltd., 1928, pp. 187-188.

Dispatches from the World

> transport bringing up new stores of ammunition, troops in support marching to repel a counter-attack or follow through the new objectives, ambulances threading their way back through the traffic, with loads of prostrate men, mules, gun horses, lorries churning up the mud in Flanders. [164]

The correspondents would interview men, read over reports at GHQ (general headquarters), and get as near the battlefields as they dared. Some of the generals would send for the correspondents on the eve of a battle and explain exactly what they wanted to accomplish, also noting the difficulties and the dangers of the plan. [165]

Following the activities of the day the correspondents would return to their chateau, the five would gather in one of their rooms and each man would summarize what he had found out during the day on that portion of the front that he covered "reserving for himself his own adventures, impressions, and emotions." [166]

It is good to bear in mind that although these men were working together they were also in competition. Everyone wanted the best story. Gibbs notes:

> Time was short while the world waited for our tales of tragedy or victory . . . and tempers were frayed, and nerves on edge, among five men who hated one another sometimes, with a murderous hatred (though otherwise, good comrades) and desired one another's death by slow torture or poison-gas, when they fumbled over notes written in a jolting car, or on a battlefield walk, and went into past history in order to explain the present happenings, or became tangled in the numbers of battalions and divisions.[167]

---

[164] Philip Gibbs, *Now It Can Be Told*, London: Harper and Brothers, 1920, p. 18
[165] Ibid., p. 49
[166] Ibid., p. 24.
[167] Ibid.

He describes Phillips as turning "pink-and-white under the hideous strain of nervous control, with an hour and a half for two columns in *The Morning Post*. A little pulse throbbed in his forehead. His lips tightly pressed. His oaths of anguish were in his soul, but unuttered.

"We gathered up our note-books and were punctiliously polite. (Afterwards we were the best of friends) . . . Phillips was first at his typewriter, working it like a machine-gun, in short, furious spasms of word-fire." [168]

As they completed writing their copy, it would go to the press officers who were the censors of what had been written. These officers also changed over time, but they were always at the chateau occupied by the correspondents. Once the censors finished with the copy, assuming there were no major revisions, it would go to the Signals area further in the rear for telegraphing to the newspapers back in England. If the piece was exceptionally long it would be carried by the King's messenger, who would catch a boat across the Channel and deliver the copy to the appropriate newspaper in London. Dinner would follow the sending off of the copy and could be late in the evening depending on the activities of the day.

Later in the evening the correspondents would gather in one of the downstairs rooms. In fall and winter they would sit back in easy chairs facing a large fireplace, perhaps smoking a pipe or cigarette, while they watched the logs turn to ash. Various topics would be discussed because these were men who had seen much of the world and much of the war. Press officers might also join the group.

Basil Clarke, one of the correspondents with the group for a time in 1916, describes the arrival of the day's mail and newspapers from England. "The post has arrived too, and there is silence while letters from home are read. Then the papers are hunted through; and dispatches written two days earlier are read through with a microscopic eye for the sins of sub-editors and printers super-added to one's own . . . For a quarter of an hour after the opening of the day's newspapers you will hear hardly a sound—or nothing more,

---

[168] Ibid., pp. 24-25.

perhaps, than a deep-toned 'damn,'" when a reader has found something that upsets him. [169]

Sometimes the correspondents would continue a pattern of activity that had them constantly on edge. In spite of this there were few conflicts between the men. Gibbs notes that in all the time he worked with Phillips he only had one argument with him.

> It was over a triviality in which I was to blame. For a few days we were not on speaking terms. For a few moments he desired to kill me, and I fingered my stick ready to strike him when he attacked. It was due to nerves on both sides—the nerve strain of two men so long together as daily recorders of enormous battles and daily witness of ruin, filth, heroism, and agony. [170]

It should be apparent that five correspondents could not cover the war taking place throughout Europe. The five mentioned above had as their focus the British portion of what came to be called the Western Front. There was also a French portion and a Belgian portion to that front, as well as an Eastern Front, an Italian campaign, a Palestinian campaign, and so forth. These were left to others.

Nevertheless, it is still difficult to understand how the correspondents could cover the Western Front of the war. This front was formed by an alignment of the German forces against the Allied forces from Belgium to Switzerland. As each tried to outflank the other the battle front was extended until it was anchored in the north by the coast of the North Sea and in the south by neutral Switzerland's Alps. It was now impossible for either side to outflank the other. The use of artillery led to the construction of an elaborate system of trenches on both sides. As a result, the only way the generals saw any solution to this stalemate was through frontal assaults, where the troops would go "over the top" charging stationary machine gun fire, and this resulted in hundreds of thousands of casualties.

---

[169] Basil Clarke, *My Round of the War*, London: William Heinemann, 1917, pp. 179-180.

[170] Philip Gibbs, *The Pageant of the Years: An Autobiography*, London: William Heineman, Ltd., 1946, p. 163.

William R. Black

The front did shift slightly to the west and then slightly to the east, but it was amazingly stable and it became apparent to any observer that the war had become one of attrition and the winner would be the one that still had soldiers left at the end. Phillips and the other correspondents could cover the Western Front, as they did, only because it did not shift a great deal during the war and because they covered only the activities in the British sector of that front.

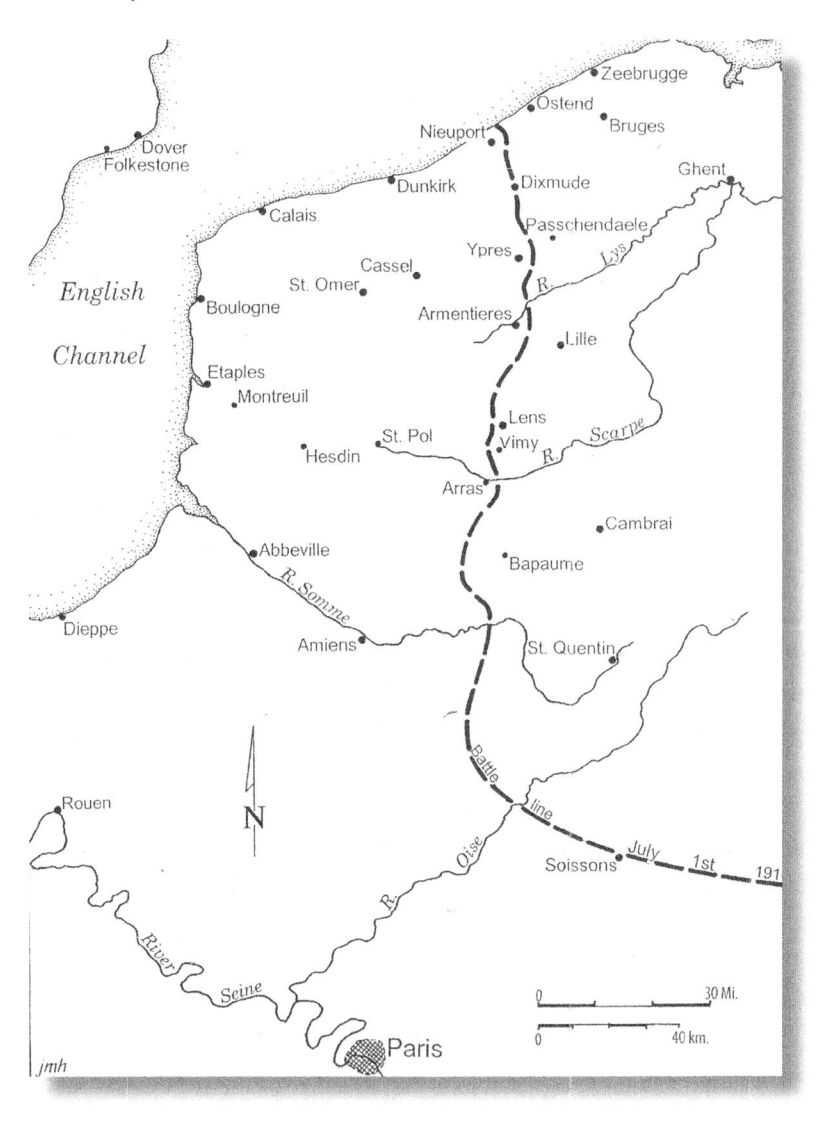

The British Sector of the Western Front.

Dispatches from the World

The level of frustration had to be high for all concerned. For every battle won today the same land would often be lost tomorrow. As a result we have the first battle of Ypres (sometimes referred to as Passchendaele), the second battle of Ypres, and the third battle of Ypres. This was repeated for nearly every battle of the war as the Western Front shifted to the east and then to the west. The ridge, the town, the wood already taken would be lost today and won back tomorrow or next week and always at a tremendous cost in human life and suffering.

One of the numerous battles that Phillips wrote about was the battle of Vimy Ridge that took place on May 15, 1916, in which he describes the craters created by the British mining an area of the ridge and subsequently taking the area. [171] At the close of the article in the *Daily Express* is the following brief clarification: "Sir Douglas Haig, in the communiqué published in the 'Daily Express' yesterday, reported the recapture of a mine crater on the Vimy Ridge by the Germans." So it was throughout the war.

A year earlier Lady Bathurst, the owner of *The Morning Post*, was very impressed with an article that was written by a "special correspondent" that appeared in her newspaper in May of 1915. She sent her praise to H.A. Gwynne, who was the editor of that newspaper at the time. He responded:

> The Special Correspondent's story of the battle of Ypres was by Percival Phillips, who does not belong to us. The arrangement that exists now is that we have to share our correspondents with other papers. Sometimes it is our turn and in that case we share with other papers. In the present instance it was the Daily Express, and I agree with you that the account is splendid. I am seeing that 12 copies are sent to the Commandant of the Red Cross Hospital at Cirencester with the passage marked.[172]

---

[171] Percival Phillips, "Battle of Vimy Ridge," *Daily Express*, May 20, 1916, p. 5.

[172] Letter: H.A. Gwyne to Lady Bathurst, 26 May 1915, in Keith Wilson (ed.), *The Rasp of War: The Letters of H.A. Gwynne to The Countess Bathurst, 1914-1918*, London: Sidgwick & Jackson, 1989.

By that summer Gwynne's interest in news of the war, or perhaps Lady Bathurst's interest, had increased to the point where he was vying for his own war correspondent. Blumenfeld apparently thought this move might be successful and would result in the *Express* losing Phillips' coverage of the war. To prevent this from happening, he entered into another agreement with Gwynne to use one month of the *Morning Post* correspondent's reports to two and one-half months of Phillips' reports. The correspondent for the *Morning Post* was H. F. Prevost Battersby and his columns began appearing in the *Daily Express* during the summer of 1915. At these times Phillips would go off and pursue other noncombat related stories.[173]

One such story took Phillips across the North Sea to neutral Sweden, in the fall of 1915. He wrote in November that upon arrival one is "startled by the unexpectedly German atmosphere in which he suddenly finds himself. It is a surprise as complete as it is distasteful." He continued, "German conversation, German literature, and German-made news; shaven-headed, raucous-voiced Prussians and their aggressive wives; portraits of Hindenburg, the wooden-faced generalissimo, and his accomplices, and the red, white and black flag of Britain's deadliest enemy are features of everyday life." [174]

He also wrote, "The first flag I saw in Stockholm as my train crawled towards the central station was a German one hung in front of a butcher's shop. (It struck me as being rather appropriate, although I do not suppose the butcher meant it that way.)" [175] The article continues, painting a rather unflattering picture of Germans and their behavior in Stockholm. This piece could be described as propaganda, but knowing Phillips concern for detail and accuracy it may have very well been an accurate description of what he observed.

---

[173] Sir Percival Phillips Album, ID Number: 99/54/1, 9066, Imperial War Museum Collections, London.

[174] Percival Phillips as quoted in "Swedish Sentiment," *The Times of India*, January 1, 1916.

[175] Ibid.

CHAPTER 12

espionage

It has been suggested that Phillips was involved in spying for the British during the World War. Although there is little to confirm this during the entire war, James Dunn, a reporter for the *Daily Mail* out of London, notes in his memoirs that he and Phillips were involved in the spy system during 1914. Phillips had moved to the Weimar Hotel in Rotterdam, Holland and he often complained to Dunn that the walls of his bedroom were too thin, implying that one could easily hear anything being discussed there. This lack of privacy was obviously a point of some concern to him.

Dunn also records an incident that occurred during the early months of the war. He notes:

> It was Christmas Eve of 1914 that Phillips and I did a rash exciting thing. We motored to a Dutch village on the Belgian frontier, entertained the Dutch guards, and the German sentries, and posing as Americans, but producing no passports—it was good entertainment—crossed the frontier![176]

They mingled with the Landsturm troops guarding a Belgian village.[177]

---

[176] James Dunn, *Paperchase: Adventures In and Out of Fleet Street*, London: Selwyn and Blount, 1938, p. 114

[177] Landsturm forces were made up of men between the ages of 19 and 45. They were the oldest of the regular forces of the German Army.

> Tankards of beer we had, and we sang "Tannebaum," the German Christmas carol with the same tune as "The Red Flag." I sang "Tannebaum" too. I have never yet understood why peace was not declared immediately. It was a great night! I hate to think that as a result of it, those poor, genial Landsturmers were sent to the front, and their places taken by young Prussians. [178]

The events noted by Dunn took place on what has come to be called the Christmas truce of 1914, which has been described very well by Stanley Weintraub in his book, *Silent Night*. [179] The emphasis of Weintraub's volume is on the truce that took place between the British and German troops in the forward trenches from Christmas Eve through Christmas Day at several locations along the Western Front. The troops exchanged beer, wine, schnapps, tobacco, puddings and various other treats, engaged in soccer matches, and carried on conversations with one another, much to the dismay and sometimes disgust of their commanders.

Phillips in his dispatch for Christmas day focused his writing on the German side of the events, similar to Dunn's comments.

> Smaller detachments of marines and Landsturm stationed at Westcapelle, Knocke, and other villages close to the Dutch border, gathered around blazing fires last night and sang songs as a prelude to to-day's feast.
>
> A description of the scene in the German barracks at the frontier town of Salzaete, on the Ghent ship canal . . . may be taken as typical of all the scenes witnessed to-day in all the depots and towns occupied by the enemy.

---

[178] Ibid.

[179] Stanley Weintraub, *Silent Night: The Story of the World War I Christmas Truce*, New York: Penguin Putnam, Inc., 2001.

Dispatches from the World

> The Christmas festivities began officially at four o'clock this afternoon with the lighting of candles on a lofty Christmas-tree erected in the main waiting-room of the railway station, adjoining the canal.
>
> The tree, which came from Cologne, was erected on Thursday, and the commandant and other officers present at its inauguration supervised the distribution of gifts. In addition to private parcels sent to the men by their families and friends, each received a box containing fifty cigars, and five ounces of smoking tobacco. [180]
>
> In some of the villages near the Dutch frontier which have not suffered from the excesses of the enemy or felt the pinch of famine, Germans and Belgians mingled in the season's jollification with a certain friendliness which, however, was more a truce of Christmas than any alteration in the feelings of the civilians towards the pillagers of their land. [181]

There is no mention in Phillips' writings of the Christmas truce between the British and German troops. If he had wanted to write about this it would have never made it by the censors. According to Weintraub there was no mention in the British press of the troops fraternizing until the *New York Times* broke the story on the last day of the year. [182] Newspapers in England and Scotland began inserting letters from soldiers describing the truce in their pages after that.

Dunn's memoir also notes that his and Phillips's names were placed on a German black list. Whether Dunn appeared on such a list is unknown, but a correspondent for *The Tyd*, an Amsterdam newspaper, noted in June of 1915 that the Germans had drawn up

---

[180] Percival Phillips, "German Orgy on Stolen Wines," *Daily Express*, December 26, 1914, p. 1.

[181] Ibid., p. 3.

[182] Weintraub, op. cit., p. 157.

a new "black list" with the names of several Belgians whom the Germans suspected of carrying out espionage for the Allies.

> In addition to these alleged spies, the name of one newspaper correspondent has been placed on the list, apparently because his dispatches have given the German military authorities much annoyance. The correspondent to whom the Germans have paid this rather exceptional compliment is Mr. Percival Phillips of the 'Daily Express.' [183]

The article also noted that the list had been communicated to German sentries on the Dutch frontier. This gave the sentries permission to arrest and shoot anyone whose name appeared on the list.

It is not surprising that Phillips name was placed on a black list by the Germans. Although at this time be was based in neutral Holland, he had sources throughout Belgium and he did not hesitate to put information from these sources in his columns that would have outraged the Germans. This would include details of pending visits by the Kaiser and troop movements. As a further illustration, the following excerpts appeared in Phillips columns on December 23 and 24, 1914.

> One report reaching me to-day from a Dutch town not far from Aix-la-Chapelle says that two reserve army corps, totaling 60,000 Landsturmers, arrived at Cologne yesterday en route for Belgium.

> Not only is a large quantity of ammunition arriving steadily near the coast, but many new machine guns have been shipped from German factories direct to the Zeebrugge defenses . . .

> I have reason to believe that the German airmen have begun using Zeebrugge as a base for aerial raids on the English coast.

---

[183] "On the German Black List. Germans Looking for Mr. Percival Phillips," *Daily Express*, June 7, 1915, p. 1.

> A reliable informant tells me that a large hangar capable of housing a number of aeroplanes has been erected near the Heyst tram station, in addition to a water plane landing stage previously reported.

These brief clippings were in the midst of news articles for just two days. It is quite possible that additional items of more importance were being removed by censors and sent directly to British intelligence analysts back in London.

According to Dunn, when Phillips was based in Holland he knew he was often being watched by the Germans. "Percival Phillips used to annoy them very much by looking most profound, and drawing maps of nowhere in particular on the back of his menu card."[184]

This sounds like the foolish behavior of a young man, the taking of unnecessary risks, but Phillips was 37 at the time. The reckless behavior is difficult to understand and one could simply say that he was courageous, but there are so many episodes during his life when he took risks that could have been avoided that one begins to think that he had no fear of dying. As noted previously he may have viewed life as a random event that could end at any time given the earlier deaths of his two brothers. If that were the case then he could go out of his way to avoid life-threatening situations, or he could take the completely opposite tact, taking extreme risks, believing that death could come regardless of what he did.

Alternatively, he may have very well understood the limits to which he could go without there being a drastic response to his actions. He had seen spies working throughout Europe by the time the Great War began. During his stay at the Grand Hotel in Stockholm in 1916, he was reminded of these earlier efforts at espionage by different nations involved in lesser wars. He wrote:

> The air of cautious activity and stealthy negotiations; the suggestion of secrets whispered over coffee; of money freely spent to achieve an unworthy end. All recall the palmy days of the Pera

---
[184] Dunn, op. cit.

> Palace Hotel, when the Young Turks were intriguing for Constantinople; the Avenida Palace at Lisbon, when rival financiers and gun-runners dealt impartially with Monarchists and Republican conspirators, and the Hotel Bulgarie at Sofia when the Balkan States were trying to sell each other without going to war.[185]

So espionage and its players were hardly new to Phillips and given his ability to recall incidents, there is every reason to believe that what he knew would be of value to British intelligence during the Great War.

As for whether Phillips actually was involved with British intelligence after 1914, there are clear indications that he was asked to do this. Perhaps none is clearer than in a letter he received from Blumenfeld in the spring of 1915. That letter requested details on German activities for the British Director of Military Operations relevant to: troop movements, their composition, direction of movement and dates, time and location; movements of supplies and materials; movement of aircraft and erection of hangars; erection of barracks; casualties sustained by the enemy; health of enemy troops; and naval movements and defenses.[186] We don't know to what extent Phillips complied with this request, but it is likely that he did all that he could since his articles, as cited above, included exactly the type of detailed material that was being requested.

It is known that his observations were highly regarded by the military for their accuracy. He had a very detached style and an excellent memory for detail. Later the War Office selected him to go to Ireland during the 1916 uprising probably because of his ability to observe details and record them.

All the while the loyalty that Phillips felt for England was becoming stronger and stronger. He was not involved in combat, but he was doing all that he could to protect what had become his adopted homeland. Some indication of his attitude comes through in his response to a column in his old newspaper back in Pittsburgh.

---

[185] Percival Phillips as quoted in, "Swedish Sentiment," *The Times of India*, January 1, 1916, p. 19.

[186] Letter, Ralph David Blumenfeld to Percival Phillips, May 12, 1915. Sir Percival Phillips Album, ID Number 99/54/1, 9066, Imperial War Museum Collections, London.

Dispatches from the World

On October 3, 1915, John Balderston, a special correspondent for the *Pittsburg Dispatch*, sent a letter to that newspaper complaining about an incident in London where he and a friend had been treated poorly because they were Americans and because the man's friend, an American of German birth, began speaking German in a restaurant. The *Dispatch* published the letter on October 18.[187] Phillips got a copy of the newspaper article and apparently felt he had to respond; his response was published about a month later (November 21).[188] He pointed out that he had lived in London for 14 years and had never encountered any anti-American feelings. He did not believe the war had changed anything in this regard. He pointed out that England was at war with Germany and this was not the time to speak German.

> I have encountered visiting Americans who were too prone to criticise Great Britain's conduct of the war in public and to emphasize their own 'neutrality' to an uncomfortable extent. Conduct of this sort naturally causes irritation. Britons do not demand that every American who enters their country should forthwith declare himself a combatant with them, but they do expect that as a matter of courtesy visitors who take no part in this life and death struggle should keep silent, if they can utter only praise for Britain's enemies.

He continued:

> More than one 'anti-English' American has come here deliberately to further the cause of Britain's enemies. Some of them—of Irish origin—have tried to intrigue in Ireland and others, of German birth and in Germany's pay, have used their American citizenship as a cloak for their designs against the allies. A prominent English politician of my acquaintance

---

[187] John L. Balderston, "Americans Sneered at in London," *Pittsburg Dispatch*, October 18, 1915.

[188] "Percival Phillips Takes Exceptions to Balderston," *Pittsburg Dispatch*, November 21, 1915.

said to me: 'There is no feeling against America, only honest resentment at the conduct of certain types of Americans who are our enemies.'

These views seem to indicate that Phillips was very supportive of the British position in the war and that he had been for quite some time. It is obvious that he collected strategic information for the British early in the war. It is not so obvious that he did this after 1914. He and others were sent back to England early in 1915 and when he returned he was an accredited correspondent, with a courtesy rank of captain, but his articles lacked the strategic details. Without a doubt these details were still observed, but they were more than likely sent directly to the British Director of Military Operations in London.

CHAPTER 13

troubles in ireland

It is easy to believe that the *Daily Express* brought Phillips back from the Western Front to cover the revolution in Ireland, but in reality, he was accredited for this assignment by the War Office, which would suggest the latter was interested in what he saw and reported.

Of course there was nothing new about the problems with Ireland. During 1913 and 1914 the Third Home Rule Bill, which would allow Ireland to more or less govern itself was under discussion in Parliament. There were two factions; one in favor of all the counties of Ireland being under the bill, and the other wishing to exclude four counties in the north (generally referred to as Ulster Volunteer Force or UVF) that were primarily Protestant in religion. The remaining counties of Ireland were predominantly Catholic.

It appeared that there would be some type of armed conflict between the two groups in Ireland at that time. Each side had secured machine guns and rifles and it was just a matter of time until a civil war would begin. In late June of 1914 Blumenfeld had sent Phillips to Belfast in the north to cover the events. He began sending back articles to London with the first of these appearing in the *Express* on July 2.

Phillips covered the developing conflict reporting the arrival of guns, heavy guns and machine guns; the willingness to have a peaceful solution, but also willingness to have a war; and the stockpiling of cartridges as well as food.

Phillips appears to have been more on the side of the Ulster group. This is perhaps not surprising given his Protestant background from Brownsville's Methodist Episcopal Church. One of the leaders of the Ulster group wrote later:

> There were many newspaper representatives in Belfast, who were always on the lookout for news. It was very difficult to be always on guard, but I quickly perceived that one man stood out head and shoulders over the rest, who could be trusted not prematurely to report, if asked not to, and not to exaggerate, distort or deliberately misrepresent. Percival Phillips was his name . . . On one occasion I accidentally "let out" that there was to be a march of the UVF, with fixed bayonets, through the streets of Belfast on the following Saturday, as a direct reply to the Government's threats. I asked Phillips not to report what he had heard. He respected my wishes.[189]

The man later gave Phillips tips on when gunrunning had taken place.

During the 1914 events Phillips was the only representative of the *Daily Express* in Ireland and he was in competition with the *Daily Mail*, which had sent nearly 200 correspondents to cover the situation developing. Lord Northcliffe, owner of the *Daily Mail* and an Irishman by birth, was determined to scoop the other newspapers and he spared no expense in an attempt to do this.

Phillips found all of this unbelievable. He wrote to Blumenfeld referring to the incredible business as the "Northcliffe Nightmare" and "an orgy of expense." He mentioned that the *Daily Mail* had purchased two motor boats and a yacht, but out of concern that these might not be sufficient Northcliffe had then bought a seagoing tug in Glasgow. To get around on land the *Mail* staff had purchased a Rolls Royce and a Mercedes in England and had them shipped over to Belfast with chauffeurs to drive each of them. He added that they had also purchased three Ford automobiles locally. One gets the

---

[189] F.P. Crozier, *Impressions and Recollections*, London: T. Werner Laurie, Ltd., 1930, pp. 151-152.

Dispatches from the World

impression that Phillips was always trying to be frugal with his expense and these actions were nearly beyond his comprehension.[190]

Of course the potential war in Ireland during the summer of 1914 did not really develop because of the events taking place on the Continent. Two weeks after Phillips' letter to Blumenfeld he was called back from Belfast and sent to Belgium. The situation in Ireland seemed to calm down, but the calm was more apparent than real.

Less than two years later, on Easter Monday, April 24, 1916, a group of nationalists began a revolution in Dublin. The rebels seized control of the post office and declared Ireland to be an independent state. A new government was created: the government of the Irish Republic.

British forces arrived and began to take over control of the area on Tuesday the 25th. There were street fights over the next couple of days, but by the 29th the British had the situation under control. Their victory was only temporary because in 1921 the Irish Free State, later the Republic of Ireland, was created which incorporated most of the island except for Northern Ireland, which remained under British administration.

The unrest in Ireland was not new as the events of 1913 and 1914 reveal, nor was it unexpected. There had been a general uneasiness in Ireland prior to the beginning of the Great War in 1914 and one could say that Britain was at war with Ireland before it was at war with Germany. But as one writer has noted the little war was pushed to the background by the big war. The British concern now was that if the revolution was successful then an independent Ireland might align itself with Germany. The British could not allow that to happen.

Phillips received a pass from GHQ in France on April 30 of 1916. He left British GHQ and was back in England on May 1. He took a train from Euston in London to Hollyhead on the Welsh coast, where he stayed two nights waiting for a way to cross over to Ireland. On May 3 a British destroyer took Phillips and several other correspondents across to Dublin.

---

[190] Letter, Percival Phillips to R,D. Blumenfeld, July 14, 1914, The United Kingdom Parliamentary Archives, London, BLU/I/1//PHI. 3-6.

William R. Black

After arriving in Ireland, Phillips was quartered in a small hotel across the street from the Northwestern Railway Station in Dublin. Along with him were Wilbur Forrest of United Press, Robert Barry of the Associated Press, James Tuohy, London correspondent of the New York *World*, Arthur S. Draper, London correspondent of the New York *Tribune*, and one of Phillips' colleagues from the Western Front, Percival Gibbons. The group was constantly under fire so it is difficult to understand how they were able to report anything. They were completely surrounded by rebels. Forrest wrote:

> Under these conditions we found it impossible to penetrate into the central part of the city, though we naturally made the effort to gather material for eyewitness stories of the revolt. Then, too, we were obliged to realize that it would be virtually impossible to communicate what we might write even though we should produce copy. Consequently, the first day was spent in observing the immediate neighborhood of the hotel. [191]

Later Phillips described the prisoners being moved through the streets of Dublin to the jail. "The people in the street watched the prisoners pass without any demonstration, save that an old woman spat at them and called them 'dirty dogs.'" He continued:

> Not until this morning were the accredited correspondents who came to Ireland last Thursday morning permitted to see anything of the besieged districts . . . Thus the information included in the following summary of damage done is the first based on personal observation. [192]

He then proceeded to describe the damage in the various streets and districts of Dublin.

---

[191] Wilbur Forrest, *Behind the Front Page. Stories of Newspaper Stories in the Making*, New York: D. Appleton-Century Company, Inc., 1934.

[192] Percival Phillips, "Scenes of Ruin in Dublin." *Daily Express*, May 2, 1916.

Dispatches from the World

On the following day Phillips watched the prisoners from the uprising being loaded onto a ship for England.

> I stood on the gangway and watched each drawn face passing under the glare of an electric lamp. They were extraordinary studies in defiance and despair. The tallyman on deck checked his recorder, and at every fiftieth man halted the procession for a moment. The fifty-first would pull up sharply, look around him with sudden apprehension in his eyes, and then, with his head bent forward, wait for what might happen. He did not know how near he might be to the firing party he expected to encounter at the end of his journey. His look was not exactly one of fear, but there was hopelessness in it, and you could see the quick bracing of his tired muscles. It was the look of a man who considered himself already on the brink of the grave. [193]

After the conflict was under control there was the problem of courts martial for the rebellion's leaders, finding the bodies of the dead and burying them, and providing food for those in Dublin, where commercial life had come to a halt. [194]

Phillips returned to Europe and submitted a story about the battle known as Vimy Ridge. It was a late filing since he was in the process of returning from Ireland when the battle took place.

The details are sketchy, but it would appear that Phillips once again became quite ill with symptoms resembling influenza, not unlike those he encountered during the 1911 durbar. Most likely this was in late May after his return from Ireland, but prior to the Somme offensive of July 1916. On July 1, 1916, we know that the dispatch for the *Daily Express* was filed by John Irvine, who had been sent to Europe to take Phillips' place. According to records at the Imperial War Museum in England, Phillips was taken to Etaples in the rear on June 25, where he received some treatment, although it seems likely

---

[193] Percival Phillips, "The Prison Ship," *Daily Express*, May 3, 1916, p. 1, 5.
[194] Percival Phillips, "Search for the Dead. Rebel Casualties Still an Unknown Number. 3,000 Prisoners," *Daily Express*, May 4, 1916.

that he was ill for some time before that. Etaples, on the coast, was where most of the ill, wounded and injured were taken. He did not remain there; he was next sent to England and taken to the 3rd London General Hospital at Wandsworth, formerly a school for orphaned girls, which had been converted into a hospital for the duration of the war. The *Daily Express* said he was in England recovering from a serious illness. [195] There is nothing to indicate that he was wounded. Assuming that he had something in the nature of influenza, then plenty of rest and trying to build up his strength would be the logical next steps in his treatment once the major symptoms were gone. In late June Phillips was staying at the Savage Club and in mid July he was at the Royal Bath Hotel in Bournemouth, on England's southern coast. He was by this time anxious to get back to the action.

Phillips felt well enough by the middle of July to return to his reporting on the Western Front and he wrote to Blumenfeld and requested permission to do this. Blumenfeld was not so sure that he was healthy enough to return to his duties. He wrote back to Phillips asking him how he actually was. His concern was that Phillips would get back to the stress of the front and "crock up." At the same time he viewed Phillips as his best and most reliable reporter at the front and one can imagine the conflict he had in deciding what to do. He could okay the return to the front, but if Phillips became ill again he might possibly be out for quite some time. It was clear that Blumenfeld was not that pleased with Phillips replacement, John Irvine. In a letter to Phillips, he mentioned that Irvine was "driving nails in his coffin."[196]

Blumenfeld and Phillips were good friends in spite of their editor-reporter roles. During the war years Blumenfeld would travel over to the British headquarters in France to visit with Phillips and members of the British General Staff. On such occasions he would take along a bottle of cognac or a box of cigars for Phillips. The editor clearly liked the material he was receiving from his war correspondent. Nevertheless, Blumenfeld withheld his permission for Phillips to return to the front until early August. He seemed to be genuinely concerned about Phillips' health.

---

[195] Martin J. Farrar, *News From the Front*, Phoenix Mill, UK: Sutton Publishing, 1998; *Daily Express*, September 11, 1916.

[196] Letter, Ralph David Blumenfeld to Percival Phillips, July 14, 1916. Sir Percival Phillips Album, ID Number: 99/54/1, 9066, Imperial War Museum Collections, London.

Dispatches from the World

Once Blumenfeld gave his permission for Phillips to return to the front, there were technical glitches of one sort or another and he did not get back to the Continent and the press chateau until September 5. His first major article appeared on September 11 and carried the following message at its beginning:

> *Readers of the "Daily Express" will be pleased to learn of the return of our special correspondent, Mr. Percival Phillips, to the British front. Mr. Phillips has just recovered from a serious illness incurred during the execution of his duties with our armies in the field.* [197]

The article that followed concerned the taking of Guillemont and it is one of the major articles that Phillips wrote about the war in 1916.

In the meantime Annie Phillips had become nervous about her correspondent son. He may not have told her of his illness. Even if he had, he had moved from France to the London hospital to various other addresses and her mail was having a difficult time finding him. She wrote to the *Daily Express* and David H. Cain, a journalist who worked for Blumenfeld, responded to her letter.

After receiving a second letter from Annie, Cain sent off a letter to Phillips in November of 1916 and enclosed Annie's second letter. Cain had explained to Annie that the mail was taking a little longer than usual and that this was the reason she had not heard from Phillips. It is not clear if Annie was aware of the fact that Phillips had been ill and Cain makes no mention of this in the letter to Phillips. Annie had mentioned that the general attitude in America with regard to the war in Europe was changing and Cain saw this as a positive development.[198]

Phillips' responses to his mother's letters are unknown, but given his general attitude toward her and the way in which he tended to treat her, he most likely wrote and apologized for any concern he might have caused her.

---

[197] Percival Phillips, "How Our Men Took Guillemont, *Daily Express*, September 11, 1916, p. 1.

[198] Letter, David H. Cain to Percival Phillips, November 16, 1916. Sir Percival Phillips Album, ID Number: 99/54/1, 9066, Imperial War Museum Collections, London.

CHAPTER 14

back to the front

For the most part being away from the demands of preparing daily columns had been a good thing for Phillips' writing and the articles he began to write had a new freshness that was missing from earlier pieces. By the fall of 1916 he had seen more than two years of the war and it is quite possible that he wrote some of the material that appeared shortly after he returned when he was recuperating. The writing seems less hurried.

Phillips wrote about the preparation for battle:

> The tense calm of the last hour before battle leaves an unforgettable impression. The preparations are finished. Everything is ready for the dawn. Expectant infantry crowd the forward trenches, rehearsing their final orders and locking home their bayonets; gunners pace idly beside their batteries, fingering their watches; empty dressing-stations put out neat piles of bandages, and skillful surgeons wait to mend the wounds of men which are still unhurt. The stage is set for the great drama, and silence, heavy and oppressive, hangs over the waiting army in the field.[199]

It is impossible to cover the war here as Phillips covered it. That would take volumes, and volumes have been dedicated to telling

---
[199] Percival Phillips, "Before the Battle," *Daily Express*, September 18, 1916.

the story of the Western Front. A conservative estimate would be that Phillips wrote a million words in his columns during the war. We can give a little attention to his writing. Phillips was generally not viewed as a literary writer, but more of a reporter in the strict sense of writing down precisely what he observed. However, some of his writing had more of a literary style. In particular, the writing that Phillips did in the last two years of the war is some of his best.

In January of 1917 following a snowfall he wrote:

> The snow has changed everything. It has shrouded the bones of dead villages and blotted out the debris strewn across the countryside in the wake of a beaten army. Trenches, ice-encrusted craters, crumbling dug-outs, broken labyrinths of rusted wire, shattered stumps of woods are overlaid with a thick mantle of white. The battlefield we know has disappeared. Even the giant howitzers and a stray derelict tank are disguised beyond recognition. The little wayside cemeteries are buried deep in the drifts piled up by the restless wind. The roads are polished glass beneath their treacherous covering, and the heavy lorries crawl carefully over them with their loads of food for the men and guns. [200]

He described the battlefield on another occasion without snow and saw a much more catastrophic scene.

> Ruin, utter ruin everywhere. Bits of brick and mortar, heaved into formless masses; gaping holes and new mounds of earth; dead men in grey, twisted machine guns, powdered concrete, broken rifles, howitzers tilted at impossible angles, blackened tree stumps, bent rails, and splintered timber. Chaos and appalling desolation. The picture cannot be imagined. The earth is convulsed and dead. [201]

---

[200] Percival Phillips, "Snow," *Daily Express*, January 12, 1917, p. 1.

[201] Percival Phillips, "Shambles," *Chicago Daily Tribune*, April 12, 1917, p. 5.

Dispatches from the World

On another occasion he described the preparations for a major battle. The British had actually constructed a model of the area where the attack would take place.

> The battle itself was rehearsed bit by bit. The infantrymen who followed the equally well trained artillerymen's barrage this morning had been drilled for their journey by practice trips far from the scene that left nothing to chance. They had a wonderful model of the ridge covering more than an acre of ground and true in every detail of contour and adornment—which could be studied for hours.[202]

On another occasion rain threatened to delay a major attack planned by the British in August of 1917. He wrote about this as well.

> The weather changed for the worse last night, although fortunately too late to hamper the execution of our plans. The rain was heavy and constant throughout the night. It was still beating down steadily when the day broke chill and cheerless, with a thick blanket of mist completely shutting off the battlefield. During the morning it slackened to a dismal drizzle, but by this time the roads, fields, and footways were covered with semi-liquid mud, and the torn ground beyond Ypres had become in places a horrible quagmire.
>
> It was pretty bad in the opinion of the weary soldiers who came back with wounds, but it was certainly worse for the enemy holding fragments of broken lines still heavily hammered by artillery and undoubtedly disheartened by the hardships of a wet night in the open after a day of defeat.[203]

---

[202] Percival Phillips, "Wytschaete, Messines and Other Formidable Positions Stormed. The Earth Rocking for Miles," *Daily Express*, June 8, 1917.

[203] Percival Phillips, "Dramatic Features of the Great Battle," *Daily Express*, August 2, 1917.

Phillips noted the muddy fields where the battles took place on several occasions. On one day, also in August of 1917, he wrote:

> I talked today with a number of wounded men engaged in the fighting in Langemarck and beyond, and they are unanimous in declaring that the enemy infantry made a very poor show wherever they were deprived of their supporting machine guns and forced to choose between meeting a bayonet charge and flight. The mud was our men's greatest grievance. It clung to their legs at every step. Frequently they had to pause to pull their comrades from the treacherous mire, figures embedded to the waist, some of them trying to fire their rifles at a spitting machine gun and yet, despite these almost incredible difficulties, they saved each other and fought the Hun through the floods to Langemarck. [204]

Phillips was very impressed with the new technology of war on the Western Front. This was the use of tanks and aircraft. He wrote about the former during the spring of 1918.

> For the first time British and German tanks have met in battle, and the victory is ours. They fought yesterday in the open fields round Villers-Brettonneux, east of Amiens, where the enemy made a determined and, for the moment, a successful attack on that town and high ground round it.
>
> The German tanks led the attack, swinging on the town from the north-east and from the south, and in their wake came infantry with their machine guns and heavy mortars and light artillery.

---

[204] Percival Phillips, "Victory in Mud. Germans Bitterly Punished by Our Guns. Fights in Cellars at Langemarck," *Daily Express*, August 17, 1917.

Although there were four or five tanks they were bulky, ungainly creatures, quite unlike the British tank in appearance, with a broad, squat turret containing quick-firing guns. Hidden in the thick mist until very close to our trenches, they crawled up in the wake of an intense barrage about six o'clock in the morning.

They concentrated their guns on one British tank, but others came to the rescue, and in the brief duel that followed one enemy tank was put out of action by an opponent of less bulk and lighter armament and the others scuttled away.

The lesson of this first engagement between German and British tanks seems to be that we have nothing to fear from the enemy despite the greater size and armament of his machine. The crews plainly showed their unwillingness to stand when invited to fight out to a finish. [205]

Some of Phillips' columns include descriptions of individuals who performed nearly super human feats. One of these involved a wounded officer, who captured several Germans and ordered them to carry him back to his lines as his prisoners. Another story concerned a young man who captured twenty of the enemy soldiers. This borders on propaganda, but one cannot say these events did not occur as described.

In the July of 1917 the King and Queen of England came over to the Western Front to visit the troops as well as the correspondents. In a letter to Blumenfeld, Phillips wrote that he had not mentioned in any of his articles that the King had formally received the correspondents since it seemed like bragging. In addition, the King would literally receive hundreds of people on such visits and he did not think it would be proper to mention the correspondents and not all the others. He did think that perhaps Gibbs had mentioned it in one of his articles.

---

[205] Percival Phillips, "Battle of the Tanks. First Fleet Action Won by British. One Enemy Machine Disabled," *Daily Express*, April 26, 1918.

Phillips mentioned that he and Gibbs had been presented to the King first since they were present at the beginning of his tour of the front. After he noticed Phillips ribbon from the Coronation Durbar, the King chatted with him about that event in India six years earlier. The King also said that he could not imagine putting in a full day observing the war and then writing about it before the day ended. He mentioned the death of Serge Basset, a well-known French war correspondent attached to the British General Headquarters, who had died from rifle fire two weeks earlier near Lens. Phillips was also impressed that the King had first received the French correspondents since they were in France.[206]

The United States entered the war in the spring of 1917, but by the end of the year less than 200,000 troops had arrived in Europe. In time U.S. troop strength would reach more than four million. Apparently Phillips was unaware that the American troops had seen combat early in the spring of 1918. He wrote the following in July:

> Vaire Wood and the battered village of Hamel, on the green slopes above the Somme, will find a place in American history, for there, in the dawn of Independence-day, British troops and soldiers of the Republic fought side by side for the first time and died together in the cause of freedom.[207]

Phillips continued:

> The American boys who came back wounded from Hamel and Vaire Wood do not try to tell you that it was their battle. They are modest—painfully modest and self-depreciative. They say: "It was an Australian show, and we were allowed to take part." Nevertheless, they are very proud of having made prisoners and killed Germans; proud of their own wounds, like the youthful corporal who has three but is able to set off

---

[206] Letter, Percival Phillips to Ralph David Blumenfeld, July 14, 1917. The United Kingdom Parliamentary Archives, London, BLU/1/17/PHI. 7-10.

[207] Percival Phillips, "How the Americans 'Made Good'", *Daily Express*, July 6, 1918.

seven dead Germans against them—two Germans for each wound and one to spare.

Their first battle involved them in all the phases of fighting so familiar to Australians and other British troops—the resistance of isolated machine-gun groups, the attacks by hidden bombers, and the sudden reappearance of enemy infantry from dug-outs after they had passed.

The majority of the Americans who took part in the attack are from the Middle West and North-West. The wounded I saw today, who had been through Vaire Wood and Hamel village, were from Chicago. All of them confess that the escorting barrage was beyond their wildest conception of artillery fire.

They went forward very determinedly, very seriously, each man with the consciousness that he might never come back, but determined, nevertheless, to "make good" before he died. One boy related quite simply this morning as he lay on his cot in a canvas tent, wrapped in bandages and pallid after a night of pain, how he and his pals of a certain platoon shook hands and said good-bye before they "went over the top" and moved forward with the same words shouted at each other, "Make good." You can imagine that little ceremony at night under the stars in the sinister calm that is the prelude to battle—these farmers' lads and city-bred boys of the Middle West, most of whom had never seen a man die, none of whom had taken a human life, set suddenly in the midst of the infernal machinery of modern war, saying farewell to each other as they might say goodnight at home, thinking only of their honour and their country. [208]

---

[208] Ibid.

One gets the impression that H.A. Gwynne, the editor of *The Morning Post*, had received some complaints about Percival's coverage of the war from Lady Bathurst, owner of *The Morning Post*, and that she had suggested more attention should be paid to the British troops fighting on the Western Front. Gwynne responded by letter on October 17, 1918:

> With regard to Percival Phillips. We do call the tune, and when I was out in France I had a long talk with him. He is not very expensive, and I told him there was too much Australians [sic] about his stuff and that he did not pay enough attention to what our own people are doing. He explained to me that that is not altogether his fault. I think it arises from the fact that Douglas Haig thinks that this war gives him an opportunity not merely of beating the Boche, but also cementing the Empire, and he is inclined to think that the best way of doing so is to boom the Australians and Canadians, I had a long talk with him also on the subject, and I told him people were beginning to feel it very strongly. I see a great improvement now. On the occasion in question the Australians really did remarkably well and you must remember that the Censorship does not always leave a free hand to the correspondent. You will have noticed the improvement.[209]

Following the armistice of November 11, 1918, Phillips was back in Belgium. On that occasion he wrote:

> Just at eleven I came into the little town of Leuze, which had been one of the headquarters nearest the uncertain front. From the windows of all the houses round about, and even from the roofs, the

---

[209] Letter: H.A. Gwyne to Lady Bathurst, 4 October 1917, in Keith Wilson (ed.), *The Rasp of War: The Letters of H.A. Gwynne to The Countess Bathurst, 1914-1918*, London: Sidgwick & Jackson, 1989.

Chateau Rollancourt, 1918
(front row is Perry Robinson, Percival Phillips with dog, and Henry Nevinson, Beach Thomas is sitting behind Nevinson and Frederic Palmer is standing at the far right) James Nisbet & Company, Ltd.

inhabitants looked down on the troops and heard uncomprehendingly the words of the Colonel as he read from a sheet of paper the order that ended hostilities.

A trumpeter sounded the "stand fast." In the narrow high-street at one end of the little square were other troops moving slowly forward, and as the notes of the bugle rose clear and crisp above the rumble of the gun—carriages these men turned with smiles of wonder and delight and shouted to each other "The war's over."

> The band played "God Save the King." None heard it without a quiver of emotion. The mud-stained troops paused in the crowded street, the hum of traffic was stilled. A rippling cheer was drowned in the first notes of the Belgium hymn; the "Marseillaise" succeeded it, and the army of each ally was thus saluted in turn. I do not think that any one heard the few choked words of the old mayor when he tried to voice the thanks of Belgium for this day of happiness. [210]

Frederick Palmer, an American, was attached to the accredited correspondents for a brief period of time. He stated "those whose business it was to observe, the six correspondents, Robinson, Thomas, Gibbs, Phillips, Russell and myself, went and came always with a sense of incapacity and sometimes with a feeling that writing was a worthless business when others were fighting."[211] Other correspondents also expressed this attitude from time to time. Some did not think they were worthy of the special treatment they received while others seemed to want to pick up a rifle and 'do their part.' As noted previously Valentine and Douglas Williams did exactly this; they stopped being correspondents and enlisted in the British army. There are no indications that Phillips thought he should pick up a rifle and join the conflict. He was perfectly content to cover the war as an observer and journalist, not as a participant.

Phillips was with the British forces when they entered Germany at the end of the war. He wrote in his dispatch to London that day:

> In Germany at last!
> British lancers and dragoons, streaming through the high street of Malmedy, sabres drawn and pennons stiff in the winter wind; horse guns clattering past the cobble-stoned marketplace led by a great Union Jack; heavy wagons and cyclists and staff cars

---

[210] Percival Phillips, "The Army Carries On. One Moments Emotion at the Front," *Daily Express*, November 12, 1918.

[211] Frederick Palmer, *My Second Year of the War*, New York: Dodd, Mead & Company, 1917, p. 226.

> passing through a silent curious crowd; shaven heads bared reluctantly to the 'contemptible little British Army'; furtive scowls partially countered by a few faint bleak smiles of conciliation; stern faces peering through half drawn blinds; gleeful children chided by apprehensive women and sullen men glowering at the troopers from their doorways—such is my impression of our entry into the first Prussian town within the British zone of occupation. [212]

Phillips had been with the Belgian forces early in the war and for the most part remained there until the fall of Antwerp. A couple of days after the entry into Malmedy, he was entering Germany with them. He wrote in one of his columns about their entrance into Aix-la-Chapelle (today Aachen, Germany).

> When the Belgium advance guard entered Aix a proclamation appeared on public buildings—strangely reminiscent of another military occupation. The inhabitants were ordered to remain indoors between seven in the evening and five in the morning—Belgian time; to furnish ten hostages; to salute all officers in public places. Cafés and amusement resorts in the city were closed until further orders, unauthorized ingress and egress were prohibited, and public meetings were declared unlawful. The German mark was written down to seven pence. Many other regulations were laid down for the conduct of the people of Aix.
>
> A man stopped beside me as I read the proclamation in Prinz Freidrich Platz this morning, and when I finished he said to me: "It is what we did in Belgium. We have nothing to complain of."

---

[212] Percival Phillips, "Our Army in Prussia," *Daily Express*, December 4, 1918, p. 1.

> That is it exactly. The people of Aix are under martial law as defined by their own war makers, for the proclamation issued by the Belgian Governor is an exact translation of those put up in Belgian towns by the German authorities. [213]

---

[213] Percival Phillips, "Hats Off in Aix. Prussians Made to Taste Their Own Medicine. Belgium's Turn," *Daily Express*, December 6, 1918, p. 1.

CHAPTER 15

war's end and its aftermath

On December 16, 1918, ten days after his proclamation piece appeared in the *Daily Express*, Phillips was in Cologne. It was a cold, damp day, made tolerable by the finality that brought him and three of the other accredited correspondents there. He, along with Philip Gibbs, Perry Robinson, and Beach Thomas were in Cologne to receive the appreciation of Field Marshall Douglas Haig, Commander-in-Chief of the British Armies for most of the war. They were not the only ones being recognized: other British, Allied, neutral, and American correspondents were also there. Haig made a short speech and then presented each of the correspondents with a Union Jack, according to *The Times*.[214] One may have the impression of a large flag, but the reality is that the flags given were of the type that small children might hold and wave along a parade route.

Beach Thomas did the write-up of the event for *The Times*. He also had a photograph taken of the four accredited correspondents standing on the Hohenzollern Bridge across the Rhine at Cologne. The photograph appeared in his book, *A Traveller in News*,[215] in 1925. Later in the day Phillips walked along the sidewalk that bordered the Rhine carrying his camera. He paused alongside two naval photographers and the three took photographs of General Haig.

---

[214] "Parting Gift to War Correspondents," *The Times*, December 18, 1919, p. 9.
[215] Sir William Beach Thomas, *A Traveller in News*, London: Chapman and Hall, 1925.

Correspondents at the Hohenzollern Bridge with Cologne Cathedral in the background, December 16, 1918. Left to right are Percival Phillips, Perry Robinson, Philip Gibbs, and Beach Thomas, (Chapman and Hall, Ltd.).

On June 30 of 1919 Phillips wrote a piece for the *Daily Express* entitled "Our Army As I Have Seen It." [216] It is an article that praises the British armies that were on the ground in Europe during the war. He wrote that what he saw from these troops was continual optimism that they would prevail, and their blindness to any possibility of ultimate defeat.

---

[216] Percival Phillips, "Our Army as I Have Seen It," *Daily Express*, June 30, 1919.

Dispatches from the World

For months during 1917 and early 1918 Phillips' articles would usually be found in the very center of the front page of the *Daily Express*. But as the war came to a close in the fall of 1918 his articles began to slip to the back pages of the newspaper. He was a war correspondent, it was a label that he enjoyed, but it also implied some type of a back bench position once there was no war to report. There had been other times during the war when naval battles dominated the news, but even at those times he was rarely squeezed off the front page. It is hard to say exactly how he felt about this, but more than likely he was able to cope with it.

Phillips remained on the Continent until July of 1919 as part of the Army of the Rhine, returning to London on the 4th. He was welcomed back by staff at the *Daily Express*, who wrote they were "proud to be his colleagues." [217] The newspaper ran a piece about his accomplishments, while at the same time taking credit for some of what he had done. They wrote:

> More than half of his forty years have been spent on the battlefields of the world, and during eighteen of those strenuous years he has given millions of "Daily Express" readers vivid clear-cut pen pictures of war and the happenings which stir continents.
>
> From the earliest days of the war Percival Phillips' despatches established a reputation for soundness of judgment, intelligent anticipation, absolute reliability, and brilliant literary style.
>
> His passion for accuracy, amazing grip of detail, and deep understanding of the meaning of the movement of battle enabled Phillips, of the "Daily Express," to assemble from the intricate mass of jig-saw pieces of information pouring in from many points of the battle line a finished picture—a masterpiece of war dispatch.

---

[217] "Mr. Percival Phillips. Return of the Famous War Correspondent." *Daily Express*, July 5, 1919.

> During the first weeks of the war it is known that the British GHQ in France turned to Phillips' despatches as the quickest and surest means of gaining reliable information regarding the movements of German troops at the front—a remarkable tribute to the accuracy of the Daily Express. [218]

There are writers today who take issue with the way in which Phillips and the other accredited correspondents reported the war. They are blamed for not being honest and for misleading the populace back in England about the war and its progress. This fails to recognize the environment of the readers or the correspondents. If you lived in England from 1914 through 1918 you knew how the war was progressing. Your sons, brothers and father or the sons, brothers and fathers of your neighbors were dying in the war. The wounded were being returned to England and walking (if they could) on the same streets as you. The daily newspaper listed the number and names of the casualties—killed, missing and wounded.

As for the correspondents' situation during the war, whatever they wrote had to be approved by the censors or it would never see the printer's ink. Valentine Williams noted that while he was at the St. Omer press chateau he was not to write about: the strength, composition or location of forces, the movement of troops and operations, the state of supply and transport, the casualties, important orders, criticisms and eulogies of a personal nature, or the morale of troops. [219] The British General Staff was also reluctant to have the correspondents write about the darker side of the war for fear of its impact back home.

So while the accredited correspondents were quite capable of writing about what they observed, the various rules, regulations and dictates prevented them from doing this. They saw eager young men moving forward, anxious to face the challenge of combat and test their manhood, but at the same time there were others moving to the rear with the look of death in their eyes from having been

---

[218] Ibid.
[219] Valentine Williams, *World of Action*, Boston: Houghton Mifflin Company, 1938, p. 274.

Dispatches from the World

at the front for far too long. The correspondents were there on pleasant days with birds chirping in a nearby wood as troops moved forward, but just as often the artillery had frightened away the birds and the roads to the front were deep in dust, which surrounded the troops with clouds of the same. On other days the roads had turned into mud pools caused by days of rain and too much traffic and the boots of the replacements sank into the deep mud that was once the road. The troops sometimes moved forward in a peaceful and tranquil solitary line on a road leading to the front, but just as often the road was congested with ambulances or trucks loaded with armaments and supplies moving to the areas of combat. They would see the injured and the dead returning from what was now their destination and soon would be the destination of their replacements. After the use of mustard gas, there would be long lines of injured soldiers, eyes bandaged, following each other in a single file, a hand resting on the shoulder of the man in front of him, each leading the man behind him toward the rear. If the troops were moving through lands that had already been contested, there were the shattered remnants of trees, appearing to be upright bundles of sticks without binding, not looking much like trees since all had been shelled, and off the road to the right or left there would be the occasional dead horse or mule, bloated in the heat of summer or covered by the snow of winter. But the correspondents were not to write of such things.

Once at the front the soldiers were in the trenches, perhaps those built by the unit they replaced, or just as likely those built earlier by their enemy. Trenches were gained and lost in the battles. These were foul places with rats scurrying quickly from one area to the next. There were odors of human waste. Then there was the stench of the dead. Bodies were always collected and moved to the rear, unless they laid in the contested "no man's land," but shelling is not kind to the human body, and parts were always left behind for the rodents. But these things too were not to be written about by the correspondents either.

So was it right for the military to censor what was being written? In time of war it is almost mandatory. The telegraph made it extremely fast for the outcome of battles to get to the newspapers, but it could also get to your enemies almost as quickly. So censorship was necessary. The Great War of 1914 did not start the censoring of correspondents as some have suggested. Phillips encountered this in Greece, Turkey, Japan, Russia, and the Balkans prior to 1914. Before the arrival of the telegraph in areas of combat, censorship was not necessary, it would take a horse and rider to relay information and these were slow enough that censorship could be kept to a minimum.

Of course today the telegraph has been surpassed by numerous innovations that facilitate audio and visual communication. Even the least developed parts of the world today have an abundance of cell phones and these, as well as the internet and its social networks, have made censorship obsolete, but it was viewed as necessary in the 1914-1918 war. It more than likely was.

But what of the non-strategic news? Once again the British General Staff thought if someone painted an accurate picture of the war and what the troops had to endure, it would turn the populace back in England against the war, and they were probably right. So this also had to be censored from their point of view. But this was not the fault of the accredited correspondents.

Was this the type of "war correspondent" that the young Percival had wanted to be? Probably not. His dream was to wonder into a remote telegraph office and send in his story. There was nothing in that dream about running it by a censor first. But the world of MacGahan and Forbes was gone. Things would never be the way they were during wars of the late 1800s again. Phillips realized this and tried to do the best job that he could under the circumstances that prevailed.

Following his arrival back in England, Phillips took a break from reporting for the better part of July 1919. He knew what was coming and that was an official tour of Canada followed by his "unofficial" tour of parts of the United States. On August 5 the Prince of Wales (later King Edward VIII) sailed out of Portsmouth for a voyage that would take him to Canada, and Phillips was onboard covering the trip for the *Daily Express*. As usual the Prince of Wales was on the *H.M.S. Renown* for the trip across the Atlantic. Another vessel accompanied them; it was a light cruiser, the *H.M.S. Dragon*. The *Renown* arrived at Conception Bay, Newfoundland on August 11. The shorter voyage

Dispatches from the World

to St. John, New Brunswick was on the *Dragon* and it arrived there on August 15. Aside from these two cities the Canadian tour included Ottawa, Toronto, Montreal, Winnipeg, and Vancouver.

The purpose of this and several other tours after the war was so that the Prince of Wales could tell members of the new British Commonwealth that they were now equals with Great Britain, and to thank them for their participation in the war. [220]

Phillips accompanied the Prince of Wales on this and several other tours. It couldn't have been for the pressing news value of the tour, because there was very little of this. Perhaps Phillips just liked being in the presence of royalty. He filed a couple of articles: the Prince's hand became disabled from all the handshakes, a group of girls attacked his car (apparently anxious to become part of the royal family), the Prince visited a deep shaft silver mine in Ontario, the Prince became an honorary Indian chief of the Six Nations, but these articles were hardly consistent with the writings of a man who had spent four and one-half years reporting the events of the Great War. [221] Perhaps the assignment was a relief after that experience.

Phillips was with the Prince most of the time, but he also took advantage of the proximity to go and visit his mother in Brownsville. Around the third week of October he telephoned her to let her know he would be by for a visit near the end of the month. [222] He wanted to inform her that he was to receive an honor from the French government in recognition of his work as a correspondent during the war. [223]

In late October Phillips left the Prince of Wales tour and went to Pittsburgh. He visited with several of his friends from his reporting days in that city. His former colleagues with the various Pittsburgh newspapers had invited him to attend a luncheon at the Pittsburgh

---

[220] Prince of Wales, "Address by His Royal Highness the Prince of Wales at the Empire Club, November 4, 1919," *The Empire Club of Canada Speeches 1919*, Toronto: Empire Club of Canada, 1920, pp. 384-391.

[221] Percival Phillips, "Prince of the Magic Smile," *Daily Express*, August 30, 1919, p. 1; Percival Phillips, "Prince a Victim of 'Grip,'" *Daily Express*, September 1, 1919, p. 1; Percival Phillips, "A Kiss for the Prince," *Daily Express*, September 4, p. 1; Percival Phillips, "The Prince in a Silver Mine," *Daily Express*, October 17, 1919; Percival Phillips, "The Prince's Indian Dance," *Daily Express*, October 22, 1919.

[222] "Got His Early Training in the Valley," *Charleroi Mail*, October 22, 1919.

[223] Untitled, *Charleroi Mail*, November 12, 1919.

Press Club on the 30th of October as the guest of honor. He did attend and after that he went to Brownsville to see his mother. About the middle of November he left for New York where he boarded the *Caronia* for the trip back to England. He arrived at Plymouth on November 21.

While in America it was announced that Phillips would receive the Cross of the Legion of Honor from the government of France "for valuable services during the Great War." [224] This would make him a Chevalier of the Order. The other four accredited correspondents also received the honor. Receiving the recognition involved Phillips going by the French embassy back in London and having the French Ambassador, Monsieur Cambon, making a little speech, followed by his pinning the cross to Phillips chest and the traditional French kiss on both cheeks. There would be no audience, and it is not known if anyone attended the brief ceremony with Phillips.

Following the war, Phillips service on the Western Front was also recognized by the British government. He was awarded the 1914-1915 Star Medal, the British War Medal, and the Victory Medal. He received these in 1921.

The *Daily Express* sent Phillips to the Middle East following his return from the Canadian tour with the Prince of Wales. During this mission he visited Italy, Egypt, Palestine, Syria and Constantinople. Phillips was in Damascus when snow began falling in early February. His dispatch to the *Daily Express* that day began:

> Snow lay thick on the bare brown slopes of Jebel Kasynn when Emir Feisul looked from his bedroom window . . . Muffled half-frozen figures picked their way over treacherous, ice-coated streets; in the bazaars shivering merchants huddled round their braziers of glowing charcoal. The beggar outside the door of my hotel was too benumbed to ask for his morning alms.

---

[224] "Mr. Percival Phillips. Honor for the Famous War Correspondent." *Daily Express*, November 10, 1919, p. 1.

Dispatches from the World

> It is the first snowstorm here in ten years.
>
> All the fascination of Damascus has fled before the gale which sweeps down from Mount Hermon and the barren hills hemming us in on three sides. Sunshine alone—for which all pray devoutly—will bring back its charm.
>
> There is no other city in the East quite like it. Constantinople—Tunis—Cairo—Tripoli—none of them has quite the same atmosphere of mystery and romance as pervades this great nerve centre of the Moslem world. [225]

A few days later Phillips was on a ship en route to Palestine. He was going to Palestine to see the extent of the snow there since snowfalls in that region were very uncommon. Ordinarily a land route would have been chosen, but due to the snow a sea route was selected as probably being safer and faster.

On February 9, Jerusalem received 27 inches of rainfall followed by what many thought would be a brief snow shower. But the snow did not stop for 36 hours and in the end the snow was on average 40 inches deep with drifts up to 10 feet. About forty houses were crushed by the snow and a battalion of Yorkshire troops garrisoned in the city helped them dig out as the city had no snow plows or snow shovels for that matter. [226]

During this same mission Phillips had occasion to be onboard a ship in the Mediterranean off the coast of Jaffa (also Joppa) in Palestine (part of Tel Aviv today). He wrote the following on that occasion:

> From the cheerful saloon to the main deck amidships was a walk of perhaps thirty yards. In such a brief interval I descended into another world.

---

[225] Percival Phillips, "A City of Sinister Charm. Blending the Past and the Present," *Daily Express*, March 5, 1920, by-line February 10.

[226] Otis A. Glazebrook, "Tremendous Snowstorm in Palestine, February 9-11, 1920," *Monthly Weather Review*, 48, 2, February 1920, p. 80.

Unwashed humanity filled the narrow space from bulkhead to bulkhead, and overflowed across the battened hatches. Men, women, children, lay around me, with only a thin blanket between them and the hard deck. The dim light shone on pallid, weary faces; on mothers with children at their breasts; tattered, bearded men of incredible age; young girls huddled together, with arms entwined; tin trunks and perambulators and crazy luggage tied with bits of string. The air was close and foul.

I took a step hesitantly. A mattress seamed to writhe underfoot. A touselled head rose up at my knee, stared questioningly, and sank back into slumber with a sigh. I moved aside—

"Please be careful," said a grave voice in the shadows. "Do not step on the baby."

An old man stirred restlessly and said something in a strange tongue. Another answered him, in the darkness a child cried, frightened by the rattle of the winches. Soothing words came from some one at my feet. What a scene for a painter! The misery and the wretchedness so dimly revealed by the faint yellow lamps seemed no less than a glimpse into the inferno of Dante. Thirty yards away in the cheerful saloon an English girl was playing the latest London waltz.

"They are Jews," said a ship's officer, "poor Jews going home to Palestine."

In the morning sunlight they looked even more miserable and forlorn. They appeared to have been at sea for years, and to have lost all hope of ever reaching port. They still sat or lay in their bits of padded sacking, staring dully at the unpainted deck beams. Occasionally they raked out bits of stale food

Dispatches from the World

from greasy paper parcels and ate them without haste or appetite. The children never smiled. A fragment of a newspaper in Hebrew was read and reread and passed from hand to hand among the younger men. An air of dejection, of meek resignation pervaded these travellers to the Promised Land.

The steamer swung into Jaffa roadstead—which is no more than the open sea. Arab boatmen swarmed around the companion ladder. A soldier in British khaki with the device of the seven branched candlestick—the mark of the Jewish Battalion—on his cap, followed the passport officer aboard. Slowly the pilgrims and their papers were sifted through the examination which admitted them to Palestine.\They went ashore in little boats, tossed about like chips on the long rollers that break against the rockbound coast. The women wept in sheer fright, and some of them collapsed—seasick and inert—at the feet of the native oarsmen. They were hoisted up the steep, slippery steps of the quay. Their tin trunks and perambulators and drenched mattresses were tossed after them. Dazed and bewildered they stood about staring stupidly at the bales of merchandise and crates of oranges and blundering camels. The last I saw of them they were trudging up the steep winding way that leads to the market place of Jaffa.

Such a scene can be witnessed on the arrival of nearly every steamer from Europe at the ports of Jaffa and Haifa. Jewish refugees are streaming back to Palestine after four and a half years' exile. Jewish immigrants—new settlers in the Promised Land—fill the available remaining space in these coastwise ships. They come with dreams of a new Zion which will set them again among the nations of the world. Most of them, I am sure, expect to find their dreams already fulfilled.

> Disillusionment awaits them. They realise, before they have been many days in the land of their fathers, that the claims of Zion are bitterly opposed. They find little sympathy save among their own kind.
>
> For it must be said frankly, the Zionist movement has many bitter enemies. I cannot go deeply now into the reasons for the antipathy, but it will be admitted by everyone who has visited Palestine and the remainder of Syria that the movement to repopulate the country with Jews from other parts of the world has roused great antagonism. It is increasing steadily.
>
> Meanwhile, the ships still come with their cargoes of poor, hopeful pilgrims, who cling to the illusion that they have left all suffering and persecution behind them, and that when they sight the rocky heights about Jerusalem their wanderings and their troubles are for ever ended.[227]

Phillips concludes his piece with "I have no anti-Jewish feeling. I simply state the facts from direct observation."[228] In spite of this proclamation, reading this and other pieces that Phillips wrote suggests that he was anti-Semitic. He may have been, but so was the majority of the Anglo-American world. Freidel has noted with regard to America:

> While there was little of the virulent anti-Semitism in the United States that wracked parts of Europe, there was widespread prejudice, which excluded Jews from some residential neighborhoods, resorts, and clubs, and made it difficult for them to obtain work in some occupations.[229]

---

[227] Percival Phillips, "Returning to the Promised Land. On Board Ship—and After." *Daily Express*, March 22, 1920.

[228] Ibid.

[229] Frank Freidel, *Franklin D. Roosevelt: A Rendezvous with Destiny*, Boston: Little, Brown and Company, 1990, p. 295.

Dispatches from the World

As for the situation in Britain, George Orwell, writing in 1945 noted, "One would then find that though anti-Semitism is sufficiently in evidence now, it is probably less prevalent in England than it was thirty years ago."[230] With regard to the news media, it has been noted that the owners of newspapers such as the *Daily Express* and the *Daily Mail* were either privately or openly anti-Semitic. This had little notable impact on the former newspaper during the first twenty years of R. D. Blumenfeld's term as editor as he was Jewish.

As for Phillips' views on whether it made sense to have Palestine occupied by the Jews, this is open for debate, and it has been debated for decades. He was correct in his interpretation of the mood of Syria and other nations in the region. They opposed this eighty-five years ago as many of them do today.

After his arrival in Jerusalem, Phillips looked up another correspondent, Ernest Smith, and they wandered around the city, with Phillips taking photographs. Two of these were published in a book by Smith. The book was entitled *Fields of Adventure: Some Recollections of Forty Years of Newspaper Life*.[231] The photographs by Phillips were of the Boutmi, the Turkish gallows tree in Jerusalem and the other was of the garden of Gethsamene. Smith notes that tradition had it that as long as the gallows tree stood the Turkish Empire would continue. Branches were torn from the tree by the snowfall, while the partition of Turkey was being discussed in London.

On March 31, 1920, the *Daily Express* published the "war service honors," the list of those to be recognized by the King as knights, dames, and so forth.[232] "Sir Percival Phillips" was mentioned in the various headlines of the article and within the text were the names of the other four accredited war correspondents. In Phillips' case the announcement of the pending knighthood did precede the actual event by several months. This was due to the fact that Phillips was in

---

[230] George Orwell, "Anti-Semitism in Britain," *Contemporary Jewish Record*, April, 1945.

[231] Ernest Smith, *Fields of Adventure: Some Recollections of Forty Years of Newspaper Life*, Boston: Small, Maynard and Company, 1924, p. 88 and p. 116.

[232] "War Service Honors. An Interesting List. 108 New Knights. Sir Percival Phillips, of the 'Daily Express.' Dame Clara Butt." *Daily Express*, March 31, 1920.

Constantinople for the *Daily Express* during the intervening time. He returned to London in September.

Tuesday, October 12 (1920) began with a mist and fog in London that cleared as the day went on. The rain that was a possibility had confined itself to the west over Cornwall and it seemed unlikely it would occur in London. The day was clear when Phillips arrived at Buckingham Palace prior to eleven in the morning.

He was there to receive The Most Excellent Order of the British Empire, more commonly referred to as a knighthood, from the King. Of the five newspaper reporters that were accredited by the British government during the War, the other four—Philip Gibbs of the *Daily Mirror*, W. Henry Thomas of the *Daily Mail*, H. Perry Robinson of the London *Times*, and H.W. Russell of Reuters News Service—had all received their knighthoods. Only Phillips had not.

The recommendation that the five should be so honored had come from the War Office. None of the five knew exactly why. Beach Thomas and Gibbs had discussed the forthcoming knighthood in Groom's Café on Fleet Street in London soon after they heard of it.

Gibbs had said, "What do you think about this knighthood idea? I should like to get out of it."

Beach Thomas had responded, "I wouldn't mind refusing it, but it's too late now, I imagine."

Gibbs' major problem with the knighthood was that he thought there were many other men who deserved the honor far more, but they were not being recognized. [233]

It is not known if Phillips shared these feelings. It seems unlikely. For one who had always loved journalism and who had come to love England, this should have been a very happy occasion. However, it is unlikely that he could avoid thinking of his brother, Smith Phillips.

Nearly a month earlier, on September 25, Smith was injured in an automobile accident. His vehicle collided head-on with a truck near Castle Shannon, a Pittsburgh suburb. The incident itself was reported by the *Pittsburgh Post* and the *Pittsburgh Press*. Two days later the *Press* reported that Smith was in St. Joseph's hospital in Pittsburgh

---

[233] Philip Gibbs, *The Pageant of the Years: An Autobiography*, London: William Heinemann Ltd., 1946, p. 244.

"in critical condition with a fractured skull." They further noted that he had not recovered consciousness since the accident.[234] On Friday, October 8, 1920, he died while still in the Pittsburgh hospital.[235] His funeral in Brownsville occurred on Sunday, two days before Phillips was to be awarded the knighthood.

After Phillips' arrival at Buckingham Palace in top hat and a tail coat, he was coached on the procedure that would be followed. When his turn came, he knelt with one knee on a velvet cushion and held his top hat in one hand as the King approached him. He was touched on the shoulder with a sword, received a silver star, which was affixed to his coat, and had a cross and ribbon placed round his neck. The King would have probably said something to him, because like most of the other correspondents so honored, he also knew Phillips from their travels together and when the King and Queen had visited the Western Front during the war. He had to also be familiar with Phillips' writings about that latter visit.[236]

It was an unusual event, but most of the world, including many reporters, thought of Phillips as an American living in London and working as a journalist for a British newspaper. He would not be the first American to be knighted. Members of the U.S. military had received the honor previously, but he would be the first American newsman, although not the last. It was for this reason that the newsman became the news.

When the announcement of the forthcoming knighthood was made in England the previous spring, it also appeared in several American newspapers, including those of Fayette and Washington County, Pennsylvania.[237] Haydn Church, writing for the *Los Angeles Times* during the following summer dwelt on the fact that Phillips

---

[234] "Bank Cashier Hurt in Auto Accident; Two Others are Victims of Cars," *Pittsburgh Post*, September 26, 1920; "Three are Dead and Four Injured in Auto Accidents," *The Pittsburgh Press*, Monday, September 27, 1920.

[235] *The* (Uniontown, PA) *Morning Herald*, October 11, 1920.

[236] Percival Phillips, "Twelve Days with the Troops: The King and Queen at the Front," *Daily Express*, July 16, 1917, p. 1, 3; Percival Phillips, "Investiture Amid Ruins." *Daily Express*, July 18, 1917, p. 1; Percival Phillips, "The Queen at the Front," *Daily Gazette*, July 19, 1917, p. 1.

[237] "Brownsville Boy Knighted by the King," *Charleroi* (Pennsylvania) *Mail*, April 24, 1920; "Knighthood Conferred by King George on Percival Phillips of Brownsville," *The* (Connellsville) *Daily Courier*, April 28, 1920.

was an American citizen, as he was at the time.[238] However, unbeknownst to most reporters was the fact that Phillips gave up his U.S. citizenship after that summer and became a British subject.[239] This occurred only four days before he was knighted. For the most part he kept this information to himself. He did confide it to one other reporter that we know of and that was Dewitt Mackenzie. Writing for the Associated Press several months after Phillips' death, Mackenzie stated that Phillips "had become a British subject shortly after the war."[240] He added that Phillips had told him at the time:

> I would like you as an old friend to know why I am abandoning American citizenship. I have spent most of my working days in England. I intend to live the rest of my life here. This country has given me my living and my security. I feel that it would be wrong for me to accept these things without giving my allegiance to the British flag.[241]

Most of Phillips' fellow reporters thought it was improper for him to subsequently use the by-line: Sir Percival Phillips. Actually, the *Daily Express* did this on the very day that his forthcoming knighthood was announced.[242] However, the criticisms of his colleagues were based on the assumption that he was still an American citizen, and the title of "Sir" would be appropriate only for a British subject. We don't know if he ever addressed these criticisms, but it seems unlikely that he would have done so. He was not one who invited confrontations with others.

One must wonder how the rest of England viewed the knighthoods offered to the correspondents that had covered the war. For the mass of the population that had read their newspaper columns day after day from 1914 through 1918, they probably thought

---

[238] Haydn Church, "First American Made a Knight," *Los Angeles Times*, July 18, 1920.
[239] Certificate 7,264, issued October 8, 1920, National Archives, London
[240] Dewitt Mackenzie, "British Press Will Respect Private Lives," *The Lima* (Ohio) *News*, September 20, 1937.
[241] Ibid.
[242] "War Service Honours. An Interesting List. 108 New Knights. Sir Percival Phillips, of the 'Daily Express.' Dame Clara Butt." *Daily Express*, March 31, 1920.

the recognition was well-deserved. Those more closely tied to what can only be called the aristocracy and upper classes in Britain were less likely to recognize them.

Lord Louis Mountbatten was the great grandson of Queen Victoria, who reigned over the British Empire from 1837 until her death in 1901. Mountbatten, who accompanied the Prince of Wales on his 1920-1921 tour of the East, referred to Phillips, Robinson and Russell as the "Press-Knights" in his diary.[243] At the same time he found Phillips to be a charming man. Mountbatten was not as charmed with Russell or his behavior on the tour.

Phillips appears to have wanted to be associated with royalty, but it is hard to say how much of this was due to his various editors who saw in him someone perhaps more cultured than other correspondents of the day. One of his earliest assignments was accompanying the King on a trip to Ireland in 1903, he made numerous trips with the Prince of Wales, and he covered the major events (e.g., the Durbar of New Delhi) involving the royal family, if he was available.

While some Englishmen may have been critical of him, he did not approve of their behavior on numerous occasions. In 1934 he offered some advice in the form of a list of "Don'ts" to those from his adopted country in the pages of the *Daily Mail*.

Phillips suggested that those traveling across the English Channel should not do so with a superiority complex. He added that "civilization does not stop at Calais." He further suggested that if those on holiday were going to be visiting the cities on the Continent, it might be best not to wear plus fours and sports shirts, but rather the kind of clothing one would wear in London. Phillips had probably heard many tourists claiming that the prices were too high or that they were being robbed, and he suggested that such outbursts did not have the slightest influence on the franc or the guilder. He further suggested that when abroad you should not tell your hosts how much better things are done in Great Britain, since they won't believe you anyway. He also suggested they should remember road traffic goes to the right everywhere else and if they narrowly escape

---

[243] Philip Ziegler (ed.) *The Diaries of Lord Louis Mountbatten 1920-1922: Tours with the Prince of Wales*, London: Collins, 1987, p. 175.

being killed they shouldn't blame the host country. They should also not complain about tea abroad since they might very well hear that our coffee is worse. He further stated that one shouldn't complain loudly about the manners and appearance of people around you, many people in Europe speak English. Finally, don't forget that your slight knowledge of a foreign language is not improved by raising your voice.[244]

Phillips could also be critical of Americans. In the early days of the Great War he was in Boulogne, France, when Americans who had been in Belgium arrived. They were attempting to flee the approaching Germans. "Their joy at seeing the British mailboat and hearing a tongue they can understand is almost pathetic." [245] As noted previously, indications are that Phillips could speak most of the languages of Western Europe and he obviously thought others should be able to do this as well.

He was often critical of American life styles. The heavy emphasis on work, money and rushing from place to place was the subject of different articles that he would send back to England during his visits in the 1930s. He found the pace of life in Britain much more to his liking.

One gets the impression that Phillips took off from work for the entire month of his knighthood. He had no by-lines in the *Daily Express* during that time. A little over a month later he appears in Geneva for the first general assembly of the League of Nations, which consisted of 41 nations. The League was the creation of U.S. President Woodrow Wilson and among other things it was supposed to prevent the recurrence of a war of the type that had been experienced from 1914 to 1918. Although Wilson won the Nobel peace prize in 1919 for this and other components of his 14 points, the U.S. Senate never ratified that country's participation in the League, and the U.S. was not represented at the Geneva general assembly of November 15, 1920, except for some correspondents.

Phillips wrote about the situation in Geneva the night before the first session with a suggestion of skepticism.

---

[244] Sir Percival Phillips, "Don't for Tourists Abroad." *Daily Mail*, August 16, 1934.
[245] Percival Phillips, "Distressing Scenes Near Battlefield," *Philadelphia Inquirer*, August 25, 1914, p. 2.

Dispatches from the World

> All the diverse elements of the League of Nations, which begins its survey of this troubled world tomorrow, had drifted to their proper niches in over-crowded Geneva by this evening, and the tons of luggage and official documents which are apparently essential to the success of this expensive undertaking, had been sorted and put in order for the opening session.
>
> Two special trains brought the British, French, some Japanese, and a mixture of lesser powers yesterday morning, and the ordinary railway services added their quota of more or less optimistic pilgrims from the end of the earth. The profiteers of Geneva had a warm welcome for all of them, and the flag of every country which is helping to enrich this one in the interest of peace was generously displayed in hotel windows and on the flocks of luxurious motor-cars without which these zealous workers for the welfare of the world are unable properly to fulfill their mission. [246]

He added:

> Prices have soared again, and before nightfall anguished hotel proprietors already full to the roof, had to refuse, almost tearfully, offers from latecomers to take beds at double prices, thereby enabling, in one instance, representatives of San Salvador and Sweden to gaze complacently at the ineffectual pleadings of some tardily arrived colleagues from France. [247]

---

[246] Sir Percival Phillips, "Geneva the Hub of Nations." *Daily Express*, November 15, 1920.
[247] Ibid.

Phillips remained in Geneva for the formalities of the first day, leaving soon after that, but not before filing his story on the day's activities. [248]

Within a week Phillips was on board the *Leopolis* near Corfu, a Greek Island in the Ionian Sea. The occasion was the return of ex-King Constantine to Greece. Indications were that the people wanted their king back. The problem was that some of the Allies from the war were upset that he was returning. Part of the reason for the Allies position was that the King was to supply 60,000 troops as part of the Gallipoli peninsular campaign during the war and he failed to do this, but this was only part of the reason why the Allies failed to capture the peninsula.[249] Nevertheless, that failure to help the Allies occurred at a critical point and because of this they (specifically Great Britain, France and Italy) did not believe he should be returned to Greece as its monarch. They went so far as to suggest certain economic sanctions if he did return. [250] Nevertheless, he did return and he continued as king until September of 1922 when he abdicated and went into exile.

---

[248] Sir Percival Phillips, "March Past of the Nations. Ballot Parade of the League at Geneva. Miniature Babel," *Daily Express*, November 16, 1920.

[249] William Manchester, op. cit., pp. 534-536.

[250] Sir Percival Phillips, "Greece Wants an Explanation. Minister Puzzeled by the Allied Note. Tino Defended." *Daily Express*, December 6, 1920; and Sir Percival Phillips, "Greece Drops Tino. Urged to Abdicate by the Athens Government. Allies Feared." *Daily Express*, December 8, 1920.

CHAPTER 16

prince of wales tour of the far east

It is difficult to characterize the tours in which Phillips participated during the first third of the 20th century. There were several of them and here we will only discuss the 1921-22 tour with the Prince of Wales. As a summary, Phillips' words will suffice:

> The tour began on October 26, when the *Renown* left Plymouth at sunset with her band playing "Auld Lang Syne" and the Prince looking down from his saluting platform above the bridge on an impressive and very moving farewell scene. Calls were made at Gibraltar, Malta, Port Said, Suez, and Aden. Bombay was reached on November 17. Four months later to a day, the *Renown* sailed again from Karachi for Japan. During the voyage the Prince paid visits to Ceylon, the federated Malay States, the Straits Settlements, and Hong Kong. The homeward journey began at Kagoshima on May 9, and calls were made at Manila, Labuan, Jesselton (now Kota Kinabalu), and Brunei (Borneo), Penang, Trincomalee, Great Hamish (for oil), Suez (hence his Royal Highness went to Cairo), and Gibraltar. The *Renown* arrived at Plymouth late on

the afternoon of June 20, and the Prince proceeded to London by special train the next morning. [251]

There is considerable detail known about this particular trip because it resulted in a small volume entitled *The Prince of Wales Eastern Book: A Pictorial Record of the voyages of H.M.S. "Renown" 1921-1922*. Phillips was responsible for writing the accompanying text for what was essentially a book of pictures. The volume was actually published for St. Dunstan's, a hostel for blinded soldiers and sailors, and if there were profits from the book this is where they went.

Herbert Russell, who was also one of the knighted correspondents, was on the *Renown* for the tour and he published a book on the tour which was released in July of 1922, four months before the work by Phillips.[252] It is hard to say if this created any ill-will between Phillips and Herbert. It is also hard to say which of the men began their project first, but each had to be aware of the other.

The various trips that were made by the Prince of Wales were to let those living in distant parts of the British Empire know that they were not forgotten. In some cases there were conflicts between London and the colonies and it was believed the trips did help with such conflicts by lowering the tensions that existed. In other cases where visits were made to non-colonies, the purpose of these visits for the most part was purely for diplomatic reasons.

The India portion of this trip was to be of the most significance. It was to be a public relations event and negative reports were not encouraged. To say that the organizers would have liked to censor all outgoing news would probably be accurate. Phillips would not participate in a charade of that nature; this was not a war. While *The Times* was reporting that happy crowds greeted the Prince, Phillips' articles proclaimed "Bayonet work in Madras. Leinsters scatter the Gandhist rioters. Grim scene of the royal route." [253]

---

[251] Percival Phillips, *The Prince of Wales Eastern Book: A Pictorial Record of the Voyages of H.M.S. "Renown" 1921-1922*. Published for St. Dunstan's by Hodder and Stoughton, Limited, London, 1922.

[252] Herbert Russell, *With the Prince in the East*, London: Methuen, 1922.

[253] Chandrika Kaul, *Reporting the Raj: The British Press and India, c. 1880-1922*, Manchester: Manchester University Press, 2003, p. 238.

Dispatches from the World

If trouble was anticipated at different destinations, these sites were bypassed. If necessary, "popular welcomes" were arranged. "Phillips noted that in Lucknow, Agra, Delhi, and Lahore, where the population observed a day of mourning, the 'imposing crowds' were largely due to the efforts of authorities to prevent a repetition of the dismal picture of deserted thoroughfares.' "In some cases, 20,000 to 50,000 villagers were brought by train to give the appearance of great support along the royal route. [254]

In Bombay where the *Guardian* was claiming the city "creates a record for enthusiasm" and the *Mail* was reporting about "five miles of festive streets," Phillips "spoke of 'the Bombay battle zone.' "According to Kaul, as Phillips was touring the city in an armored car, he found it 'seething' with unrest; in the 'native quarters' the scene was one of constant rioting and attacks on Europeans.[255]

The cause of all the unrest was in part related to the nationwide movement of non-violent protest initiated by Mahatma Gandhi against British control of India that later became the Non-Cooperation Movement. During the time that the Prince of Wales was in Bombay there were incidents led by those who believed in Gandhi's ideas, but lacked his ability to follow non-violence as an approach. It was primarily these latter individuals that were responsible for the violence that occurred during the Prince's tour.

It is questionable whether this particular tour did much to help relations with India. Phillips expressed his views on the matter:

> In my opinion the prince's visit has not influenced the political situation, one way or another. There is undoubtedly a great feeling of relief among officials now that it is over and that the anti British elements have not gone nearly so far as they intended in trying to wreck it. [256]

---

[254] Ibid., p. 240.
[255] Ibid., pp. 243-244.
[256] Robert J. Prew, "India Unchanged by Prince's Visit," *The Washington Post*, March 18, 1922, p. 13.

Phillips understood this, although it is unlikely that he felt any sympathy for the movement because it would negatively impact Britain.

    A few months later following his return to England Phillips was nominated for membership in the Royal Geographical Society. The nomination was put forward by George MacKenzie of Inverness and also by Lord Ronaldshay, the president of the society at the time. The society's file on Phillips notes that Sir Percival had just returned from a tour with the Prince of Wales; this was the trip to India and the Far East. Phillips was elected as a Fellow of the Royal Geographical Society by their membership at the annual meeting on November 13, 1922. Without a doubt Phillips had probably seen more of the world than any geographer living at the time. He had also developed a little ledger that gave him the quickest route and manner of travel from anyplace to anyplace in the world. There was also a fondness for maps and his habit of never going anywhere without maps of the place with him. Finally, there is the fact that he had also written substantially more than most of the RGS members by that time. He was clearly deserving of the honor.

    Back in the States Smith Phillips' widow, Lucille, married a man named Isaac Mathias and the family moved to the Cleveland, Ohio, area. Lucille still had sisters living there. Although there are no records of Percival ever visiting this new family, he did have a couple of assignments that took him to the Cleveland area and he would have most likely visited them on these occasions. There are indications that he kept in touch with his nephews.

    The death of Smith and the movement of Lucille and her only grandchildren to Ohio had to have a devastating effect on Annie Phillips. They were the last of her immediate family in Pennsylvania. All of her sons had died except for Percival and most of the time he was more than half a world away.

    Toward the end of November in 1920 Annie Phillips decided that she should draw up a will. Her mother had died two years earlier and perhaps she thought it was the right thing to do in order to avoid any confusion later. Her son, Smith, had died the previous month and this had to make her even more aware of her own mortality. The will was prepared. She had two neighbors who lived across the street from her on Church Street, Mrs. Jessie Browning and Browning's sister Miss Mary Cunningham, witness her signature. She named William F. Knox of Pittsburgh as executor of her will. He was the son of her uncle of the same name who had passed away five years earlier. The will was then put away for safe keeping.

Within a year, Annie's uncle Philander Chase Knox, U.S. Senator Knox at the time, also died, quite unexpectedly. He was two months younger than she was. The loss of so many family members in so short a period of time had to take its toll on Annie. Combining this with Lucille and her grandsons moving to Ohio was to create a situation that was too difficult for Annie to cope with.

CHAPTER 17

with the *daily mail*

It is not clear exactly why Phillips left the *Daily Express* and its owner William Maxwell Aiken (Lord Beaverbrook) to go and work for Harold Harmsworth (Lord Rothermere), the owner of the *Daily Mail* and the *Daily Mirror*. In terms of circulation, the *Express* sold more copies each day. It was also seen as somewhat more reputable, at least in comparison to the *Mail* and the *Mirror*, which were seen as tabloids at the time. It could be that Lord Rothermere wanted someone who had been knighted and he was willing to pay for this in terms of a larger salary. It could also be that Phillips wanted assignments or commissions that would keep him in one place for a longer period of time. This was to happen with the *Mail*, which gave him assignments in Italy, Iraq, China, Russia and India.

There is another possibility and that is that Phillips had always wanted to work for the *Daily Mail*, but when he approached Alfred Harmsworth (later Lord Northcliffe) in 1901 he failed to get a job with the *Mail*, much to his disappointment. Alfred was a joint owner of the *Daily Mail* with his brother, Harold Harmsworth (Lord Rothermere), but the former ran the *Mail*, and Harold ran the *Daily Mirror*. In August of 1922 Lord Northcliffe died. It will be recalled that Phillips had thought Northcliffe very eccentric during the 1914 Ireland episodes in terms of his expenditures and he was quite negative about Northcliffe in his letters to Blumenfeld at that time. When Northcliffe died, Rothermere took over and within three months Phillips was working for the *Daily Mail*. There is only one piece of evidence to support this view: Annie Phillips said in 1901 that her son had gone to England to work for Alfred Harmsworth, a name she would not have known in 1901 unless Phillips had told her this was his goal.

It is a little misleading to say that Phillips was working for the *Mail*. Since Lord Rothermere also owned the *Daily Mirror*, Phillips' by-line could also be found on rare occasions in the *Mirror*, or in the dispatches that these newspapers sent out to other news outlets. Nevertheless, the bulk of his reporting was for the *Mail*.

Shortly after joining the *Daily Mail* in November of 1922, he was sent to investigate the British occupation of Mesopotamia, better known as Iraq today. His first article on the situation appeared on November 10 of 1922. This was also the first article that he wrote for London's *Daily Mail*.

Phillips' investigation resulted in his being in Iraq for nearly six weeks. The substantive results of that investigation appeared in the *Mail* through the first week of December, with some human interest articles appearing after that date. The investigative articles were also collected and bound as a slim little book entitled "Mesopotamia."[257] The report was not favorable to the British administration of Mesopotamia as reflected in the chapter headings: The Millstone Round the Taxpayer's Neck, Tax-Collecting by Bomb, The Bill for Mesopotamia, "The House of Cokkos," The Vast Aerodrome in the Desert, The Swarm of Officials, "We Must Be Helped," Britain's Bad Railway Bargain, The Army With Everything Except Soldiers, The Palace that Fell into the River, "Glaring Examples of Waste," and "Withdraw to Basra."

It should be noted that Mesopotamia was part of the Ottoman Empire that had been an ally of Germany in the World War. The armistice of that war resulted in the distribution of lands to the victors and this resulted in Great Britain taking 'possession' of Mesopotamia, or Iraq. It was soon apparent that Great Britain had secured an albatross that was causing it more problems than it could handle.

There is little need here to recite the entire contents of Phillips' inquiry since some of it has little or no relevance today. Instead,

---

[257]   Sir Percival Phillips, *Mesopotamia: The 'Daily Mail' Inquiry at Baghdad*, London: Carmelite House, 1922.

Dispatches from the World

some of the observations that Phillips made are relevant even today. These are as follows:

> We have created a native State there (called officially Iraq) and provided it with a cumbrous and costly organisation in which British military and civil elements are intermingled and intended to serve as a prop to the new Government until it can stand on its own. [258]
>
> A dispassionate survey of present conditions shows that the results so far obtained do not justify the time and money lavished upon the enterprise. [259]
>
> There is an artificial kingdom ruled by an unpopular King, Feisal, and a doubtful Ministry, without the confidence of the people and dependent on a native population which is either suspicious or apathetic. [260]
>
> Their efforts to infuse a vigorous love of country into the detached tribes which form the population of Mesopotamia have not succeeded. A feeling of pessimism, which in some cases is tinged with despair, pervades the little community of British advisors. [261]
>
> More than half the population of Mesopotamia are fanatical Shiahs (a Moslem sect), who are opposed to all forms of civil power. [262]
>
> The self-dependent tribes in the desert have as little love for the King at Baghdad as for taxation in their homes and for military service. They pay

---

[258] Ibid., p. 11.
[259] Ibid.
[260] Ibid.
[261] Ibid., p. 12.
[262] Ibid.

taxes reluctantly, when they pay them at all. The financial crisis this year has been largely due to the Government's inability to collect the revenue from the land and from other sources. Bombing aeroplanes have been used repeatedly as tax-gatherers in backward districts. [263]

King Feisal's army at present consists of 400 officers and fewer than 4,000 men—the latter for the most part the dregs of Iraq's population. [264]

The immature State is jealous of its independence; it listens but does not necessarily follow the course indicated. The military expenditure proceeds merrily.[265]

The British taxpayer must decide whether it is worthwhile continuing to pour money into Mesopotamia for an indefinite period in order to maintain this purely artificial kingdom. [266]

We are asked to stand ostensibly in the background, somewhat in the attitude of a rich benevolent uncle who has been made responsible for the actions of an undisciplined, immature youth suddenly given unlimited freedom. [267]

If we take the bit in our teeth and spend money we can 'make a go' of it. Otherwise not. The Arabs cannot maintain law and order themselves. That is certain. It is equally certain that if we leave someone else will come in—probably the Turk. [268]

---

[263] Ibid.
[264] Ibid., p. 13.
[265] Ibid.
[266] Ibid., p. 21.
[267] Ibid.
[268] Ibid., p. 23.

Dispatches from the World

In November of 1922 Mr. Bonar Law, the prime minister of Great Britain at the time, expressed his feelings on the Iraq situation by stating "I wish we had never gone there."[269] Bonar Law died the following year from throat cancer and the problem of Iraq passed on to his successor, Stanley Baldwin, for the remainder of the decade. The policy recommended by Phillips after completing his study was "withdrawal from all of Mesopotamia except the small area around Basra, which could be cheaply held, and which would safeguard the single important British oilfield—that acquired well before the war in South-Western Persia." [270] It was to be nearly another decade before the British could get out of Iraq, and they accomplished this with a treaty in 1930 promising military support for Iraq if it needed it.

The situation of the British in Iraq in 1922 is not the same as the situation that the United States found itself involved with from 2004 to 2011. This time there was a civil war between the Sunni and the Shiah groups and a war that had the United States, Britain, and others combating insurgents. But many of the problems encountered by the British in 1922 were also encountered by the powers that are in Washington, D.C., and the U.S. should have anticipated these, if they had taken the time to do any background research prior to their invasion in 2003.

Among the various factors that have not changed is the creation of a central government that is of little or no significance to the populace. While there is no longer a king that the people support, the existing government and its prime minister seem to have little support of the population. The tribal society that existed in the 1920s continues today. It is uncertain whether the Shiahs of today differ from those of that earlier era. Today they appear to reluctantly serve in the military. The Iraq of today is a somewhat similar creation to the country that existed in the early part of the 20st century. Just as the British decided it made little sense to continue their financial support of this artificial kingdom, the U.S. decided the conflict no longer merited its support in terms of its financial and human costs. The British were willing to commit long term military aid to simply

---

[269] Ibid., p. 7.
[270] Ibid., p. 8.

get out from under their support of this country, so the Americans have pledged military support to the country into the future. The U.S. has also created an embassy in Bagdad that has 16,000 employees as of the beginning of 2012. And, if the bombings of 2012 are any indication, the country is still unable to maintain law and order. So in some ways the U.S. is repeating the errors of the British, although they seem to be slower to recognize this fact.

Before the final articles on Iraq appeared in the *Mail,* Phillips was in Italy to investigate and report on the activities of Benito Mussolini. His articles on "Il Duce," as he would later be referred to, appeared through the remainder of 1922.

If Percival Phillips can be cited for any major blunder, it was with regard to his position on fascism. Of course there were many examples of fascism around the world in the 1920s, but the one that developed in Italy with the rule of Benito Mussolini was the one of interest to the *Mail.*

One must try to understand the situation that developed in Italy after the Great War of 1914-1918. The country was without leadership, chaos reigned, and along came the son of a blacksmith, a journalist, who wanted to change all that. It was an easy dream to follow, and Italy did, and so did Phillips. Phillips saw the existing chaos, and he saw the actions being taken in the 1920s by Mussolini to correct these problems. There were mandatory (or forced) resignations from positions, or encouragement to resign with extreme threats. If this involved the death of current office holders, this was unfortunate, but acceptable. Phillips saw only chaos and he saw Mussolini as a cure for that problem. There is every indication that he was aware that Mussolini's black shirts were "crossing the line," but this did not seem to matter to him. His recognition and understanding of the various events in Italy under Mussolini in the early 1920s are recited in detail in "The Red Dragon and the Black Shirts," [271] which was published in January of 1923 and based on the series of articles he had prepared for the *Daily Mail.* The basic thesis of the articles was that communism is a far worse menace than the extremism of fascism and if embracing the latter helped to improve the situation this was acceptable, at least to Phillips.

---

[271] Sir Percival Phillips, *The Red Dragon and the Black Shirts*, London: Carmelite, 1922.

Dispatches from the World

There was also a certain amount of admiration that Phillips felt for Mussolini. There was always the possibility that the Italians could stop the move toward communism without switching over to Mussolini's fascism, but that seemed unlikely to Phillips. He believed that Italy needed an extremely strong leader to prevent this and to remove the communists that had already infiltrated various governmental units in Italy ranging from small villages to the national government. He also believed there was a need for a benevolent dictator, it was rightly or wrongly the way he viewed the world. Favoring a dictatorship that "kept the peace" was a position that he would return to later with the China situation of the late 1920s.

It should be noted that Phillips was in many ways a supporter of the philosophical position of the newspaper he was working for at the time. Lord Rothermere carried on a mail correspondence with Adolph Hitler and praised him repeatedly, and he supported Benito Mussolini and his fascist government. Therefore, since Lord Rothermere was very much in favor of Adolph Hitler, as well as Benito Mussolini, Phillips may have felt his proper position was to support the position of his newspaper's owner. [272]

One can look back on the events surrounding the rise of Benito Mussolini and wonder how anyone could be so naive. However, Phillips was not alone. Five years later Churchill met Mussolini in Italy and passed along his views on the leader to *The Times*. He wrote, "I could not help being charmed, like many other people have been, by Signor Mussolini's gentle and simple bearing and by his calm, detached poise in spite of so many burdens and dangers. Secondly, anyone could see that he thought of nothing but the lasting good, as he understood it, of the Italian people, and that no lesser interest was of the slightest consequence to him." [273] While Churchill may have believed what he stated, one should not lose sight of the fact that Mussolini was struggling to rid Italy of communists and Churchill, as well as Phillips, saw communism as far more of a threat to Europe than fascism at the time.

---

[272] S.J. Taylor, *The Great Outsiders: Northcliffe, Rothermere and the Daily Mail*, London: Weidenfeld & Nicholson, 1996, p. 278.

[273] "Mr. Churchill on Fascism," *The (London) Times*, January 21, 1927, p. 14.

Phillips did not keep these views forever. By the late 1930s, he was beginning to see the problems that Mussolini posed, or perhaps it was after leaving the *Daily Mail*. In any event, Sir Robert Laird Borden met Phillips while both were on their way to the dedication of the Vimy War Memorial in July of 1936. Borden notes, "I had an interesting conversation with Sir Percival Phillips, who was a war correspondent in Ethiopia and who had just returned from attending the presidential conventions in the United States. In his opinion, Mussolini is a greater peril than Hitler, but no greater than the men behind Hitler." [274] More than likely his view of Mussolini was changed by what he had seen in Ethiopia the previous fall and spring. At that time Mussolini's armies invaded Ethiopia with nearly 500,000 troops. They also used mustard gas against a virtually defenseless Ethiopian Army. An estimated 6,000 Ethiopians died from the gas bombs, which were dropped from aircraft.

Phillips early view of Mussolini was very positive, but by 1935 he came to realize that "Il Duce" had managed to stamp out all opposition to his regime during the previous nine years. In 1926 any Italian was able to voice his opinion of the regime and its policies. "Repression really began after the attempt on Mussolini's life in 1929, at Bologna. The police almost overnight proclaimed measures which effectually killed all opposition, however slight, to the established Government. Passports were annulled, all non-Fascist public meetings were declared illegal, non-Fascist parties were dissolved, and public licences were withdrawn from all newspapers and periodicals that did not support the regime." [275]

If Phillips was aware of these shortcomings dating from as far back as 1929, one can wonder why he did not voice his concerns or views before 1935. The answer has to recognize that the policies of Lord Rothermere of the *Daily Mail* were very favorable toward Mussolini and Hitler. Phillips views changed most dramatically after he joined the *Daily Telegraph* and was out from under the former editorial views and positions of the *Daily Mail*.

---

[274] Henry Borden (ed.), *Letters to Limbo*, Toronto: University of Toronto Press, 1971, p. 275.

[275] Percival Phillips, "An Iron Hand: The Fascism of Italy," *The* (Wellington, NZ), *Evening Post*, May 31, 1935, p. 9.

Dispatches from the World

At the same time Phillips was quite aware of Hitler's abilities. "Herr Hitler does not lose his hold on the nation. He can ascend a platform surrounded by a docile and inwardly lukewarm crowd, and instantly electrify it by merely opening his mouth. His hearers are thrilled, not so much by what he says as the way he says it, and the effect is sheer intoxication." As noted above he thought that Hitler was being directed by those around him. "The Fuhrer may be hampered by ill-advised and dangerous advisers, but in the eyes of the nation he is a sacred figure capable of no wrong. An irreverent foreigner who appreciates his good qualities expressed it to me in another way: 'Hitler is a mascot. Who holds him holds Germany.'" [276] Given what we know of Hitler today, one could argue that he was in control, but that he was not very capable as a military strategist.

Phillips' investigations of Iraq and Italy took less than a month and a half each, which does not appear to be enough time to get a thorough grasp of the situation in either situation. On the other hand he seemed to completely understand both cases even though one can find faults with his analysis and conclusions with regard to fascism in Italy.

One cannot accuse Phillips of making short shrift of the events that developed with the French occupation of Germany in 1923. The situation that brought the French Army into the Ruhr area of Germany did not receive a great deal of attention in the U.S. The "invasion" was due to Germany's failure to make payments in accord with the Treaty of Versailles, which ended the Great War. That treaty had a reparations clause that called for Germany to make payments for war damages, for their occupation of countries and for the pensions of all wounded men. The idea was for Germany to be forever a poor country. However, a poor country could not possibly make the payments, particularly after much of its industrial infrastructure was destroyed. The country's failure to make reparations led to the French sending in the Army to make sure that goods were produced that could be sold in order to make the payments. The French were unsuccessful at this.

---

[276] Percival Phillips, "Popular Move; German Re-armament," *The* (Wellington, NZ) *Evening Post*, June 24, 1935, p. 11.

Phillips was sent to the Ruhr to cover the situation for the *Daily Mail*, even though the French actions were opposed by the British. While Phillips was in Germany there was an incident involving the probable courts martial of some individuals by the French courts in Essen. An attorney out of London was sent to represent the individuals and to request a postponement of their case. The attorney was Patrick Hastings, later Sir Patrick Hastings.

The journey of Hastings was to be done in secret, and he was not even sure who had requested him to go and represent the individuals. He made arrangements for the trip in secret and even used a different name. Prior to leaving he was approached by a man named Thomas Marlowe, who told him every detail of what he thought were his 'secret' travel plans. Marlowe asked Hastings to allow him to make the travel arrangements and told him that he would be met at the German border by a *Daily Mail* car. Hastings later wrote:

> At this time the *Daily Mail* was all-powerful in that district. They were understood to be strongly pro-French and had a regular correspondent at Essen in the person of Percival Phillips. Not only was Phillips a man of great personality and universally respected, but the authority and influence of the *Daily Mail* were greatly feared and, as I discovered later, Phillips was the only person who had absolute liberty of action and movement throughout the whole of the military territory. [277]

Phillips met Hastings with a car that trailed a six-foot flag with *Daily Mail* printed upon it. Phillips was surprised to see that Hastings had made it to the meeting point; he assumed he would be stopped prior to reaching the frontier. They continued on their way and were stopped several times by sentries. During the drive Phillips explained the reasons behind the precautions with regard to his visit.

---

[277] Sir Patrick Hastings, *The Autobiography of Sir Patrick Hastings*, London: William Heinemann Ltd., 1948, p. 206.

> He said that my visit was well known, and the authorities were quite determined that I should not attend any courts-martial; he told me that as long as I was physically in his company my position would be perfectly assured, but that if at any time I was away from the protection of the *Daily Mail* my stay in Germany would be extremely short. [278]

They arrived in Essen, registered at the hotel, went for a walk and returned to find that all of Hastings' bags had been opened and searched, papers were untied and read as well. The two went to dinner. At the next table were three well-dressed ladies, and Phillips grinned.

"I know those three," he said. "They are always used for this purpose. I'll get rid of them."

He went to their table, spoke to them in a very polite tone in French, explaining that Hastings was dining with him. The ladies left. Phillips explained that a brief chat with them would have gotten him thrown out of the country.

The following day Hastings went to court accompanied by Phillips. After some delays the court finally agreed to the postponement. Phillips took him back to his hotel and the two then traveled to Cologne where he said good-bye. Phillips told Hastings he did not think he would have to return for a trial. As it turned out, the defendants were discharged. There never was a trial. [279]

The primary reason for mentioning this incident is that it begins to appear that Phillips once again was doing more than newspaper work. It would appear that he may very well have been doing some work for the British government, as well as the *Daily Mail*. These are not quite the tasks that one would expect of a correspondent. If that is the case, the newspaper must have been aware of it since Thomas Marlowe was the editor of the *Daily Mail* when he visited Hastings in London.

Aside from this incident Phillips devoted most of his time to the straight reporting of the events in Germany for nearly the entire year.

---

[278] Ibid., p. 207.

[279] Ibid., 208-214.

There was rampant inflation and food shortages, strikes and the general refusal of the German miners to work for the French, riots throughout Germany, railway strikes, passive resistance throughout the work force, suspected plots by everyone, separatist movements, and concerns that the communists would end up taking over the country. Phillips left Germany just before Christmas for a much needed break.

He took some time off from his reporting for the *Mail* during January of 1924. It would appear that he may have taken a holiday in the Western Isles, a series of islands off the northwest coast of Scotland, although this can hardly have been a pleasant place in the middle of winter. He wrote one article regarding the possible famine in the islands and this was all. [280]

On January 24, 1924, Nikolai Lenin died in Moscow. With Phillips' return from his holiday, the *Mail* sent him to Russia primarily to assess the impact of Lenin's death on the nascent communist state. There was a belief in some quarters that this would bring about the end of Bolshevism, perhaps even the hope of this on Phillips' part, but this was not to occur for several decades. He returned to England after several articles appeared in the *Daily Mail* for February.

Another break from his reporting duties occurred in March, but by the end of the month Phillips had started reporting on the forthcoming British Empire Exhibition to be held at Wembley, England, beginning April 23. He covered the opening ceremonies involving the King. Sir Edward Elgar directed the choirs on that occasion.

The Empire was weak (some would say it was disintegrating) at this point due in large part to the 1914-1918 war, and the exhibition was an attempt to pull everything back together, to remind everyone of the Empire's former greatness. Fifty-six countries (or colonies) participated in the event which cost in excess of £10 million to produce and it attracted more than 25 million visitors. But the British Empire would never return to its former status, those days were gone forever.

Phillips wrote his last article on the Exhibition, one dealing with plant growth, on May 8. He then took a train to Liverpool where he boarded the S.S. *Baltic* of the White Star line for a trip to the United

---

[280] Sir Percival Phillips, "Western Isles: Famine Peril," *Daily Mail*, January 17, 1924, p. 6.

Dispatches from the World

States. He arrived in New York on May 19. In all likelihood he visited with his mother in Brownsville and then returned to New York.

Phillips had gone to the U.S. to accompany a group of American and Canadian cowboys back to England where they were to perform at Wembley. The cowboys were to put on the world's greatest rodeo with international competition between the U.S. and Canada. Phillips was also to write articles about the personalities and methods of the rodeo for audiences back in England.[281]

Two ships had been chartered for the purpose of bringing the various "rodeo" participants to England. The first vessel was the *S.S. Menominee* and it was to carry 150 cowboys, 15 cowgirls, 100 vicious bucking ponies and 40 wild horses. Although the events planned would most often use Texas cattle, these were excluded due to a government embargo. In their place were Canadian cattle, 170 of them, on the *S.S. Turcoman*, which had sailed earlier. Canadian cattle were larger than U.S. cattle and it was thought this might create some unexpected outcomes.

After a day at sea 130 of the cowboys were seasick; only a few of them had ever been on a vessel before. Phillips said that most of the cowboys confessed they were utterly defeated in their attempt to "rough ride the Atlantic." After a week at sea the cowboys were trying to lasso porpoises, which is suggestive of the high level of boredom that prevailed on board the *S.S. Menominee*.

The cowboys were very excited when the tip of England emerged out of the fog several days later. They were also happy to hear the Lizard foghorn a little later. By late on the fifth day of June the cowboys had arrived at Tilbury, near London. Phillips had sent out wireless stories to the *Mail* throughout the trip (May 24 to June 5) so many people back in England were looking forward to the contests at Wembley that were scheduled to last two weeks.

In July Phillips covered the arrival and visit of Ras Taffari, Prince Regent of Abyssinia, to England.[282] For all practical purposes the Prince Regent was the leader of that African nation, which had

---

[281] Charles B. Cochran, *I Had Almost Forgotten..*, London: Hutchinson & Co., Ltd, 1932, p. 49.
[282] Phillips' articles appeared in the *Daily Mail* on July 10, 11, and 12 of 1924.

recently joined the League of Nations. This would appear to be just another visit of an unimportant dignitary to London, but this was not the case. Ras Taffari would become the Emperor Haile Selassie by the end of decade. He would also invite Phillips to his coronation as his personal guest and later be in part responsible for him receiving a major news story. It is reasonable to conclude that they got along well during their initial meeting.

Phillips wrote of the Prince Regent's visit to a London hospital and the London zoo. The following day he visited the law courts, St. Paul's Cathedral, and the exhibitions at Wembley. Visits to Westminster Abbey and Windsor Castle were also included as part of his itinerary. Phillips wrote about the Prince Regent in very flattering terms and it was obviously something that would prove very favorable to Phillips in later years.

September found Phillips back in Germany following stories on British loans and trade, but by the end of the month this was completed and we once again see his by-line virtually absent from the *Mail's* pages except for two articles in October on Russia and one in December on the Ruhr occupation.[283] There appears to be no record of what Phillips was doing during the last two months of the year. Even the articles noted would not have required his presence in Russia or the Ruhr area.

It is known that he was in Germany by the end of the year and he remained there well into January. Phillips had gotten word of an attempt by Germany to rearm itself. Under the Treaty of Versailles Germany was allowed to maintain an army of 100,000 men for home defense; this army was known as the Reichswehr. Phillips noted that after their training many of the men were discharged as being medically unfit or otherwise unqualified to serve in the army. "The gaps thus created are filled with new recruits. The discharged men carry with them into civil life a military permit equivalent to a mobilization card."[284] Phillips wrote several articles on this for the *Mail* during January of 1925; several of these articles were picked up

---

[283] Sir Percival Phillips, "Russian Women Under Soviet Regime," *Daily Mail*, October 11, 1924, p. 9; Sir Percival Phillips, "Russian War on Religion–Christianity Abolished," *Daily Mail*, October 13, 1924, p. 13; and, Sir Percival Phillips, "Ruhr Occupation–Evacuation–Cologne Views," *Daily Mail*, December 29, 1924, p. 9.

[284] Sir Percival Phillips, "Warlords Build Great Army of German Youth," *The Syracuse* (New York) *Herald*, Sunday, February 15, 1925.

Dispatches from the World

by other newspapers as well, but nothing was done by the world's nations to stop the practice.

In the spring of 1925 Phillips went to Doorn, Holland, to interview Kaiser Wilhelm, the head of Germany during the World War. The Kaiser had been living there in exile since the end of the war. A reporter for another newspaper, Robert Henrey, had received a cable from his newspaper to go immediately to Doorn in Holland, to also interview the ex-Kaiser. As Henrey would write later:

> I feared this assignment from the start, for the exiled monarch was impossible to approach. When, two days later, I reached the little dolls'-house village that is Doorn, I found the position even worse than I had expected. Sitting quietly on the balcony of the little blue and white hotel, smoking his pipe, was Sir Percival Phillips.
>
> The tranquility on his face told its own story. He had already been there three days and had written a brilliant account of the ex-Kaiser . . . I was no match against Sir Percival Phillips at the best.[285]

Phillips had gotten a story about how the former kaiser of Germany spent his days sawing wood in Doorn; he apparently did this in an attempt to stay fit. At the same time there is no indication that Phillips was able to interview the former German leader based on the article published.[286]

In late May of 1925 Phillips began suffering from hay fever. This was not a new ailment, but it was one that tended to recur. A colleague suggested that he see a nose and throat specialist and so he did. The physician whom he saw was one Mr. William Lloyd. Phillips hay fever was cured and he was so pleased by this outcome that he wrote a piece on hay fever for the *Daily Mail*. "The article

---

[285] Robert Henrey, *A Century Between*, New York: Longmans, Green and Co., 1937, pp. 293-294.
[286] Sir Percival Phillips, "Ex-Kaiser Sawing," *Daily Mail*, April 27, 1925.

began by stating that suffers from hay fever could take hope for the future, for a prominent West End specialist had at last found an absolute cure for this distressing malady."[287] The article appeared on June 5 and the by-line simply listed "By our special correspondent." The physician's name did not appear in the article.

Hay fever suffers who read the article called the newspaper's editor asking for the name of the "special correspondent." This was passed on and the individuals began writing to Percival requesting that he pass along their name to the physician and asking the same whether he would be willing to see them by appointment. The *Daily Mail* passed this along to William Lloyd and he saw the patients. News of this activity reached others who informed the medical council that this sounded far too much like advertising, something which doctors were forbidden to do by the Britain's General Medical Council. As a result William Lloyd's name was removed from the *Medical Register*.

News of this reached members of Parliament and during some discussion led in part by Neville Chamberlain, then Minister of Health, it became clear that the procedures used by the General Medical Council needed to be reviewed. For example, if a physician writes a book and he is then interviewed by a newspaper, isn't this also a form of advertising? It is not clear what discussions occurred outside of the published minutes of these various groups, but on November 28, 1927, nearly two and one half years after the article appeared, *The Times* published a brief article on page 11 stating that William Lloyd's name had been restored to the *Medical Registry*.

Earlier that year the Empire Press Union announced that there would be an Imperial News Conference in Australia. Phillips was one of the 30 representatives selected to attend the conference as a representative of Great Britain, but there were also representatives there from Canada, New Zealand, South Africa, India, the British West Indies, Singapore, and Malta. It would appear that the major purpose of the conference was to acquaint the newspapers of the Empire with Australia and New Zealand.

---

[287] "General Council of Medical Education and Registration, Winter Session 1925," *The British Medical Association, Supplement to the British Medical Journal*, December 5, 1925, p. 193.

Dispatches from the World

The majority of the conference representatives from Great Britain sailed to Canada on the *Empress of France*, which departed in early July. Phillips sailed across the Atlantic with the other correspondents, but he left the party and crossed into the United States, taking a train from Buffalo, New York, to Pittsburgh, he arrived there on July 15, and went to visit his mother, Annie, who was ill at the time. On July 19 he took his mother to a sanitarium for the chronically ill near Ligonier in Pennsylvania. [288] Later on the same day he took a train to Toronto and joined the others for a train trip to western Canada.

A special Canadian Pacific Railway train was used to cross Canada. The conference group arrived in New Zealand on August 17 and remained there for ten days (until August 28). They left New Zealand in order to arrive at the official reception in Melbourne, Australia on September 1. They remained there for two months touring every state of Australia, before leaving toward the latter part of October. [289]

Rather than returning to England Phillips sailed to China by way of Singapore on board the *Marella*, which was scheduled to arrive at the destination on Saturday, October 24. The ship was about five miles out of Singapore when Phillips heard a whistle blow. At the time he was having tea in the saloon. As he looked out the starboard windows he saw another ship, the *Conus*, three or four ship lengths away, but headed for the *Marella*. Neither ship was damaged that much by the collision, but the plates on the side of the *Marella* separated and the ship began to take on water. There was five feet of water in the engine room twenty minutes later. The ship began to list several degrees to the starboard and the order was given to enter the lifeboats. Being as close to port as they were, there were several other boats that came to their assistance. Most of the passengers were quite relieved when they finally reached port. The *Marella* was beached to keep it from sinking and the following day after some repairs it was towed into port. The *Conus*, a British oil tanker, continued on its voyage after the incident. [290]

---

[288] "Great Journalist Visits His Aged Mother," *The Charleroi Mail*, July 20, 1925.

[289] "Imperial Press Conference, The Visit to Australia," *The Times*, June 9, 1925, p. 11.

[290] "Marella in Collision," *The Singapore Free Press and Mercantile Advertiser*, October 26, 1925, p. 8.

On the following Tuesday Phillips sailed for China on the *Haruna Maru*. His objective in going to China was to assess the extent to which the Soviet Union was becoming involved in what was for all practical purposes a civil war. Phillips was able to get material for two major stories, but he was then called back to England, before the second appeared in the Singapore newspapers. [291]

It was during this trip back to London that Phillips was to encounter an individual and a vessel that would be significant in his future. The first was James Grant Anderson, a stage actor and repertory theater manager, who was on the same ship as Phillips on that trip home. Phillips would later become a close friend of both Anderson and his sister. The vessel was the *S.S. Ranchi*, which would take him back to England by way of Marseilles. Phillips would encounter this P&O vessel in the twilight of his life although he could not have known that in 1926.

Stanley Baldwin, Prime Minister of Great Britain, stated to an audience of 10,000 people on January 27, 1926:

> I venture to think that no trade union leader could do better service to the cause he represents than by investigating closely what the methods are that enable American workmen to enjoy a better standard of living than any other working people in the world, to produce more, and at the same time to have so much higher wages. [292]

The *Daily Mail* saw this as a reasonable suggestion and began organizing such a fact-finding tour of the United States and several of its key industries. Those workers selected for the tour were a machine man, an iron worker, a pattern maker, a fitter, an iron moulder, a turner, a blacksmith, and a tool fitter and turner. Fenton McPherson of the *Daily Mirror* was sent along as an organizer to make

---

[291] Percival Phillips, "Bolshevised Canton," *The Singapore Free Press and Mercantile Advertiser*, February 1, 1926, p. 6; Percival Phillips, "China's Curse," *The Singapore Free Press and Mercantile Advertiser*, March 8, 1926, p. 11.

[292] Sir Percival Phillips, *The Daily Mail Trade Union Mission to the United States*, London: Daily Mail, 1926, p. 3.

Dispatches from the World

sure that the workers were taken care of and to make sure they were able to meet with the appropriate industrial, labor and government representatives. Phillips was also sent along; he had been abruptly called back from India to go with the tour and to cover its various activities and to document its findings.

On February 27 the group sailed from Liverpool aboard the R.M.S. *Carmania*. The Cunard liner was delayed somewhat by fog and it reached New York on March 9 of 1926. When interviewed by the *New York Times* about the purpose of the tour Phillips said, it was "to give them an opportunity of informing themselves at first hand regarding working conditions, hours, wages and the use of up-to-date machinery in representative American industrial establishments."[293] The British workers examined among others a General Motors plant in Detroit, Buick and Chevrolet plants in Flint, Michigan, steel mills in Pittsburgh and Gary, Indiana, the Western Electric Company in Chicago, as well as electric and hydroelectric plants in the U.S. In all, the group visited industries in thirteen cities and covered 12,000 miles.

The British visitors concluded that the Americans were more productive than workers in England. They were of the opinion that this productivity difference was attributable to the American worker being "far better equipped for his job, both in knowledge and tools he had." [294] The final report that was issued by the group and written by Phillips actually had much more to say than this. They concluded that the workers in Britain were not being paid enough in comparison to their American counterparts and that increasing salaries and giving workers more equipment to help them perform their jobs would increase productivity and lead to greater local consumption of the goods produced. They also saw much less class structure in the U.S. industry in comparison to the British case and noted that this seemed to yield better ideas coming from workers to management. [295]

---

[293] Sir Percival Phillips as quoted in "British Labor Men Here Today on Your," *New York Times*, March 9, 1926, p. 14.

[294] "Finds Workers Here Excel British Labor," *The New York Times*, March 12, 1926.

[295] Sir Percival Phillips, *The Daily Mail Trade Union Mission to the United States*, London: Daily Mail, 1926.

Today these findings seem obvious, but this was not the case in 1926. On the whole, the tour and its final report yielded some very good findings and advice. But the late 1920s were not a very stable time in British industrial-labor relations, and it is hard to say if any of the recommendations were implemented at that time.

The group sailed from New York on the Cunard liner *Ascania* on Saturday, April 10, and arrived at Plymouth on April 19. They then went on to London for a series of luncheons, dinners and speeches regarding the tour.

CHAPTER 18

far vistas

Phillips remained in England for most of the spring of 1926, taking a leave from work during the summer months that followed. On September 18 he left London for Southampton where he boarded the *Mauretania*. Six days later he arrived in New York. He remained in the US for a very brief time and by October he was in Canada writing several pieces on that country for the *Daily Mail*. He next left Canada from the West Coast and sailed for Shanghai, arriving there on November 27 aboard the R.M.S. *Empress of Asia*. The *Daily Mail* had commissioned Phillips to investigate the general situation in China.

The problem seemed to be that Chinese in the northern part of that country had been indoctrinated into the communist view by Cantonese and Russian advisors, but the advisors had gone too far. The Chinese had become extremists, making demands that could not possibly be met. Writing from Hankow, China, in December, Phillips stated, "The Communists have created a Frankenstein monster through excessive agitation and seem unable to control it."[296]

At year's end the situation was still unsettled and several of the newsmen that had gone to China to cover the story posed for a photograph in Hankow that later appeared in Chicago's *Tribune*. Among those present were Charles Dailey of *The Chicago Tribune*, W. Turner of Reuters News Agency, David Frazer of *The Times* of London, and Phillips. In the photograph Phillips is the tallest of the four and he is wearing a bowler, which makes him appear significantly taller. He is also holding his walking stick, but he has changed considerably

---

[296] "Says Soviet Loses Grip on Chinese," *The New York Times*, December 10, 1926.

in appearance in the six years since his knighthood. He is only fifty years of age at the time, but he looks much older.

A military campaign had begun in southern China and it was moving toward the north. It was made up of the Kuomintang (the Chinese National Party) and the Communist Party of China (CPC). The goal of this campaign was to create a revolution that would remove the warlords from control of the country and remove the feudal system that existed there. Nations of the west were seen as supporters of the warlords and became an easy target for the revolutionaries.

Several conflicts and treaties over the years had given various nations special privileges in China. Specifically, these nations were granted leaseholds on Chinese territory in most major cities. The areas covered by these grants were referred to as concession areas and they were under the complete control of the foreigners, the individuals and businesses that occupied them. These foreign interests included, among others, British, French and Americans.

It was quite clear to the Kuomintang that if they were successful in overthrowing the existing government all treaties would be cancelled. Followers of the movement recognized that the concession areas represented foreign imperialism and they directed their anger toward all of the concession areas, but later focused their anger on the British.

The Chinese invaded the Hankow international concession where foreign embassies, residences and businesses were located and Phillips reported, "I am reliably informed that all women and children have been instructed by the foreign consuls to leave Hankow." [297] The British women and children left the following day followed by the American women and children. [298]

Nearly everyone moved to Shanghai, including Phillips. It seemed unlikely that the French, British and American concessions there would be able to prevent the storming of the area. As Phillips wrote, "It is obvious that the manning of the military defense line around the international settlement and the French concession, certainly by the British and possibly by other troops, cannot much longer be

---

[297] "Hankow Near An Upheaval," *The New York Times*, January 6, 1927, p. 1.
[298] "American Women Quitting Hankow," *The New York Times*, January 7, 1927, p. 5.

delayed."[299] The Kuomintang and the CPC did take Shanghai and this event seems to have precipitated the evacuation of foreigners from China. Business concerns were liquidated, missionaries moved out, as well as nearly all foreign residents.

Rather than leaving China, Phillips moved on to the next site of activity, Nanking. He sent dispatches from that city throughout March and April. He followed this with reports and dispatches from Tientsin in May, June and July. Various other dispatches followed from Nanking, Shanghai and the Yangtse valley region in August and September. A necessary break, which took Phillips to Java, was taken in October and November. From there it was on to Singapore and then back to India.

To provide some closure to this situation it should be pointed out that the leader of the Kuomintang, Chiang Kai-shek, broke ties with the CPC and their supporters from the Soviet Union. He ruled China as a dictator for nearly twenty years, although constantly in conflict with Communists. The Communists would later drive out Chiang Kai-shek in the years following the Second World War. He and his supporters sailed across to Formosa, better known as Taiwan today, and established an independent state there, although China has never recognized this newly created state.

By December Phillips was on his way back to Europe. He met King Amanullah and Queen Soraya of Afghanistan in Bombay and accompanied them on their tour of Europe. The king and queen had left their country in early December and reached Karachi on December 11, 1927. They then proceeded to go by ocean liner stopping at Bombay and Cairo arriving at the latter on December 28. A train trip to Paris, followed by visits to Brussels, Berlin, and London followed. They arrived in England on March 13, 1928. The party continued their tour visiting the Soviet Union, Turkey, and Iran.

It is notable that most of the nations visited were impressed by the king and his queen. It is also worth noting that the king and queen were duly impressed with what had been accomplished by these more developed nations. They were so impressed in this regard that upon their arrival back in Kabul, Afghanistan, they began

---

[299] "Shanghai Prepares for Battle," The New York Times, February 24, 1927, p. 4.

taking certain actions that would modernize the country. This did not sit well with the thousand or so tribal leaders there and within six months the king and queen were forced to leave the country and go into exile in Italy. King Amanullah died there in 1960 and Queen Soraya died there in 1968.

Later in 1928 Phillips was sent to Russia to investigate what the Bolsheviks were up to in Africa and Asia. It should be obvious that Phillips was an avid anti-Communist. He saw Russian Communists trying to take control of nearly every country during the 1920s and 1930s: Italy (prior to Mussolini), Germany (after the World War), Afghanistan, Palestine, China, Java, India, the Malay States, Egypt and others. Was he being overly careful? Probably, but at the time Phillips had little doubt that the Soviet Communists wanted to control the world, and he was probably right.

Phillips followed his Russia trip with a series of articles on Rumania and its economic problems. In July and August he changed his focus completely and went to Amsterdam to cover the Olympic Games.

One of the interesting things that began in earnest in 1928 and continued for a couple of years involved Phillips writing of feature articles that were not tied in any way to local events. He wrote about twenty of these in 1928 and about thirty in 1929. Topics varied from traveling in sleeping cars to animals being caught for zoos, from changes he saw in London to the catacombs of Palermo. Correspondence from the readers of these articles thanked Phillips for "taking them" somewhere they would not have known about otherwise.

In the spring of 1929 a decision was made that the Prince of Wales and his brother the Duke of Gloucester would go on safari in the fall of that year. Phillips was sent along to cover the events of this expedition for the *Daily Mail*. They left London on September 6 for what was supposed to be a five-month vacation. They went across France by train and reached Marseilles on September 7. They next sailed across the Mediterranean to Alexandria. Over the following several days they visited Cairo, the Pyramids, and the Suez Canal, arriving in Mombasa, Kenya, on the September 29. They left for Nairobi the following day on the Uganda Railway. Arrangements for

Dispatches from the World

the safari were in the hands of Captain Denys Finch-Hatton. He would also be in charge of the elephant hunt, but he wanted someone other than himself to lead the lion hunt. He got Bror Blixen to handle this part of the safari and everything was ready when the party arrived. Finch-Hatton became a little upset with Blixen for promising the Prince of Wales that he would guarantee him a lion, but aside from this, the safari went well.[300] They began with some elephant hunting and visits to Entebbe and Kampala in Uganda. This was followed by some lion hunting in northern Tanganyika (now Tanzania). By this time it was nearing the end of November.

Plans were to go by motor car across parts of Northern and Southern Rhodesia (now Zimbabwe and Zambia) and to arrive in Capetown by Christmas. The Prince of Wales' brother had gone ahead planning to meet the Prince in Northern Rhodesia. It was at about this time that a somewhat bothersome chest cold of King George back in England developed into what was called pleurisy. There was genuine concern that the King would die.

As the Prince of Wales scurried around the savanna and jungles of British East Africa attempting to increase the quantity and variety of the wildlife he could shoot, his mind was undecided as to whether he should return to London, or whether he should continue the safari. Various telegrams were exchanged between the Prince of Wales and Buckingham Palace. The safari continued. Then, very abruptly, the Prince of Wales decided he should return to England. Whether he did this out of love for his father or out of a sense of obligation (as the future King) is unknown even today.

It was expected that the Prince's return trip would take eleven days, but the Prince of Wales was actually there in nine and one half days. This was due in part to a train trip across Europe from Brindisi in Italy to Calais in France, after their ship arrived at the Italian port city. The Duke of Gloucester also returned to England, but since he was close to Cape Town he went the entire route by sea along Africa's west coast.

Although Phillips was unaware of it at the time, his father, Hibbard had also taken ill. It is hard to believe that Phillips would

---

[300] Judith Thurman, *Isak Dinesen: The Life of a Storyteller*, New York St. Martin's Press, 1982, pp. 262-263.

feel any concern for his father or his father's second family. At the time it would have been more than forty years since Hibbard left Annie and their three sons in Brownsville to fend for themselves. It would be hard to feel much attachment to a father who had done such a thing.

In the end the King survived the illness, but it certainly did not appear that would be the case and the return to England made sense. While the King did survive his illness, Hibbard did not. He died on November 12, 1929, less than a week after becoming ill. There are no indications that Phillips did anything about the death. Instead he returned to England and awaited his next assignment.

The Prince of Wales had missed out on a genuine adventure, and on January 3, 1930, he left England to give his African safari another try. Following some official visits in Capetown, the Prince of Wales proceeded to Mombasa in the Kenya Colony. From there it was on to Nairobi and then elephant hunting with Baron von Blixen, and lion hunting with Captain Denys Finch-Hatton, both of these hunters had been involved in the earlier safari. The Prince of Wales spent a considerable amount of time on this tour taking motion pictures of the animals and peoples of East Africa.

The Prince of Wales also visited the Belgian Congo (now the Democratic Republic of the Congo) and the Sudd on this second safari. He next flew from the latter area to Khartoum in Sudan. This was followed by a flight to Cairo from Khartoum. He then sailed to Marseilles from Port Said, and then flew from Marseilles to his residence at Belvedere Fort in England.

A conflict between the Chinese and the Russians began when the Chinese raided the consulates of the Russians in Manchuria. They said that they found evidence that railway officials were using their offices to distribute Communist propaganda to the people. "They detained many Russians and expelled others from the country, seizing the railway." [301] There were skirmishes between the Russians and the Chinese, with the Russians generally being successful in these incidents. As a result they occupied part of Western Manchuria.

---

[301] "Moscow and Mukden Sign Railway Truce," *The New York Times*, December 23, 1929, p. 1.

Dispatches from the World

It began to appear that there would be some type of truce arranged so Phillips left China. He passed through Singapore and moved on to Colombo, Ceylon (now Sri Lanka), en route to India. He was interviewed there by a representative of *The Times of Ceylon*. Asked about the situation with the railway, Phillips said, "In my opinion the whole thing will fizzle out. One hears a good deal about battles on the frontier, but these amount to nothing more than frontier skirmishes, in which both sides are—to use a Chinese expression—'saving face.'"[302]

The Times of Ceylon correspondent then asked Phillips his views on the general internal situation in China. Phillips smiled at this and he responded wryly, "It is two weeks since I left Shanghai, and anyone who is two weeks out of China is out of touch with the situation. Events change with startling rapidity, new men spring up, old men disappear and fresh factors arise to influence the course of affairs."[303] He did explain the situation as it existed at the time of his departure, which was that the anti-British feeling that was so strong in 1927 seemed to be gone.

Eventually a protocol or treaty of sorts was constructed regarding the railway situation. This essentially returned everything to the way it was prior to the initial incidents which occurred in May of 1929, with the exception that the railway was to be jointly operated by the Russians and the Chinese. [304]

The spring of 1930 found Phillips covering stories from the Cape to Cairo with articles about the communist influences in South Africa, other articles about Rhodesian wheat as well as plans to drive the British out of Egypt. By the end of July Phillips had sailed to the U.S. and crossed into Canada to cover the British Empire Games of 1930 in Hamilton, Ontario. He wrote five stories about the games for the *Telegraph*; the games were dominated by Britain and Canada. On August 5 he crossed back into the U.S. at Buffalo. He remained in the

---

[302] "The Manchurian Quarrel," *The Singapore Free Press and Mercantile Advertiser*, December 2, 1929, p. 3.

[303] Ibid.

[304] "Moscow and Mukden Sign Railway Truce," *The New York Times*, December 23, 1929, p. 3.

States until the 12th of September when he sailed for England on the *Olympia*. Seven days later he arrived in Southampton.

On the last day of October in 1930 Phillips was in the port city of Djibouti, French Somaliland, boarding a train for Addis Ababa, the capital of Ethiopia. The train would take him to the coronation of Haile Selassie as Emperor of that country. This was not a random reporting job; he was attending the coronation at the personal invitation of the soon to be emperor. He was the only correspondent honored in this way.

At the time the train trip from Djibouti to Addis Ababa was long, slow and tedious since the track zigzagged in a very circuitous manner to go from sea level to an elevation of more than eight thousand feet where the capital of Ethiopia was located. The train stopped from time to time and the air became cooler compared to Djibouti as they moved higher. The trip took parts of three days. "On the afternoon of the third day," Phillips noted, "we are again coated with dust, the scene changes: the train has reached a fertile plateau and is running through farmland dotted with grass-roofed huts and grazing flocks." [305] Arriving shortly afterward at Addis Ababa, Phillips entered what he described as a medieval world. There were various festivities that took place in relation to the coronation and Phillips was usually seated with the emperor and empress at these events.

The coronation was to take place in St. George's Cathedral, modeled after an English cathedral with a central dome and Romanesque windows, but done on a much smaller scale, and far too small to hold the many attendees. As a result the coronation required the construction of a tent next to the cathedral to hold the assembled multitude of attendees and this is where the coronation took place.

Phillips described one scene after the coronation:

> Whiskered chieftains whose accouterments flash like jewels in the clear air ride shoulder to shoulder twenty or thirty abreast, their faces like portraits of the prophets come to life and their eyes turned

---

[305] Sir Percival Phillips, "A Medieval Pageant in Black," *Far Vistas*, London: Methuen, 1933, p. 53.

sternly to the Emperor above. They flow past in eddies of yellow dust, followed by led chargers in heavy mantles of gold and silver cloth and standard bearers staggering under the weight of gigantic flags and banners as varied in design as the insignia of knights assembled for a crusade. [306]

Night closes in on the medieval scene… The silence of the African night is only broken by the mutter of distant drums calling drums still more distant and by the howling of unseen dogs. The curtains have fallen again on the Middle Ages. We are back in a forlorn little hotel drinking English beer and waiting for the train that will carry us back to today. [307]

---

[306] Ibid., p. 60.
[307] Ibid., p. 62.

CHAPTER 19

india and gandhi

On January 26, 1930, the Indian National Congress, led by Mahatma Gandhi and Jawaharlal Nehru, issued a Declaration of Independence intended to remove India as a colony of the British Empire.

Over the next two years, Gandhi and his followers began nonviolent protests or passive resistance, referred to as *satyagraha* by Gandhi, regarding salt and the taxes on the same, and on whether it was necessary to import cotton goods for Indians from Britain. This was not the first time that Gandhi used this approach. He had used it earlier in 1907 in response to a registration law, and his awareness of the approach may have stemmed from seeing Emmeline Pankhurst's suffragette movement in London in 1906. [308]

Gandhi had been serving time in jail because of his civil disobedience activities, but the Viceroy of India released him on January 28, 1931, as a gesture of good will. Gandhi responded by putting forward eleven demands or rights that he wanted for the people of India. They were:

1. The right of peasants to make their own salt (illegal at the time).
2. The right to boycott and picket.
3. Prohibition of the "toddy" (a pungent native drink fermented from palm sap).
4. A reduction of rupee exchange rate from 1s. 6d. to 1s. 4d.

---

[308] Arthur Herman, *Gandhi & Churchill: The Epic Rivalry That Destroyed an Empire and Forged Our Age*, New York: Bantam Books, 2008, p. 152-153.

5. A reduction of land revenues by 50 per cent.
6. A reduction of military expenditure by 50 per cent.
7. A reduction of salaries of high-grade Government employees by 50 per cent.
8. An increase in the protective tariff against foreign cloth (intended to make British cotton goods non-competitive).
9. Passage of Coastal Reservation Bill (aimed at British shipping).
10. The abolition of criminal police.
11. The right of citizens to use firearms for personal defence.[309]

The several monetary measures were intended to have Indians retain more of their income. If these demands were met by the British government of India, then Gandhi would call-off the civil disobedience and non-cooperation movement that was then underway.

All of this was occurring in early 1931 and at the same time the *Daily Mail*, perhaps anticipating something on the scale of a revolutionary war, sent Phillips to India to cover whatever developed. He remained there for 16 months. The salt episodes had occurred earlier in 1930, but the cotton boycott would occur later. One of Percival's major stories after his arrival was with regard to this boycott of English goods—particularly cotton—and Gandhi's plan to replace these with cotton textiles made in India.[310]

One can almost sense the anger in Phillips when he reports that the Viceroy of India has agreed to Gandhi's terms.[311] Of course this was not the end of anything; it was more like the beginning in a battle that had as its long term goal the independence of India. Gandhi was to have problems not just with the British, but with the Moslems in India and the untouchables of the Indian caste system. There would be no simple solutions.

In between Gandhi's demands and the Viceroy's agreement, Phillips covered the inauguration of New Delhi. Having covered the

---

[309] "Gandhi's Demands," *Daily Mail*, January 29, 1931.
[310] "Correspondent Attacks Accord," *New York Times*, March 5, 1931, p. 5.
[311] Sir Percival Phillips, "British in India Amazed at Viceroy's Surrender," *Daily Mail*, March 5, 1931, p. 8.

durbar of 1911, he was familiar with the reaction of most Indians to such ceremonies. However, attitudes toward the British were quite different in 1931 due in part to Gandhi's activities. Phillips described the inauguration as a "quiet, in some senses almost depressing ceremony." It lacked the brilliance of past events as well as the enthusiasm displayed on those occasions. "No crowd of Indians was lining the street or pressing against barriers to witness the pageant such as they delight in. It was more like a semi-private function."[312]

A second major story by Phillips was in response to Gandhi's plan to claim $6.3 billion from Britain for India's aid to the Empire since the reign of Queen Elizabeth I in the 16th century. In a dispatch to the *Daily Mail*, Phillips broke down the sum. Of the total, the amounts in terms of U.S. dollars were $3.6 billion was a refund to India of monies charged by the East India Company; $200 million was claimed as the cost of the Indian mutiny of 1857; and another $200 million was restitution for the wars that India fought in for the British Empire between 1857 and 1900. The World War had the empire charging India about $950 million for the war at its outset and an additional $850 million for the cost to India of that war. The remainder was interest on money owed to India.[313] The article received a considerable amount of attention at the time it was published. [314] It also led to Percival receiving the Gordon Selfridge Award for the best foreign correspondence.[315]

On the second anniversary of India's declaration of independence there were major demonstrations in Bombay and the setting of major bonfires fueled with British cloth. The Associated Press sent out the following story the next day:

> Sir Percival Phillips, American-born correspondent for a British newspaper, narrowly escaped violence

---

[312] As quoted in Reginald Reynolds, *The White Sahibs in India*, London: Secker and Warburg, 1937, p. 393.

[313] Sir Percival Phillips, "Indians Plan $6.327,000,000 Claim on Britain for Aid to Empire Since Queen Elizabeth," *New York Times*, July 13, 1931, p. 6.

[314] Sir Percival Phillips, "Gandhi's £1,265,000,000 Bill," *Daily Mail*, July 13, 1931, pp. 11-12.

[315] "No Scoop," *Time Magazine*, Monday, August 15, 1932.

when he was mistaken for a police official because he carried a club for self protection. He was saved only by intervention of natives who pleaded with the rioters to remember Gandhi's injunction against injuring foreigners. [316]

More than likely the "club" was a walking stick that Percival had taken to using during the 1914-1918 war in Europe.

To say that Phillips disliked Gandhi is to understate his actual feelings. Some of Gandhi's supporters had created problems for the Prince of Wales during his 1921-1922 tour of India. Phillips was on that tour and covered it for the *Daily Express* as noted previously. Gandhi's move to take India out of the British Empire was the basis for Phillips' strong dislike of him and what he proposed. He was also leery of Jawaharlal Nehru, Gandhi's second in command. Phillips saw him as a Bolshevik and pawn of the Soviet Union.

Phillips had heard Gandhi speak once when he was in Bombay. Gandhi had been asked to speak at the dinner of a radical young group known as the "Young Europeans" in June of 1931. Gandhi entered the dining hall wearing his usual *dhoti* and shawl and "sat down on a table, cool and relaxed, and proceeded to tell the Young Europeans, formal in dinner jackets and starched shirts, that complete and utter independence, and "Socialism" for India were his fixed goals. Most of them were shocked." [317]

Phillips and the other British correspondents that were in Bombay at the time boycotted Gandhi's speech. He told Edgar Snow, another correspondent, "I've got a job of work to do here." He added "The *Mail* is for the protection of British interests, first, last, and always. We can't do business with this blackguard Gandhi."[318] Snow stated, "Nevertheless, Phillips pride as a journalist got the better of his dignity as a knight of the realm. 'I couldn't resist having a look at the little leper,' [Phillips] admitted, 'I stood on a chair outside the door and heard every word through

---

[316] Associated Press, "Violence Marks Anniversary of Indian Revolt," *Lima (Ohio) News*, January 27, 1932.
[317] Edgar Snow, *Journey to the Beginning*, New York, Random House, 1958, p. 81.
[318] Ibid.

Dispatches from the World

the transom.'"[319] He also saw Gandhi as a wrecker and a dictator, based on the articles he had written. For one known to be objective and analytical, his views in this case were extreme and not without bias.

Phillips would be infuriated by the notion of India getting complete independence since this would be a severe economic blow to the British Empire. He was not alone. Winston Churchill was adamantly opposed to giving in on any of Gandhi's demands for fear of what it would do to the Empire. The *Daily Mail* shared his views. But the Empire was in the process of crumbling and although this would finally occur in the decades following World War II, there were many who tried to prevent it.

The story of Gandhi's efforts has been the subject of many other studies. In the present context, it is clear that the man was able to simply infuriate Phillips unlike anyone else that he encountered in his life and it is for that reason that it is included in this summary of some of Phillips' activities in India. He would remain there, covering Gandhi's activities until the middle of 1932.

Phillips' mother had been ill since the early 1920s. It is not known exactly what the ailment was, but it could have been a mental ailment related to the loss of three of her four sons. The latest of these was Smith, who had died in the automobile crash in 1920. Annie's mother had died in 1918 and her brother, David Knox Miller had died in August of 1920. Phillips visited her on numerous occasions during the early 1920s in Brownsville and then at Ligonier, probably in an attempt to comfort her.

Without other children or a husband, Annie's care was also his personal and financial responsibility. During one of the visits he transferred his mother from the sanatorium near Ligonier to the Hillsview Sanatorium on the southern tip of Main Street in Washington, Pennsylvania. It would appear that this was between 1926 and 1929. She was also suffering from numerous ailments related to her age. Her condition worsened in February of 1931 and she was taken to the West Penn Hospital in Pittsburgh. She died there on March 13, 1931; she was six days short of her 78th

---

[319] Ibid.

birthday.[320] A funeral service was held at the First Methodist Episcopal Church just down the street from her house on Church Street in Brownsville. Percival was in India at the time and because of the distances involved was unable to attend the services. Following the service the funeral procession went up the old National Road to the Redstone Cemetery where Annie Phillips would be buried. This is also where three of her sons were buried before her.

For a private music teacher she had acquired a large estate for the time. She left her silver and jewelry to Phillips. Four thousand dollars went into a trust fund for Smith Phillips' two sons. Her piano went to Ester M. Pollock, the five-year-old daughter of her niece Mary Kate Pollock (a daughter of her late brother, David Knox Miller), while other goods and clothing went to Mrs. Lillian McClain Miller, the widow of her brother. The rest went to her son, Percival, which in this case included her property and house on Church Street in Brownsville.[321]

Following Phillips return from India, the *Daily Mail* sent him to the United States in August of 1933 to study the National Recovery Act of the Roosevelt Administration. He visited numerous cities during the tour that covered most of the country from Boston to Los Angeles. In general his reports were considered balanced and fair, but he nevertheless saw some problems. In particular, he saw cases where prices were increasing significantly, and this was at a time when people would have had a difficult time purchasing goods at the former low prices.[322]

He also expressed some criticisms about the general pace of life in the U.S. after his return to London. He wrote, "Life within these frontiers appears to an Englishman accustomed to the easy pace of Europe to be a mad race around an alarm clock, with no

---

[320] "Mrs. Herbert (sic) Phillips: Mother of British War Correspondent Dies in Pittsburgh," *New York Times*, March 14, 1931; "Mrs. Anna Phillips Succumbs," *Brownsville Telegraph*, March 14, 1931.

[321] Estate Records, Mrs. Anna C.M. Phillips, Fayette County Courthouse, Uniontown, Pennsylvania.

[322] Sir Percival Phillips, "English View of the Price Boost in this Country," *Lincoln Sunday Journal and Star*, October 22, 1933, A12.

fixed goal in sight but the grave."[323] He admired the speed of some services, such as laundry, luggage, telephone and telegraph message delivery. But he added, "Meals are bolted in a way that shows no mercy for the delicate machinery dedicated to food. The intent of occupants of public restaurants is to rush in to refuel; they never really lunch or dine." [324]

Also in 1933 Phillips had a series of his articles that he had prepared for the *Daily Mail* published in a book by Methuen. The book was entitled *Far Vistas* and the articles included could be described as travel pieces, but that doesn't describe them very well.[325] Yes, the articles were of places, incidents, and situations that Phillips encountered in his travels, but Phillips was not the typical traveler. For example, few of his readers would venture into China and watch a public beheading in the 1920s. It is not known if the book was a commercial success; only three brief reviews of it are known. [326] *The Times Literary Supplement* notes that the articles had appeared in the *Daily Mail* and added:

> . . . given their purpose, they could hardly be bettered—the collection might serve as a text-book for young journalists . . . One conceives [Sir Percival] as descending upon any port of call and summoning it in the name of the *Daily Mail* to deliver a story.

"But it is when he is not thus assisted by the place . . . that we recognize his gifts most clearly."

Today much of the material described in the book is dated. It would appear that most of the pieces were written in the 1920s and early 1930s. Even if one had an interest in the subject matter, time has changed much of what he wrote. But there are a few pieces that

---

[323] "'Jove!—Those Americans Are Alarm Clocks!' Britisher Finds," *The Washington Post*, December 19, 1933, 11.
[324] Ibid.
[325] Sir Percival Phillips, *Far Vistas*, London: Methuen and Co., Ltd., 1933.
[326] Reviewed Works, "Far Vistas by Percival Phillips," *The Geographical Journal*, Vol. 83, No. 2, pp. 164-165; "Far Vistas," *The Times Literary Supplement*, October 5, 1933, p. 669; "Far Vistas," *Scottish Geographical Magazine*, Vol. 50, 1934, pp. 119-120.

would be of interest to anyone who is curious about how we got to where we are. In other words they have an interesting historical value even today.

One of these articles deals with the pageantry of the coronation of the "Lion of Judah." This was the coronation of Emperor Haile Selassie of Ethiopia in 1930, perhaps told better by Phillips than any other correspondent on the scene at the time. It is said that Haile Selassie thought Phillips had done the best job of covering the coronation.

Two other articles deal with the ocean liners from the early part of the 20th century. The first is a beautiful piece about the ships that Phillips sailed on during his career ("Liners that are Ladies—and Some Others"). His writing of this piece may have been prompted by Phillips sailing on a ship in Asia that reminded him of another ship he had sailed on in 1907 on his way to Jamaica; it actually was the same ship. This would have been the *Port Kingston* that had been adopted by Asian interests and was found ushering soldiers up and down the coast of China in the late 1920s, only to sink later in the Pacific. If the reader has ever visited the *Queen Mary* in Long Beach, California, this article clearly points out that there are worse places for the ocean liners of an earlier era. The second piece, "The Town That Goes to Sea," discusses the ocean liner as a mobile community and it is of interest.

If the reader has any interest in environmental impacts on animal life there are two chapters that should satisfy such an interest. One of these is "The Last Day of Freedom in the Jungle," and the other is "The Zoo in the Jungle." The first of these chapters focuses on elephants in Asia being captured for zoos in the West. The second chapter includes the other animals that eventually find their way to zoos in the United States and Europe. This was not exactly a new thesis for Phillips since he had addressed the zoo question in his other writings. [327]

Most of the forty articles included in the collection have lost their relevance in today's society with television channels that include important events in history, and channels that include all sorts of

---

[327] Sir Percival Phillips, "Where the Zoo Begins," as cited in "An Animal Inferno," *The Charleroi Mail*, March 13, 1930, p. 4.

Dispatches from the World

wild animal programs. In fact one can find a show that meets almost any interest that one has. However, that was not the case in the early 1930s and if we view the collection within the context of those days they were probably of considerable interest to newspaper readers. Today they might prove interesting to the cultural anthropologist with an interest in Asia, the historian, or an environmentalist, but few others.

Following his return from the U.S. in the fall of 1933 Phillips took time off for a holiday as was his custom. He was also missing from the pages of the *Daily Mail* for the early months of 1934, but in all likelihood he was in Asia. He wrote the occasional article on China or Siam in the spring, but by the time they appeared in print he had left these areas. He left Tokyo on April 27 and sailed to San Francisco on the *President Hoover*. He was in the U.S. for ten days before he sailed out of New York on the *Acquitania* for England.

Arriving back in London he took the recommendation of his foreign editor and interviewed himself regarding what he described as his fourth trip round the world. Actually it was his fourth trip at the expense of the *Daily Mail*. In his "interview" Phillips mentioned the highlights of the last trip. A couple of observations are worth noting here. As Phillips wrote, "Singapore I found suffering from the disease known in the United States as 'the jitters.' All the talk in clubs and offices was of war—impending, horrid war, out of the East. When, how, why, nobody seemed to know." [328]

The ambiguity of Phillips' response is somewhat confusing. Two years earlier he had written a column addressing the tensions between the U.S. and Japan. "The Japanese ask, if America opposes war, why does she insist on maintaining a great fleet within striking distance of Japan?" The question, which he received in Tokyo, was specifically directed toward the naval operations at Honolulu. Phillips interviewed several people in the Hawaiian Islands at the time and wrote, "I found the American community of Honolulu full of rumours of the possibility of war which they believe Japan will start in the

---

[328] Sir Percival Phillips, "I Interview Myself about My Fourth Trip Round the World," *Daily Mail*, June 6, 1934.

Pacific." [329] These are amazing statements for nine years before the attack on Pearl Harbor.

While he was in Japan he was very impressed with the railways stating:

> We have something to learn from Japan. Her railways are the most efficient I have found anywhere. I was told that if a train is more than five minutes late the driver is shot. This is obviously an exaggeration, but the statement could not be tested as I never found any train—express, omnibus or suburban—as much as a minute late. Yokohama and Tokyo are joined by an electric line with open cars of the London Underground pattern that run 20 minutes apart with the precision of a watch.[330]

Phillips continued writing articles for the *Daily Mail*, but at a very slow pace compared to his war years. There were less than two dozen articles for the year of 1934. This may be compared to nearly one every other day during the 1917-1918 years. It was not an age problem since he had maintained a very productive pace during the 1931-1932 period in India. Apparently, there was just very little of interest to him or his newspaper in the midst of the worldwide economic depression that merited him being assigned to different parts of the world, but that would soon change.

Rothermere may have sensed that Phillips was no longer happy being a correspondent for the *Daily Mail*. As the year 1934 was drawing to a close, he arranged to have Phillips' portrait painted by one Phillip Ledoux. This took place around November 22 at Phillips apartment on Chancery Lane. At the time Phillips was writing up a story on John Dillinger, the American gangster, based on his earlier travels through America. The Dillinger article appeared in the *Daily Mail* on November 29 of 1934, and it was his last article published prior to leaving that newspaper. It is not known if the painting was ever completed.

---

[329] "Eyes on America," *The* (Wellington, NZ) *Evening Post*, October 24, 1932.
[330] Ibid.

Dispatches from the World

*Sir Percival Phillips sitting for a portrait by Philip Ledoux
(Daily Mail, London)*

CHAPTER 20

with the *daily telegraph*

When Sir Percival Phillips left the *Daily Mail* in 1934, he never explained why. One can suggest several reasons. He had received the 1932 Selfridge Award for best foreign correspondence for the *Daily Mail* article he had written on "Gandhi's Bill." He also had a major collection of his writings for the *Daily Mail* published in the book entitled *Far Vistas*. Perhaps he felt he was underpaid for one as visible as he had become. There is a suggestion that he had a major argument with his editor at the *Mail* (based on a novel that was written by Evelyn Waugh entitled *Scoop*), but that has never been confirmed. It has also been suggested that there was a disagreement with Lord Rothermere, the owner of the *Daily Mail*, and possibly there was some disenchantment "with the erratic policies" of the *Daily Mail* involved in his departure.[331]

There is a very real possibility that Phillips came to fully disagree with Lord Rothermere's political leanings. Lord Rothermere was a friend and supporter of both Adolph Hitler and Benito Mussolini and he saw nothing wrong with Nazism or fascism. It has already been noted here that Phillips was pro-Mussolini in the early 1920s. This was the time when Lord Rothermere took complete control of the *Daily Mail* following the death of Lord Northcliffe. However,

---

[331] This is suggested by W. F. Deedes, *At War with Waugh: The Real Story of Scoop*. London: Macmillan, 2003. Deedes appears to be confused about when Phillips worked for the different London newspapers suggesting that he had worked for the *Telegraph* earlier.

while Phillips began to see the problems of Mussolini's fascism over time, Lord Rothermere's became a more extreme supporter of the political ideologies and leaders of Italy and Germany. [332] This may very well have been Phillips' primary reason for leaving the *Daily Mail* and moving over to the *Daily Telegraph*, but we cannot be sure of this based on the documents that have survived.

At this time Phillips did not generally cover political developments in Europe. However, in 1935 he briefly covered such developments from Vienna. He followed the rise of Hitler and the Nazi party and in that year he wrote:

> The Nazis, after months of despondency, are again raising their heads. The return of the Saar to Germany, and Germany's denunciation of the Treaty of Versailles have given them new courage. They are saying in effect that Hitler has shown them the way. By lifting his voice and banging his fist on the table, he has compelled his enemies abroad to respect, if not fear, Germany, and they propose to follow the same tactics.
>
> Terrorism being out of question at present, as they have no arms, they have turned to intensive propaganda. Despite the vigilance of the Government, their activity has increased enormously.
>
> The Socialists have kept together and are likewise engaged in a lively propaganda offensive. Far from being cowed, their publicists boast of a good fight made against Fascism in defense of the Republican Constitution. They point to the vast model housing schemes, which have been realized in the industrial outskirts of Vienna and the improved condition of the working classes as practical results of a Socialist policy.[333]

---

[332] S. J. Taylor, *The Great Outsiders: Northcliffe, Rothermere and the Daily Mail*, London: Weidenfeld & Nicholson, 1996.

[333] A quotation from the Daily Telegraph that appeared in *Living Age*, Vol. 348, 1935, p. 382.

Dispatches from the World

One of Phillips other early assignments with the *Telegraph* in 1935 took him to Greece to cover a rebellion. Of course there was nothing new about revolutions in Greece; they were almost something to be expected. *The Times* reporter saw the rebellion differently, referring to the event satirically as "the best organized revolt of recent years in Greece." [334] The revolt was over within less than two weeks with casualties listed as nine dead and 94 injured. The failure of the rebellion was attributable to numerous factors, but a principal one was that "it had no national basis or justification, but was inspired entirely by personal ambitions." [335] Phillips had covered the story, but within a short period of time he was back in London.

On May 30, 1935, Phillips sailed for the United States on the *Normandie* out of Southampton, England. It was the maiden voyage for this ocean liner and it crossed the Atlantic in very good time arriving in New York on June 3.

The *Telegraph* had sent him over to the States to cover the two national political conventions, the Republican convention held in Cleveland from June 9 to 12, and the Democratic Convention held in Philadelphia from June 23 to June 27. It is likely that Phillips visited with the family of his former sister-in-law and her two sons while in Cleveland, but no record of such a visit has survived.

Phillips was to write a series of articles on President Franklin D. Roosevelt's New Deal. The *Telegraph* was not concerned with the New Deal programs, since these were covered earlier by Phillips in a series of fair and impartial articles for the *Daily Mail*. The newspaper's concern was whether the New Deal programs were unpopular enough that they could lead to Roosevelt losing his reelection bid in November. Writing in early July, Phillips asserted that Roosevelt appeared to have the support of agriculture and industry, with the possible exception of the steel industry.[336] He suggested that it

---

[334] "Greek Revolt Ended," *The Times*, March 13, 1935, p. 14.

[335] Ibid.

[336] Sir Percival Phillips, "Farmers Still Supporting Roosevelt. Best Allies in Middle West. Opposition from Small Traders." *Daily Telegraph*, July 8, 1935, Sir Percival Phillips, "U.S. Industry Still Behind Roosevelt. Tribute to Work for Recovery. Radio Priest's Wage Campaign. Call for Minimum of £430 a Year." *Daily Telegraph*, July 10, 1935; Sir Percival Phillips, "Steel Critics o Roosevelt. Employers and Men Dissatisfied. Huge Coal Strike Still Possible," *Daily Telegraph*, July 13, 1935.

looked as though Roosevelt would be reelected unless there was a serious domestic problem, such as a major coal strike, before the election.

Phillips also noted that the northern cities had seen a major increase in blacks who had moved there from southern states. Legislation had been passed in some northern states, notably Pennsylvania, that provided for equal rights and nondiscrimination. This was causing some friction between the races and Phillips wrote that this friction could lead to a revival of the Klu-Klux-Klan.[337] In this regard, Phillips was perhaps naive; the Klan had really never gone away.

While in the U.S., he spent time in Chicago, Cleveland, Pittsburgh, Detroit, Washington, D.C., New Orleans, Philadelphia, and Boston. His plans were to return to Europe on the 17th of July. When he applied for a sailing permit, he was told that he would have to obtain an income tax clearance. He cut his stay in Washington short so that he could supply the Collector of Internal Revenue in New York with a statement of his earnings in the U.S. and then pay taxes that were due on these. He did this under protest, obtained his clearance and sailing permit and returned to England on the *Europa* on the 17th.

Phillips wasn't just anyone and the incident drew more and more attention as it pertained to newspaper reporters since it was quite common for U.S. reporters to travel abroad and not necessarily be taxed in foreign countries.[338] Several months later the U.S. Treasury decided to revise the tax regulations as they pertained to visiting correspondents, but there are no indications that Phillips ever benefitted from this change.[339]

The exact same taxation-sailing permit problem happened to R.D. Blumenfeld, Phillips' editor during part of his time at the *Daily Express*. The situation is a bit more ludicrous than the Phillips' case. In 1922 Blumenfeld came to the U.S. to buy some printing equipment for his *Daily Express* operations in London. He purchased the equipment

---

[337] Sir Percival Phillips, "Race Feeling in the U.S. Political Power of the Negro. Fear of Revival of Klu-Klux-Klan," *Daily Telegraph*, July 18, 1935.

[338] "Washington Upholds Actions," *New York Times*, August 16, 1935, p. 13; "An Expensive Tax," *New York Times*, August 29, 1935, p. 20.

[339] "Treasury Plans to Revise Tax Regulations to Stop Levy on Visiting Journalists," *New York Times*, March 10, 1936, p. 2.

for approximately $200,000, a huge sum for the time. As he went to secure a sailing permit the Collector of Internal Revenue also wanted him to pay tax on that portion of his income earned while in the U.S. In this case the major protest came from the American Manufacturers' Export Association.[340]

Phillips was in his late fifties at this point and he may have had the desire to pass along some of what he knew to other journalists. In any event it was during this time that he offered advice to Francis McCullagh and Noel Monks. Phillips had known McCullagh for at least 25 years, dating back to their coverage of the war in Tripoli in 1911, when he wrote what appears below. Monks was new to the trade and was working for the *Daily Express* at the time.

Monks wrote about the Ethiopian period to be discussed later in this chapter and stated:

> Looking back now, to such men as Sir Percival Phillips, the most loveable man it has ever been my luck to call colleague, we must have seemed a pretty green lot. Percy, as he insisted we call him, had received his knighthood for his services as a war correspondent in the First World War. He was in his sixties, yet he still lived in the age of enthusiasm, which was why he was still one of the world's top newspapermen. When a newspaperman loses his enthusiasm, he has arrived at the hack stage of his career, and should give up journalism before it gives him up.
>
> Percy's title gave him a decided advantage over his colleagues on occasions, particularly when we were dealing with the British Embassy, but Percy himself never traded on it. "I'm Phillips of the *Daily Telegraph*," was how he always introduced himself. His twinkling blue eyes exuded friendship and sincerity. From the many sessions on world affairs and the job of a foreign correspondent I had with Percy Phillips

---

[340] "Blumenfeld Taxed Wrongly on Salary," *The New York Times*, June 11, 1922.

in his room at the Imperial Hotel, I gathered a rich harvest of knowledge that was to stand me in good stead in the years ahead.

It was he who taught me, for instance, the importance of protocol to a foreign correspondent. "Whenever you arrive in a foreign land, check your baggage at your hotel, then jump in a taxi and start dropping your cards," he advised. Through that simple practice, I was to gain more contacts and make more friends in foreign parts than had I letters of introduction. For the signing of an Ambassador's visitors' book or placing of your card on a Minister's salver can set up a chain reaction of invitations and meetings with people who matter sufficiently to put any visiting fireman 'in the picture.' Another thing Percy taught me was the extreme importance of the 'thank you' cable or letter to officials and people who had helped you during your assignment. "You never know when you will pass their way again," he said. "Anyhow, it's good manners. And they always remember your newspaper, even if they should forget you." In retrospect, I would say that, apart from the mechanics of the job, these are two cardinal rules for a successful foreign correspondent. My paper and I have friends all over the world to prove it. [341]

Phillips also had long discussions with Frank McCullagh during the Spanish Civil War about balance in reporting. He said:

Most of the British and American correspondents came here full of admiration for Franco and his men. As you know yourself, the first canon of the war correspondent is to tell the truth, and the second is to identify himself with the side he happens to be on. Good old Charlie Hands of the Daily Mail expounded

---

[341] Noel Monks, *Eyewitness*, London: Frederick Muller Ltd., 1955, pp. 41-42.

Dispatches from the World

> that second canon to me over thirty years ago, when I was lamenting, at one of my first wars, the fact that I couldn't get the views of the other side so as to draw an impartial picture. [342]

> 'That's your editor's business, damn you!' said Charlie. 'It's your business to take up the cudgels for this side, and this side only. Your paper has got a man on the other side, who will take up their quarrel, so that it will get both sides. Work yourself into a state of enthusiasm for the people here, otherwise you'll write milk-and-water stuff that won't be worth printing! Glory in their cavalry charges, and their night marches, and their triumphal entry into the captured towns.' [343]

Much of what Phillips had written during the World War was criticized because he did not reveal troop movements, fatalities and wounded, and the units involved. One could do this in 1914 and he did so. Then later in 1918 when victory was within sight, it was also possible to report the details. But from 1915 until mid-1918 one could not be so cavalier with strategic details. He altered his style as indicated in an article by the man in charge of the press coverage of war operations in Europe for part of the time, the Hon. Neville Lytton:

> There are many ways of describing operations. It is possible to try to give an idea of the sufferings and hardships of the men who were killed and wounded by hundreds and thousands every day along the huge battle front, or to pass over the tragic element, which is never absent, and adopt the attitude of a well-trained staff officer, who gives you the

---

[342] Charles Hands joined the *Daily Mail* shortly after it was formed in 1896. He became a war correspondent and covered the Spanish-American War in Cuba, the Boer War, and the Russo-Japanese War. He retired from journalism in 1921.

[343] Captain Francis McCullagh, *In Franco's Spain*, London: Burns Oates & Washbourne Ltd., 1937, pp. 125-126.

> evolution of facts with mathematical precision. The latter manner was adopted by Percival Phillips, and during the course of the war he made a great name for himself, and will go down in posterity along with Henri Bidon of France and Signor Barzini of Italy as the greatest of war critics.
>
> Phillips was a perfect map-reader, and the balance of his judgment was such that out of chaos and confusion he made logic and common sense. Our French friends knew that every word that he wrote could be trusted; the wives and families of our soldiers at home knew that he gave them facts without sentiment.[344]

Monks, McCullagh, and Lytton give us an inkling of how Phillips worked as a journalist and how he was perceived by others.

Each of Phillips' colleagues viewed his approach to reporting the war quite differently. Gibbs saw him as a scholar of war who understood the motivations and goals of the various generals and their individual approaches to the war. Nevinson saw him as detached, unsympathetic to the plight of the soldiers in the trenches. The contradictions in these views are probably due in part to when the observations were made. Gibbs was with Phillips through a good part of the war. Nevinson came to cover the war in August of 1918 when Gibbs went on a month's leave. Nevinson was covering the war for a brief period and this was near its end after the censors would allow the correspondents to write about the hardships of the soldiers. Phillips had been covering the war since the invasion of Belgium in 1914. If Phillips was concerned over the human dimensions of the war, the censors would not allow him to write about this. In addition, he would have had to discard such views by 1918, or gone mad. It is true that Nevinson knew Phillips from a previous conflict in the Balkans, but that little war was comparable to a morning's battle during the Great War.

---

[344] Hon. Neville Lytton, "A Great Witness. Sir Percival Phillips' Work at the Front." *Daily Express,* March 31, 1920.

CHAPTER 21

the "scoop" and ethiopia

During the summer of 1935 it was becoming evident that Benito Mussolini of Italy was probably going to go to war with Ethiopia. The dictator saw resources that Italy could use and he apparently thought Ethiopia was his for the taking. The only question seemed to be when this war would happen. Newspapers of London sent several reporters to Addis Ababa to monitor the situation. Among those on board the ship to Djibouti, French Somaliland, were James Mills of the Associated Press, Evelyn Waugh of the *Daily Mail* and Phillips, representing the *Daily Telegraph*. Waugh, an established novelist at the time, had been hired as a correspondent by the *Mail* when Phillips left that newspaper. Also on the ship was one Francis M. Rickett, unknown to the others and believed to be an agent of some sort.

At the time there were two types of train trips from Djibouti to Addis Ababa, Ethiopia's capital in the 1920s and 1930s. One took two days and the other took three days. The group opted for the two-day trip since it was leaving first. They stopped overnight at Dire Dawa and then continued on the following day. The climb to the plateau where the capital was located was slow. On the three-day trip they would have stopped for the night at Awash and stayed in a hotel lit only with candlelight. Awash was near the Awash Gorge created by the river of the same name. On this occasion they just continued with the trip. There were other stops along the route with natives offering fruits and vegetables to passengers on the train.

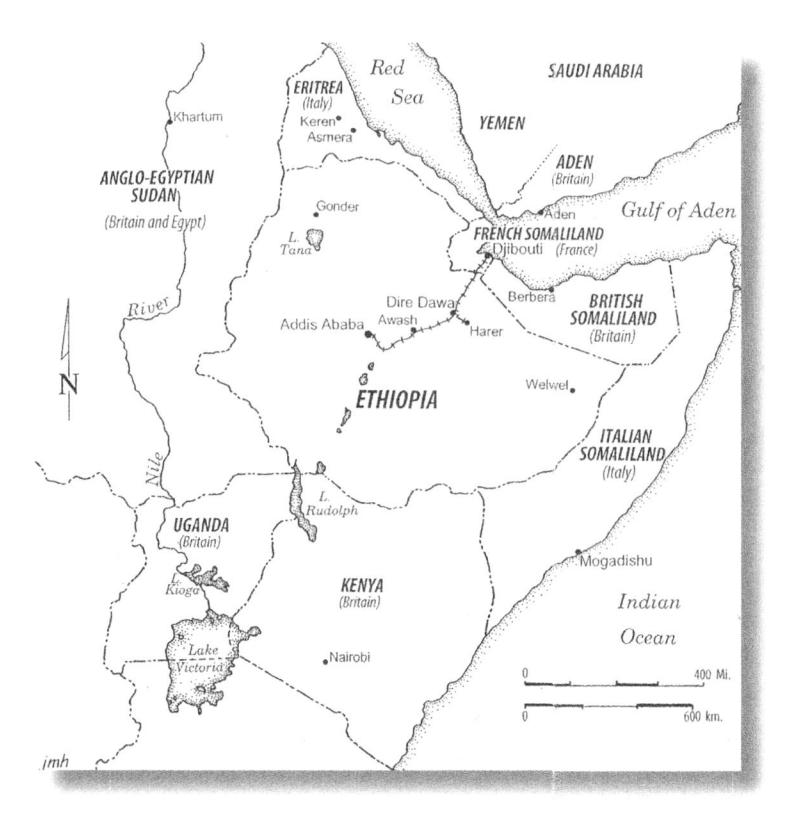

Ethiopia and Neighboring Countries and Colonies (1935).

During the trip to the capital Lawrence Stallings or Emile Pierre, both were motion picture photographers with Fox MovieTone in Ethiopia at the time, photographed much of the scenery along the way and then turned his camera on the very attractive Fay Gillis Wells, a reporter with the *New York Herald Tribune*, who had married Linton Wells in April of 1935.[345] He was also a reporter for the *Herald Tribune* and the two spent their honeymoon covering the Ethiopian conflict. The camera operator then turned his camera on Sir Percival Phillips sitting next to a window and wearing a light-colored suit. He

---

[345] Fay Gillis Wells was scheduled to participate in an air show in Detroit and then take a flight across Alaska and Siberia to Moscow with Wiley Post. She cancelled those plans and flew to New York where she joined her husband for the assignment in Ethiopia. The Moscow flight she was to take with Post crashed killing him and Will Rogers. See Linton Wells, *Blood on the Moon: The Autobiography of Linton Wells*, Boston: Houghton Mifflin Company, 1937, p. 370.

Dispatches from the World

was very busy typing using the "hunt and peck" system. Although touch typing would have been invented by the time Phillips learned to type in the 1880s, it apparently had not reached Pittsburgh by that time.[346]

From Djibouti to Addis Ababa the temperature cools as the elevation increases along the rail line. Waugh notes:

> Most visitors to Addis Ababa arrive feeling ill. The sudden rise from the coast level to eight thousand feet, the change of temperature from the heat of the Red Sea to the cold nights and sunless days of the plateau in rainy season, the food and, if they are imprudent, the water they have consumed at the railway buffets during the ascent, all contribute to disturb the hardiest constitution.[347]

There were two hotels in Addis Ababa at the time. The principal hotel was the Imperial, a barrack-like structure run by a Greek. The hotel had a lounge that was "bare like a station waiting room. There was a notice board and posters on the wall and a billiard table with barefooted Abyssinian waiters, serving drinks: gin and whisky and cognac and Abyssinian beer. At meals you drank Chianti" until someone remembered it was an Italian wine and the stores of it were destroyed.[348] The other hotel was the Europe Hotel, which was superior to the Imperial, but it was far from the center of the town, so few correspondents stayed there.[349]

Phillips was well known to the Emperor, Haile Selassie, from the interview in the early 1920s in London and the coronation in 1930. He was also known to merchants and proprietors in Addis Ababa. He and James Mills had lodgings held for them at the Imperial Hotel. Others had tried to get these rooms prior to the arrival of Phillips and Mills, but the proprietor had merely laughed at these offers. When the

---

[346] Ethiopia, 09/28/1935–10/08/1935, MT-MT-T-207, National Archives, Washington, D.C.

[347] E. Waugh, *Waugh in Abyssinia*, New York: Methuen, 1984 edition, p. 73.

[348] Patrick Balfour, "Fiasco in Addis Ababa." in Ladislas Farago (ed.), *Abyssinian Stop Press*, London: Robert Hale & Company, 1936, p. 58.

[349] Ibid., p. 59.

two correspondents did arrive on or about August 19 of 1935 they pulled their resources consisting of six competent journalists and one or two assistants and began trying to determine who Francis Rickett was and why he was in Ethiopia. They were aided in this effort by daily cables they received from their offices in London and Geneva. This also made them valuable to Ethiopian authorities who had access to the cables and this is part of the reason they were such welcomed guests. [350]

Evelyn Waugh had assumed Rickett was an arms dealer intent on supplying the Ethiopians with weapons for its eventual conflict with Italy. [351] Apparently Phillips and Mills thought there was more to him than arms and there is a suggestion that Phillips may have had him followed after his arrival in Addis Ababa. It soon became apparent to the two correspondents that Rickett was representing certain oil development interests. He had been responsible for opening up 45,000 square miles of oil fields in Iraq and it was known, at least in certain sectors, that he had been meeting with Emperor Haile Selassie for at least eight months regarding some sort of an arrangement. [352] Although it was initially reported that Rickett represented a group of Anglo-American interests, it later became apparent that these interests were entirely American. [353]

Although there was a major concern for determining who Rickett was, Phillips continued to turn in daily dispatches during August with the by-line indicating they were coming from Addis Ababa. These were primarily concerned with the preparations for an eventual war that were being taken in Addis Ababa and Ethiopia in general. [354]

---

[350] W.F. Deedes, *At War with Waugh: The Real Story of Scoop*, London: Macmillan, 2003, p. 47.

[351] Ibid., p. 28.

[352] Frederick T. Birchall, "British Ask Delay in Ethiopian Deal," *New York Times*, August 31, 1935, p. 1.

[353] Will Barber, "Claims Ethiopia Oil Venture is 100% American," *Chicago Daily Tribune*, September 2, 1935, p. 2.

[354] The following are the titles and dates of Sir Percival Phillips dispatches from Addis Ababa as they appeared in the *Daily Telegraph*: "Abyssinians Unaffected by Crisis," August 20; "Addis Ababa Volunteers," August 21; "The Emperor's Concern at Lack of Arms," August 22; "Drama of Shot Italian Consul in Abyssinia," August 23; "Italy's Plans Checked by Consul Mishap," August 24; "Emperor's War Warning to Abyssinia," August 26; "Italy's Legation Archives Leave," August 27; "Munitions for

In the meantime it became apparent to Rickett that he was being followed. He confronted Mills and Phillips stating, "You two have been following me for over a week now. In another day or two the rest of the reporters are going to wake up to the fact. That is apt to spoil everything—for you as well as for me. What I have to do here makes it imperative that I act quietly and unobserved." [355] In response to this, Mills was indifferent and Phillips said nothing. Then Ricketts said, "I have a proposal to make. If you'll stop shadowing me, within a few days I'll give you one of the biggest stories that ever happened." [356] The two reporters agreed not to pursue the story for several days.

A few nights later Rickett gave Mills and Phillips a copy of the agreement that had been worked out with the Emperor. The agreement that Haile Selassie had his minister sign with Rickett gave the African Exploitation and Development Corporation a 75-year lease to develop oil and mineral deposits in Ethiopia.

Haile Selassie's motivation seems clear enough. Whether he was seeking a deal with the Americans or the Americans and British, his intent was to make Mussolini hesitate for fear of upsetting one or the other of these two nations and eventually bringing them into any conflict that might develop with the Italians on the Ethiopian side.

Phillips and Mills spent the next several hours writing their stories and wiring these to their home offices. Phillips' article in *The Daily Telegraph* began:

> A few strokes of an ordinary black fountain-pen this morning performed one of the most momentous and far-reaching acts in the history of Ethiopia, bringing her out from the Middle Ages and setting her squarely on the road to the twentieth century.[357]

Abyssinia's Southern Army," August 28; "Moslem Aid for Emperor of Abyssinia," August 29; and, "Merchants Urged Not to Leave Abyssinian Capital," August 30.

[355] Oliver Gramling, *AP: The Story of News*, Ann Arbor: University Microfilms, 1968, p. 408.

[356] Ibid., pp. 409.

[357] Sir Percival Phillips, "Abyssinia's £ 10,000,000 Deal with British & U.S. Interests," *The Daily Telegraph*, August 31, 1935, p. 1.

He went on for more than 2,000 words explaining what had occurred.

The proposed concession would give the development corporation control over the valuable and very rich oil fields of Aussa-Jigjigga. Exploration had revealed these fields to be comparable to the oil fields of Iraq. To remove the oil, a 300 mile long pipeline was proposed that would move the oil to the coast. Construction costs were expected to be about 3 million British pounds. Annual payments to Ethiopia would allow the Emperor to further develop his country.

Everything was proposed to begin at once, with geologists, drillers and related personnel to arrive within a few weeks. After further exploration, machinery and related equipment would arrive. Roads would also have to be constructed and eventually a railway would run parallel to the pipeline.

Phillips also noted that other negotiations were underway that would seek to conserve the waters of Lake Tsana, the source of the Blue Nile. The control of this project would involve interests representing Ethiopia, Sudan and Egypt. This project would involve building pumping stations that would guarantee an adequate water supply for Sudan and Egypt. Water supply had always caused friction between Cairo, Khartoum and Addis Ababa.

As Frederick Birchall of the *New York Times* wrote:

> Whatever the ultimate outcome of Mr. Rickett's present deal, he has provided one of the outstanding journalistic scoops of the present London season. Sir Percival Phillips, special correspondent of *The Daily Telegraph* at Addis Ababa, seems to have been in the confidence of one or other parties to the deal, and his paper alone in London had the news of it, to the extent of about three columns. His nearest competitor is touring Ethiopia, and the others were peacefully sleeping when his dispatch was printed. There was a lot of perturbation in rival newspaper establishments today. [358]

---

[358] Frederick Birchall, op. cit., p. 14.

Dispatches from the World

Noel Monks, working for the London *Daily Express* at the time, recorded events that occurred later:

> In the crummy dining hall of the Imperial Hotel we feted Sir Percival with a dinner that night. 'Scooped' though we were, we had no hard feelings, and anyhow it was a pleasure to be 'scooped' by such a delightful person. Sitting next to me at that dinner was a little man who had already had his foot well and truly on the literary ladder, if not the journalistic one—Evelyn Waugh. [359]

All of the correspondents in Addis Ababa realized the significance of the "scoop" that Phillips and Mills had obtained. Monks view was similar to others. He wrote: "Not in all the twenty years I have been a foreign correspondent have I known such world-wide repercussions to one man's story as there were to Percy Phillips' Rickett's oil concession." [360]

Of course the American and British governments were furious with what they saw as an attempt to draw them into an eventual war and the deal was delayed and then finally squashed. But the scoop remained, much to the embarrassment of Evelyn Waugh, the novelist turned correspondent who was Phillips competition, and the correspondent who was touring Ethiopia at the time the scoop occurred.

The *Daily Mail* had hired Waugh because of his reputation as a great writer of the day and a well-known author in England. He was hired explicitly to replace Percival Phillips, so the newspaper was extremely upset with Waugh for missing the story and it brought to a close their working relationship. Waugh attempted to save some face by writing a novel entitled *Scoop*.[361] The Peterborough column in *The Daily Telegraph* in 1938 noted the following:

> Mr. Evelyn Waugh, in his entertaining new novel 'Scoop,' which I have been late off the mark in

---

[359] Noel, Monks, *Eyewitness*. London: Frederick Muller Ltd., 1955, p. 44.
[360] Ibid., p. 43.
[361] Evelyn Waugh, *Scoop*, Boston: Little, Brown and Company, 1937.

> reading, is anxious to the point that the African War it describes should not be confused with the Abyssinian campaign. In this he was himself a newspaper correspondent.
>
> I imagine, nevertheless, that most readers have recognized the late Sir Percival Phillips in Sir Jocelyn Hitchcock, the famous journalist who figures in the book.
>
> It is true that while Mr. Waugh carefully gives Hitchcock a white mustache, Phillips was clean-shaven. But, with one important reservation, the portrait is unmistakable. Mr. Waugh even makes Hitchcock ascribe his success to a habit of 'getting up earlier than the other fellow.'
>
> It was in these very words that Phillips himself explained the one great 'scoop' of the Abyssinian war. This was his own.
>
> At this point Mr. Waugh does less than justice to his distinguished original. He makes Hitchcock return home early in the war.
>
> This leaves the 'scoop' of the title to be obtained by the novel's incompetent hero.
>
> Actually, as will be well remembered, Phillips' famous message from Addis Ababa to the 'Daily Telegraph' revealing the Rickett concession was not only the war's biggest scoop but one of the greatest in modern journalism. [362]

Perhaps Evelyn Waugh got some satisfaction from writing the book; he would never return to being a correspondent.

---

[362] Rose Macaulay, 'Peterborough', *The Daily Telegraph*, 2 June 1938, p. 14.

Several years later Phillip Knightley wrote the book "The First Casualty," which claims that Phillips made up news stories while in Ethiopia in 1935. Knightley's source for this allegation was O'Dowd (O.D.) Gallagher, a reporter who was also in Addis Ababa in the 1930s for the *Daily Express*, Phillips' old newspaper. Knightley includes the following in his book:

> What happens is best described by the series of cables O.D. Gallagher received from his newspaper, the *Daily Express*, soon after Sir Percival arrived.

PHILLIPS IN TELEGRAPH SAYS ABYSSINIANS SPEARMEN MASSING IN TIGRE FRONT STOP WHAT FOLLOWS UP EXYOU.

> The second read:

DANAKIL TRIBESMEN MUTILATED ITALIAN SCOUTING PARTY ACCORDING TO PHILLIPS IN TELEGRAPH STOP AWAIT ACTION REPORT EXYOU

> The third:

PHILLIPS DESCRIBES HAILE SELASSIE SQUARE AS PICCADILLY CIRCUS OF ADDIS STOP THIS GREAT STUFF STOP LET'S HAVE YOUR COMPARISONS HAILE SELASSIES CAPITAL WITH LONDON.

The fourth shows the *Express*' concern at being regularly scooped by the *Daily Telegraph*.

BEG YOU EMULATE PHILLIPS STOP YOUR LACK CABLES MOST DISCONCERTING STOP NOT ONLY YOUR JOB BUT MINE AT STAKE SAYS CHRISTIANSEN [the editor] BECAUSE EYE SENT YOU ABYSSINIA—SUTTON [foreign editor] [363]

---

[363] Phillip Knightly, *The First Casualty*, Baltimore and London: The Johns Hopkins University Press, 1975 and 2000, p. 191.

According to Knightley, Gallagher went out to check on the spear men story and the mutilated Italian scouting party. Once again, according to Knightley, Gallagher could find no one who knew anything about these incidents, except for Phillips. One is left with the impression that Phillips fabricated the stories, if the stories were ever actually published.

Gallagher also suggests that some of the best parts of Phillips' stories were paraphrased from a book by C.F. Rey (*In the Country of the Blue Nile*). [364] This particular point is difficult to believe since Rey only writes about two areas that Phillips also writes about: the train trip from Djibouti to Addis Ababa and the latter city. There are similarities between the descriptions of the train trip, but it is a single track train trip and the things observed had not changed appreciably between Rey's trip in the 1920s and Phillips trip in 1935. Incidentally, the descriptions of the train trip by Waugh and Wells are also similar; there is not much to write about that is that different. [365]

It is reasonable to assume that Phillips would refer to Haile Selassie Square as the Piccadilly Square of Addis Ababa, that was the type of hyperbole that Phillips had used many times in the past; although there is no proof that such an article was ever published. In his collection of writings that appears in his book *Far Vistas*, Phillips refers to different areas of Addis Ababa in terms of similar places in pre-Reformation London such as "Cheapside" and the Strand. However, the *Far Vistas* chapter is based on Phillips' visiting the city during the coronation of Haile Selassie five years earlier. At this point it becomes tenable that Gallagher was confused in "recalling" the events of 1935.

There are no dates attached to any of the material in the Knightley piece above. There are no dates for when the articles were supposed to have appeared regarding the massing of spear men or the mutilation of an Italian scouting party, or when the London cables arrived in Addis Ababa. Knightley says they arrived "soon after Sir Percival arrived." Phillips fabricating a story about mutilations is something difficult to fathom. It is possible that one

---

[364] C.F. Rey, *In the Country of the Blue Nile*, London: Duckworth, 1927.

[365] Evelyn Waugh, *Waugh in Abyssinia*, London: Longmans, Green and Co., Ltd., 1936; Linton Wells, *Blood on the Moon: The Autobiography of Linton Wells*, Boston: Houghton, Mifflin and Co., 1937.

Dispatches from the World

of the six or seven younger journalists working with Phillips and Mills may have written such an article, but it is doubtful that Phillips would allow it to go out under his by-line. It is possible that such an article was published, but it was not published in copies of the *Telegraph* that were preserved and microfilmed. It was also not published during the months of August, September or October of 1935 of the preserved newspaper, which under the most liberal of definitions would be "soon after Sir Percival arrived." There were other editions of the *Daily Telegraph* that have not been preserved and it is possible that the articles appeared in those editions, and were not retained.

The episodes noted earlier were apparently described by O'Dowd Gallagher to Knightley in an interview, which is also undated by the latter. We can assume it was between 1954 and 1975; Knightley met Gallagher in 1954 and Knightley's book was published in 1975.[366] In an unrelated story O.D. Gallagher also told Knightley that Robert Capa's famous photograph of "The Falling Soldier" from the Spanish Civil War was based on a staged incident. Knightley also includes this claim in his book. [367] It seems fairly certain based on subsequent research that Gallagher was incorrect. [368]

Knightley says that Gallagher's response to his editor's urging for more dispatches like those of Phillips was the preparation of a piece similar to what Phillips was alleged to have written. According to Knightley, Gallagher wrote this in association with Noel Monks, another correspondent in Addis Ababa at the time. Although Monks was to write an autobiography years later, he makes no mention of the incident with Gallagher. On the other hand he has nothing but praise for Phillips as a correspondent and as a colleague. [369] Noel Monks died in 1960.

What can be concluded about the above allegations of fabricated stories and possible plagiarism by Phillips? It seems apparent that the alleged articles may have never appeared and the general charges of plagiarism are unfounded. Of course the major problem with a

---

[366] Phillip Knightley, "Why We Still Need Serious Journalism," *Cold Type*, 2005; www.coldtype.net
[367] Ibid., pp. 227-230.
[368] Richard Whelan, "Robert Capa's Falling Soldier," *Aperture*, No. 166, 2002.
[369] Noel Monks, *Eye Witness*, London: Frederick Muller, Ltd., 1955.

definitive conclusion is that Gallagher's charges are not substantiated by any other source and Knightley does a less than satisfactory job of documenting the allegations of Gallagher.

Nicholas Rankin in his biography of correspondent George L. Steer notes that Philip Knightly repeats another story told to him by O.D. Gallagher. This story states that Gallagher faked a telegram of congratulations to Steer from the owner of *The Times* of London. "Gallagher's punch line was that its interception by the Ethiopian authorities led to Steer's first getting an exclusive interview with the Emperor." As Rankin notes "this is unlikely, since Gallagher only reached Addis Ababa a week after Steer met Haile Selassie." [370]

Overall one must conclude that the evidence in support of Gallagher's charges is non-existent. But what do we know of Phillips' attitude toward reporting events that did not occur? To answer this we must return to the time following the World War when Phillips was covering the problems with German labor in the Ruhr region of Germany. While he was there, he met a writer who had a freelance assignment with the *Toronto Star* from February of 1920 until December of 1924. The writer was Ernest Hemingway and he mentioned an interesting incident that pertained to Phillips in one of his news columns as follows:

> Percival Phillips, of the *Daily Mail*, after he had been badly letdown by a piece of French news he used which proved false the next day, said he would use no more of either (French or German) press bureau's news without labeling it from the press bureau. "My paper is pro-French," he said, "but it might not always be my paper, and I have a reputation as a journalist to sustain." [371]

This gives one a fairly good idea of what Phillips thought about anything false getting into his daily column.

---

[370] Nicholas Rankin, *Telegram from Guernica: The Extraordinary Life of George Steer, War Correspondent*, London: Faber and Faber, 2003, p. 19.

[371] Ernest Hemingway, "French Speed with Movies on the Job," *Toronto Star*, May 16, 1923.

Dispatches from the World

The Rickett oil concessions incident may have caused Mussolini to pause slightly, but after the British and U.S. disavowed the agreement, he was anxious to expand the area under his control. This could obviously not be done very easily in Europe, but Africa was a completely different situation. He already had control of Italian Somaliland and Eritrea, but lying between these two colonies was Ethiopia. He was convinced that Europe and the League of Nations (of which Ethiopia was a member) would do very little to interfere if he made a move against Ethiopia, and he was correct. There were indications that Italy had increased the production of potential military equipment for such a war, but they had these production sites dispersed and they moved the materials at night. This made it difficult to really know what was happening.

The reason why the League of Nations members in Europe, and Britain was a leader of this group, didn't do something to halt the invasion of Ethiopia was that they needed and wanted Mussolini's help in trying to control Adolph Hitler of Germany who had his own wild plans for Europe. Winston Churchill thought that Mussolini could do this. But then, Mussolini signed a pact with Hitler, and the weapons for the Italian invasion were sent to Mussolini's other two lands in the region: Eritrea and Italian Somaliland.[372]

At the time any little disagreement between Italy and Ethiopia was magnified to the point of a major international incident. But there was a general belief that Italy would not attack. This general belief was discarded on October 3, 1935 when Italian planes bombed Adowa. As Phillips reported from Addis Ababa, even the Italian Minister to Ethiopia "was startled by the suddenness of the Italian advance."[373] On October 7 a delayed dispatch from Phillips revealed that the Emperor Haile Selassie had allowed all Italians to safely leave the country.[374]

Between the advance of the Italians and the Italian legation leaving Ethiopia, a reporter for the *Chicago Daily Tribune*, Will

---

[372] Sir Winston Churchill, *The Gathering Storm*, Boston: Houghton Mifflin, 1948, pp. 165-168.

[373] Sir Percival Phillips, "Advance Startles the Italian Envoy," *New York Times*, October 3, 1935, p. 10.

[374] Sir Percival Phillips. "Ethiopians Give 28 Italians Safe Ride to Border," *Chicago Daily Tribune*, October 7, 1935, p. 4.

Barber, took ill and died of heart failure due to toxemia combined with infected kidneys and malaria. [375] The *Tribune* had no one else in Ethiopia, so they apparently made a deal with the *Telegraph* to publish Phillips' coverage of the conflict there. This is the reason why there are articles cited here from both the *Daily Telegraph* and the *Chicago Daily Tribune*.

On October 10 reporting from Dire Dawa, Ethiopia, Sir Percival noted that the war was being fought from well to well, emphasizing the importance of water in this area of Africa. [376] He also noted:

> ... the lack of authentic news about the progress of the Italian advance from government officials adds to the general anxiety and confusion of the population, The only contact with the rest of Ethiopia is through a radio station which is transmitting everything to Addis Ababa with long delays muddled by censorship. No war has been fought in modern times so far from all links with the outside world. [377]

Phillips continued to report the events in Ethiopia, but there was little that seemed to get by censors in Addis Ababa at the time and he spent considerable time discussing what appeared to be local events, even though they weren't. The Italians set up battle lines,[378] the Ethiopians lose a holy city,[379] the Italians bomb numerous towns,[380] and the Italians halt in the South and retreat in other areas,[381] but these were not decisive events.

---

[375] Robinson Maclean, "Will Barber, First to Cover Ethiopia, Dies," *Chicago Daily Tribune*, October 7, 1935, p. 1.

[376] Sir Percival Phillips, "Italians in South Fight for Water," *New York Times*, October 11, 1935, p. 16.

[377] Sir Percival Phillips, "Italians Battle for Water on Southern Front. *Chicago Daily Tribune*, October 11, 1935. p. 3.

[378] Sir Percival Phillips, "Italians Set Up Battle Lines in African Desert," *Chicago Daily Tribune*, October 14, 1935, p.1.

[379] Ibid.

[380] Sir Percival Phillips, "Italian Armies Reported 'Stuck' in Ogaden Desert." *Chicago Daily Tribune*, October 15, 1935, p. 2.

[381] Sir Percival Phillips, "Italians Reported at Halt in South, With Retreats from Some Places," *The New York Times*, October 16, 1935, p. 1.

Dispatches from the World

The rains came and Phillips sent out a dispatch from Djibouti in French Somaliland on November 1 that stated as soon as dry weather was assured the Italians under General Rudolfo Graziani would make a sustained push along the entire front.[382] In the interim the Italian troops began to suffer from shortages of both water and gasoline.[383] On November 29, also reporting from Djibouti, Phillips noted that the Italians were preparing for a major push, and although the Ethiopians continued with raids, these were largely ineffective.[384]

The Italians tried to bomb Haile Selassie over the next couple of months, but this also proved ineffective.[385] When the Italians made their move in the spring, many of the Ethiopian troops deserted and the collapse began. In the end Italy's armor and weapons overwhelmed the Ethiopians. Steps that could have been taken by the League of Nations to prevent this ordnance from getting to the combat zone for Italian use were not taken. When the inevitable became a reality, Emperor Haile Selassie went into exile in French Somaliland. The date was May 2, 1936; Ethiopia fell three days later.

Phillips had started his reporting in Addis Ababa, but found there was little information there and what was available was subject to censorship. Some writers assume that the 8,000 feet above sea level made it physically uncomfortable for Phillips to breathe and as a result he moved to Djibouti on the coast of French Somaliland. This may have been the reason for the move. On the other hand the high temperatures and high humidity of Djibouti would not provide much relief; those with heart ailments have difficulty in both environments. When Phillips did move to Djibouti on October 4, arriving there three days later, he found the French were indifferent about the events taking place in Ethiopia and whenever facts were learned Phillips did not have to worry about having those facts deleted by a censor. This may have been the reason for the move. Phillips continued reporting

---

[382] Sir Percival Phillips, "Rain Slows Up Italians," *Chicago Daily Tribune*, November 2, 1935, p. 10.

[383] Sir Percival Phillips, "Italian Armies Face Shortages of War Supplies," *Chicago Daily Tribune*, November 6, 1935, p. 9.

[384] Sir Percival Phillips, "Italians Poised for Offensives on Two Fronts," *Chicago Daily Tribune*, November 29, 1935, p. 2.

[385] Sir Percival Phillips, "Italian Flyers Aim Bombs for Haile Selassie," *Chicago Daily Tribune*, February 13, 1936, p. 11.

on the war from Djibouti until Addis Ababa fell to the Italians. At that time he returned to England.

Back in England he finished writing a piece on Djibouti for the *Daily Telegraph*. He wrote, "even in normal times sinister romance can be found behind its dingy facade. Slave traders, gun-runners, pearl smugglers, and other gentlemen of fortune have made it their port of call during years of questionable adventuring in the Red Sea." He continued, "Today Djibouti has other interests. It is the 'bottle neck' through which the backwash of war trickles down from the Abyssinian plateau. The circuitous railway ending suddenly at a sandy foreshore brings fugitives of every kind overflowing the four hotels at sea level." [386]

In late May of 1936 Phillips went to Southampton to board the *Queen Mary*, which was sailing to New York via Cherbourg on its maiden voyage. He wrote several stories about the trip while crossing the Atlantic. It was one of the few times that a colleague of his could recall his being upset. The colleague was Trevor C. Wignall, a radio journalist who knew Phillips from earlier assignments, and he was also crossing on the *Queen Mary*. Phillips was furious when he found a "story he had written 24 hours before still in the ship's radio room, unsent." [387] This is one of only a few cases known where Phillips had lost his temper. The only other documented case was an argument that he had with Philip Gibbs during the World War when they were serving as accredited correspondents. The remainder of the voyage went off without incident and the *Queen Mary* arrived in New York on June 1, 1936.

A similar situation of an article not being sent to Phillips' newspaper had occurred much earlier in his career. It was early in 1914 before the war. Phillips was sent to the Canary Islands to interview some labor agitators who had been deported from South Africa and were expected to arrive in the islands. Each of four reporters copied down their cables, most in block letters or typed, except for Phillips who prepared his in long hand. The next day he received a cable from the London office of the *Express* asking where his copy was. The clerk

---

[386] Sir Percival Phillips, "Town of Mystery," *The Evening Post*, March 7, 1936, p. 22.
[387] Untitled, *Daily Express*, January 30, 1937.

Dispatches from the World

had an easier time with the block letters and typed copy; the long hand was more difficult so he had not bothered to send it.[388]

After sailing to the U.S. on the *Queen Mary* Phillips went to Cleveland, Ohio, to cover the 1936 Republican National Convention. As one of the particularly boring morning sessions drew to a close, the delegates, while standing, began singing "America." Another reporter, Sidney Olson of *The Washington Post*, observed Phillips, Sir Wilmott Lewis of *The Times* of London, and James Bone of the *Manchester Guardian* sitting near *The Washington Post* staff seats. They were singing as well, but they were singing the words of "God Save the King," which has the same melody and from which the melody for "America" was derived.[389]

On June 24, 1936, Percival sailed for England. Once again he was on the *Queen Mary*. Little is known of the three weeks he spent in the States during this trip. His family had all died, his parents and his last brother, and he had only his former sister-in-law and his nephews left and they were living in Ohio. Whether he visited them is unknown, but it seems more than likely that he did.

---

[388] Hamilton Fyfe, *My Seven Selves*, London: George Allen & Unwin, Ltd., 1935, pp. 143-144.

[389] Sidney Olson, "Gauge of Applause Noise Gives Vandenberg Victory in Cheers," *The Washington Post*, June 10, 1936, p. 1,4.

CHAPTER 22

the spanish civil war

The next conflict was almost underway in Spain. The prime minister of that country had two military officers suspected of conspiracy against the government exiled to commands in the Canary Islands, Spanish islands located off the west coast of Africa. One of the exiled military officers was Francisco Franco.

It was an attempt by the military to overthrow the government of Spain in July of 1936, which led to the Spanish Civil War. The government (also referred to as the Republican) forces were supported by the Soviet Union and Mexico, but they also had various other communist volunteers as well as Americans willing to fight in support of their side. The rebel (also referred to as the Nationalist) forces were led by General Francisco Franco, who had now returned from exile. Franco had the support of Hitler's Nazi Germany and Mussolini's fascist Italy. The governments of Great Britain and the United States were officially neutral in the conflict, but some of the newspapers in these countries supported the rebel forces.

Phillips was on the Continent in late July of 1936 to cover the events surrounding the dedication of Vimy Ridge memorial. During the World War, four divisions of the Canada Corps were in a battle at Vimy Ridge against three divisions of the German Sixth Army. The Canadians were victorious. The memorial was in honor of the Canadians who fought and died there during the 1917 battle.

Within a month Phillips was reporting the events of the conflict in Spain; his first dispatch was dated August 3 for the *Daily Telegraph*. On that day he wrote about an encounter between the Spanish government's battleship *Jaime I* and the German battleship

Deutschland. The former was about to shell rebel-held areas when the German battleship placed itself between the two opposing forces. The government was reluctant to take on the Germans, although it was quite apparent that the latter supported the rebels. All of this was visible from Gibraltar, which Phillips used as his early base, venturing into Spain only sporadically at the beginning. Later he was based with the Spanish rebel army during much of his reporting.

Phillips was not the only war correspondent to make his way to Spain to cover the conflict developing there. Many of his colleagues from previous wars and conflicts were to go there as well, although in some cases they never ran into each other. The primary reason for this is obvious; some were with the government forces and some were with the rebel forces. Some estimates suggest that there were a thousand correspondents covering the conflict from the two sides, but this seems like an overestimate. To say there were between one and two hundred may not be far off the mark.

The most famous of these covered the government side of the action. Included in this group would be Ernest Hemingway, John Dos Passos, and George Orwell. Fewer covered activities from the rebel side and those that did were seasoned correspondents like Phillips and colleagues such as Francis McCullagh (from the Tripoli invasion), William Forest (from the 1916 events in Ireland), Webb Miller and Noel Monks (both from the Italian invasion of Ethiopia). In Phillips case he was assigned to cover the rebel side of the conflict along with Pembroke Stephens. In addition to Phillips, there were other reporters covering the war in Spain for the *Daily Telegraph*. These included Cedric Salter, who would later join the *Daily Mail*, Alan Dick, who would be active in the summer of 1937, Henry Buckley, and as noted Pembroke Stephens, who would soon be assigned to cover the Japanese/Chinese conflict.

Phillips had not spent much time in Spain prior to this. He was there just after the Barcelona rebellion in 1909, but that was nearly three decades earlier. He had been back in October of 1929 for an interview with General Primo de Rivera, who became dictator of Spain following a *coup d'état* in September of 1923. Rivera was to continue as dictator for only a little more than two months before resigning in January of 1930 and going into exile in Paris, where he died less than two months later. Phillips time in Spain for the

Dispatches from the World

rebellion and interview, as well as some holiday trips, were brief in comparison to this new assignment to cover Spain's civil war.

Phillips' reports on August 6 and 13 reflected the vigorous movement on the part of the rebels and the loss of more and more ground by the government. Rumors that the *Jaime I* had received significant damage by rebel bombers on August 13 were confirmed on August 14. Phillips suspected that the new bomber pilots were Italians or Germans, otherwise he could not quite understand the accuracy of the rebel bombers in comparison to their poor showing in previous attacks. He later confirmed that the new pilots were actually Italians and Germans.

Phillips did spend some time with his old friend, Francis McCullagh, while in Spain at this time. They had covered the Italian invasion of Tripoli in 1911; Phillips working for the *Express* and McCullagh working for the New York *World*. Now they were covering a civil war from the rebel side.

In a conversation with McCullagh at the time, Phillips said, Spain "has to import foreign mercenaries to fight for it, even in a civil war. Foreign artillery are blowing Spain to bits." Officials "won't let us mention Italians and Germans in our despatches, but they're here all the same." [390] Phillips was aware of this fact because Italian and German aviators were staying at hotels in Salamanca; he was also staying at a hotel in Salamanca at the time. He reported weapons were being delivered by the Germans to General Francisco Franco's rebel forces on the 20th of August. [391] He actually went so far as to write an article for the *Daily Telegraph* that gave the names of the German pilots and the numbers of German airplanes. [392]

Of the two countries supporting Franco's forces, Italy offered substantial aid in the form of fifty thousand troops and significant supplies of arms, tanks and planes. Germany's contribution was

---

[390] Francis McCullagh, *In Franco's Spain*, London: Burns, Oates & Washbourne. Ltd., p. 122.

[391] "March on Madrid from the South," *New York Times*, August 6, 1936, p. 2; "Revolters Launch A Drive on Malaga," *New York Times*, August 13, 1936, p. 2; "Franco's New Pilots Are Accurate Shots," *New York Times*, August 14, 1936, p. 2; "British See New Danger," *New York Times*, August 20, 1936, p.2.

[392] Monica Strauss, *Cruel Banquet: The Life and Loves of Frida Strindberg*, New York: Harcourt, 2000, pp. 221-222.

estimated to be about $125 million, a substantial amount at the time. Hermann Goring, in charge of Germany's Air Ministry at the time, was pleased to have the opportunity to evaluate and test new guns, tanks, war planes and troops in Spain. [393]

On November 4 Phillips reported that Alcorcon, seven miles outside the city of Madrid had been captured by the rebels and that from his location in that city he could see Madrid was afire. He wrote:

> Clouds of dark smoke and flames were rising from the buildings in the center of the capital, giving the impression that this area had been fired. Smoke rose also from other parts, but it was only in the center that I could see the flames. The Royal Palace, the tall Beaux Arts Club and El Retiro, the central part of Madrid, were clearly visible. [394]

He also reported that the Madrid airport had been seized that day.

During most of November Phillips remained in Salamanca, a city to the west of Madrid that had become the "capital" of the Franco forces. He spent a considerable amount of time talking with McCullagh about the general situation in Spain and the problems of moving around the country and censorship. It was apparent from their very lengthy discussions that Phillips had an intimate knowledge of the situation, far more than he could possibly get by the censors. Franco's Press Bureau would only allow the correspondents to go out to battle areas after an event and then only with them. [395]

Phillips was of the opinion that most of the American and British correspondents who went to Spain to cover the civil war were pro-Franco, but that Franco's Press Bureau had alienated most of them to the point where they had become pro-government. The individual who headed the Press Bureau was one Captain Don Luis Bustamente de Torquemada (a pseudonym that McCullagh uses

---

[393] William L. Shirer, *The Nightmare Years 1930-1940, 20th Century Journey, Vol. II*, New York: Bantam Books, 1985, pp. 264-265.

[394] "Center of Madrid Is Reported Afire; Airdrome Seized," *New York Times*, November 4, 1936, p. 1.

[395] Francis McCullagh, op.cit., pp. 106-153.

Dispatches from the World

for Luis Bolin) and he was responsible for most of the bad feelings between the Press Bureau and the correspondents.

Bustamente was not a soldier, although he wore a uniform. According to Phillips, "he dabbled in journalism in London, where he represented the *A.B.C.*, a Madrid newspaper. He also sent contributions to the London papers, but only one paper, which is extremely conservative and aristocratic, took anything from him. I asked the *Daily Mail* man why he refused his articles and he said, with the usual politeness of Carmelite House: "because they were d—d rubbish." I suppose that's the reason he's now treating the *Mail* men as if they were dirt beneath his feet, despite what Rothermere has done for Franco and all that he can still do." [396] The principal correspondent for the *Daily Mail* in Spain at this time was Harold Cardozo. It is not clear if this is the *Mail* man that Phillips was referring to in his statement. Cardozo also had an assistant, Frances Davis, an American, and she would later become famous as a foreign correspondent. Bustamente made it very difficult for the *Daily Mail* people to get their dispatches through the censors and sent off to England.

It was said that Bustamente had been responsible for getting an airplane for Franco to fly from the Canary Islands to Morocco, and that Franco had rewarded him by placing him in charge of the Press. [397]

McCullagh would later write that Phillips attitude toward Bustamente might have been due to the fact that he " . . . had been brought up in a Puritan family which regarded Spain and Catholicism with equal horror, so that a combination of both brought back old prejudices, which Sir Percival had believed to have died in him long ago." McCullagh continues, "I had not known that they had ever been alive, for this great journalist's frequent visits to Catholic countries and the warm friendships he had with many Catholics had made him so tolerant that more than one holy bishop and abbot of his acquaintance believed he would sooner or later enter the Church."[398] It is a possible argument, but Bustamente prevented so much information from leaving Franco's Spain that most of the

---

[396] Ibid., p. 106
[397] Ibid.
[398] Ibid., pp. 98-99.

correspondents serving there would later publish their observations in books after the civil war was over.

Phillips told McCullagh that he actually thought Bustamente was a very "clever man, with many good qualities. He is no good, it is true, as a propagandist: I would describe him as a preventive rather than a propagandist: he has a positive genius for preventing news from getting out." [399] In so doing Phillips argued, he had actually hurt Franco's cause.

There was no need to be so excessively hostile toward the correspondents. Phillips said that correspondents were treated much better on the government side, adding, "I have met dozens of fellows who are in Barcelona and Madrid, and they told me that though there was hopeless confusion, they were always treated like brothers. Busty's opposite number on the Government side isn't dressed up as an officer . . . as a general rule he's a real journalist wearing civilian clothes and working hard in his office, and glad to see colleagues from London and New York. No need to wait three hours for an audience, and then be told that you must come back tomorrow: you just blow in through the open door of the office, and help yourself to a drink or a cigar if the censor is busy." [400]

McCullagh was impressed with the way in which the *Daily Telegraph* kept their correspondents well-informed. Each day the newspaper cabled Phillips "a synopsis of all the news from Spain received in London that morning from every source." [401] This was not unlike the resources he had in Addis Ababa months earlier. As was true in Ethiopia, Phillips had an assistant while he was in Salamanca. This was Rowland Winn, a young Englishman who had earlier been a correspondent for Reuters in Madrid. He spoke fluent Spanish.

On the evening before Phillips was planning to leave Salamanca, he met with McCullagh. He explained that he was going to leave the following day. Phillips said, "I came here for one thing only, Franco's entry into Madrid, but now I'm convinced that Franco won't enter Madrid for another year, if ever he enters it at all, so that I'm going to clear out. I don't think however, that Busty (Luis Bolin) will let me

---

[399] Ibid., p. 116.
[400] Ibid., p. 108.
[401] Ibid., p. 51.

Dispatches from the World

clear out. He'll suspect that I've had some private information about the failure at the Front. Anyhow I'll ask him."

McCullagh suggested that he wait for the GHQ communique. Phillips replied, "No earthly use to me, their communique. It won't lie directly, but it won't give all the truth, and what truth it does give will be so worded as to convey an entirely false impression. I have had a large experience of official communiques in more than twenty different armies." [402]

The following day Phillips met McCullagh for lunch prior to leaving Salamanca. He said that he had requested a *salvoconducto* (letters of safe conduct) from Busty, but added that he had refused to give these to Phillips.

"I'll feel easier in my mind when I get across the frontier," said Phillips. "These Spaniards would be capable of doing anything to prevent news from leaking out. They would be capable of having me murdered. Didn't Phillip II have Juan Escovedo murdered? At any rate, they would be capable of keeping me here for months if they thought that I had got hold of important military secrets." [403]

It is apparent from some of McCullagh's writings that Phillips was unhappy and depressed while in Salamanca. He moved on to Portugal in part because he didn't feel quite safe in Spain. McCullagh also recognized that Phillips had some medical problems. He encountered him lying down on a couple of occasions and was convinced that Phillips had heart disease.[404] He may have had heart disease, but this is not what would later kill him, although it would contribute to his death.

At some point Phillips moved back to Gibraltar and began sending dispatches from there. On December 3 he reported a build-up in the number of Germans and German troops that were entering the rebel-held areas of the country.[405] Then on December 21 he reported that the Nazis were gaining control of much of the commercial exports from captured parts of Spain. They were taking over large

---

[402] Ibid., pp. 142-143.
[403] Ibid., p. 146-147.
[404] Ibid., p. 98.
[405] "More Germans Arrive," *Chicago Daily Tribune*, December 3, 1936, p. 12.

stocks of olive oil, oranges, wood, cork, and iron as payment for the assistance they had offered Franco and his forces. [406]

The civil war that looked so close to being lost by the government in December of 1936 would continue until April 1 of 1939, when Franco's forces were successful, but Phillips would not send any further dispatches from Gibraltar nor would he see the war's ups and downs. He had become very ill. Indications are that he may have known this during his meetings with McCullagh. Several days before their final lunch together, Phillips told him, " . . . I'm going back to Lisbon in a week or so, and shall never return to Spain."[407]

---

[406] "Nazis Capture New Trade as Result of Spanish Civil War," *Chicago Daily Tribune*, December 21, 1936.

[407] Francis McCullagh, op. cit., p. 126.

CHAPTER 23

the final days

Articles in the *Daily Telegraph* with the by-line of Sir Percival Phillips became less frequent. Perhaps he was tired or fatigued, which would not have been uncommon symptoms for one suffering from nephritis, a potentially fatal disease of the kidneys given the level of medical knowledge at the time. The disease would be accompanied by chills and fever, and pain on one or both sides of the back in the position of the kidneys. However, there are no indications that Phillips was aware of what his ailment was.

Phillips had been gravely ill before. There was the time when he had to quit one of his early jobs in Pittsburgh and go back to Brownsville to recover. There were the two influenza attacks: one at the durbar in 1911 and the other during the 1914-1918 war. Years later he was always trying to prevent illnesses by avoiding certain foods, by wearing his cholera belt, or by constantly drinking cod-liver oil. His health improved, but then he developed a tendency to get hay fever. This was the situation noted earlier where the physician involved was dropped from the Medical Register by the General Medical Council in England, but was later reinstated.[408] What Phillips had now was not due to a bad meal or to pollen in the air, or to a case of the flu. What he had now was much more severe than those ailments.

Phillips condition was getting worse so he went across the Straits of Gibraltar to Tangier in Morocco, most likely for better medical care. The trip would have been more difficult than it sounds

---

[408] Untitled, *Daily Express*, January 30, 1937.

since the distance is 30 miles and the water is often very rough. A decision was made, probably by him, to return to London. He was taken to the *S.S. Ranchi*, a relatively new British passenger and cargo carrying ocean liner built a decade earlier at Newcastle-upon-Tyne and operated by the Peninsula and Oriental (P&O) Steam Navigation Company. The ship was large enough, but the berths were small with no difference in the size of the two and three berth cabins, the third berth being located above the second.

The *Ranchi* was known to Phillips. The P&O used the vessel on the route from Bombay to London via Marseilles and Phillips had sailed on her at least once before in 1926, but in that case he sailed from Bombay, not Tangier.

It is doubtful that Phillips left his cabin since his pain was now more intense. He was in enough discomfort that someone decided a nurse should accompany him on the trip back to England. The nurse was referred to as Sister Stemp and she was "a charming little brown-eyed nurse" according to Bernard Falk, a colleague of Phillips who was editor of the *Sunday Dispatch* from its beginning in 1918 to 1931.[409] The nurse's actual name was Maud Florence Stemp and she was 37 years of age. Her daughter Daphne, a student in Morocco, accompanied her on the trip back to England. Both were British citizens who lived in the Herne Hill area of London when in England.

The *Daily Telegraph* still needed the news covered and for this purpose they also had Pembroke Stephens in Spain covering the civil war from the Nationalist side. He began covering both sides as best he could. Stephens had been a lawyer and an official of the League of Nations before becoming the *Daily Express*'s "man in Berlin." The Germans expelled him in 1934 for reporting some construction underway in a forest near Dessau. The construction was most likely related to an expansion of the Junkers aircraft company by the Nazis. After leaving the *Express*, he joined the *Telegraph*.[410]

---

[409] Bernard Falk, *Five Years Dead: A postscript to 'He Laughed in Fleet Street,'* London: The Book Club, 1938, p. 75.

[410] Following his coverage of the civil war in Spain, Pembroke Stephens was sent in August to cover a Chinese-Japanese conflict. He died in November of 1937 from machine gun wounds inflicted by Japanese forces.

Dispatches from the World

Reporters of the day picked up on the story of Phillips' illness and on January 15, 1937, *The Times* of London noted Sir Percival was "stated to be seriously ill on board the liner *Ranchi*, which called at Plymouth yesterday on its return from Tangier."[411] The *Ranchi* actually took Phillips to Tilbury, on the north bank of the Thames, near London. Landing at Tilbury, Phillips immediately thought of his job. To a colleague, who met him at the docks, he remarked, 'Tell the office everything's paid up-to-date.' He had an extraordinary brain for organizing his affairs smoothly. If he were being sent to China or Peru, he would merely say to the Foreign Editor. 'Please see that £ 500 is paid into so-and-so bank; I will do the rest.'[412] As ill as he was, he was still functioning as the correspondent.

By the following day *The New York Times* noted that on the 14th he had been taken to a London hospital. It continued "he is suffering from acute nephritis and his condition is causing anxiety."[413] A few days later his condition was said to show "a slight improvement."[414]

Phillips was looking forward to returning to his rooms in London. It is unlikely that he spent more than two or three months of the year there on the average. In some years, such as during the World War, the stays were clearly less than that. For more than thirty-three years he lived at 60 Chancery Lane in what was called the New Stone Buildings. Chancery Lane is accessed on the north from High Holborn and on the south by Fleet Street. When he took space there, he worked for the *Daily Express*, which was just down the Lane, left on Fleet Street and then about a half-mile further to Shoe Lane or St. Bride Street, both of which provided access to the newspaper offices.

---

[411] *The Times*, January 15, 1937, p. 12.
[412] Bernard Falk, *Five Years Dead: A Postscript to 'He Laughed in Fleet Street.'* London: The Book Club, 1938, p. 75.
[413] "Sir Percival Phillips is Ill," *The New York Times*, January 16, 1937, p. 3.
[414] *The Times*, January 18, 1937, p. 12.

*Sir Percival Phillips
working in his rooms, 1934 (Daily Mail, London)*

His rooms consisted of a flat up five flights of stone steps; there was no elevator or lift. The steps had to be difficult for him to climb at the end of a day of work in London and considering that in his later years he apparently suffered from heart disease. Friends tried to convince him that he should move to other quarters, but he would not hear of it. [415] The fact that he was quite close to Fleet Street and the newspaper offices was probably to his liking.

The flat was decorated with an etching by Joe Simpson and Japanese prints which Phillips collected. It was filled with the rarest of books and curios, which he had gathered on his travels. There were also photographs from his travels. One of these was a photograph of him sitting on the throne of an empress of China. There would have been a slight odor of pipe tobacco in the rooms even though he had a housekeeper, Mrs. Wauman, who took care of the place whether he was in, or out of the country for months on end. Now he spoke

---

[415] Bernard Falk, *Five Years Dead: A Postscript to 'He Laughed in Fleet Street,'* London: The Book Club, 1938, p. 75.

Dispatches from the World

hopefully of entertaining his friends with an exhibition of films he had picked up in Spain, but he was never to return to his rooms. [416]

Instead, he was moved to the Empire Nursing Home, Vincent Square, Westminster, perhaps with the belief that nothing more could be done for him. On the 29th of January Kenneth George Stacy Hatfield, an engineer and close friend of Phillips went to the nursing home. It was apparent that Phillips was extremely ill, but he wanted to make out a will and state the disposition of his estate. He asked Hatfield to write down what he was about to dictate. Hatfield wrote down each provision and repeated it aloud to Phillips, who approved each one.

A more formal statement of the will and its terms was written and Phillips signed it only with a cross or an X. Three nurses at the home witnessed the signature. Phillips then told Hatfield, "Now Kenneth, you know what I want, and you will see these things are done." [417] About an hour after making his will Sir Percival Phillips died. Newspapers on both sides of the Atlantic carried word of his death. [418]

Signor Arnaldo Cipolla, a distinguished Italian journalist at the time published the following about Phillips in *Il Messaggero*:

> He was always in the front line, and his loss has affected and shocked me like the loss of a brother. I do not remember when I first met him; it seems that I must have known him all my life.
>
> I saw in him a modest man, but a maker of miracles. He was an up-to-date encyclopaedia on the world, the living history of the last quarter of a century, with a memory of iron. He had seen and described the most varied and different events.

---

[416] Ibid., p. 76.

[417] "High Court of Justice Probate, Divorce and Admiralty Division, The Late Sir Percival Phillips Estate, Hatfield v. Phillips and Another," *The* (London) *Times*, February 25, 1938, p. 4.

[418] "Obituary Sir Percival Phillips War Correspondent" *The* (London) *Times*, January 30, 1937, p. 14; "Percival Phillips, Journalist, Dead," *The New York Times*, January 30, 1937, p. 17.

> This great reporter was the friend of crowned heads and chiefs of States. He was the confidant of Chinese satraps, of despots over tens of millions of men. People would have covered him with gold if only he would have agreed to spread news in favour of their designs.[419]

Editors throughout the U.S. and Europe offered similar tributes. From Asia an interesting tribute came from *The Times of India*.

> Probably the only American-born journalist ever to have received the honour of a British Knighthood, Sir Percival Phillips was generally recognised as one of the most brilliant descriptive writers and war correspondents of the age. In forty years of almost uninterrupted travel in every quarter of the globe there was hardly any event or movement of major importance, right up to the present struggle in Spain, which he did not witness or report upon first hand. In fact the record of his movements since 1897 reads almost like a political and military history of the world.

The article next summarized his reporting history and goes on to note: "It was while he was in Spain this year reporting the civil war that he contracted the illness which ultimately led to his death." It concludes with the following:

> His professional brilliance is shown by the fact that despite his uncanny flair for news gathering and the large number of exclusive stories which he managed to obtain for the newspapers he served, he aroused no hostility and made few, if any, enemies. On the contrary, he was liked wherever he went and

---

[419] "Sir Percival Phillips: An Italian Tribute," *The Daily Telegraph*, February 4, 1937, p. 13.

>exceedingly popular among all with whom he came into contact.[420]

Most of the newspapers indicated that Phillips had died of nephritis, the *Telegraph* added heart failure to the causes of his death. Generally, if the kidneys fail this will cause a strain on the heart and the cause of death would be heart failure. This was not much different from the cause of Will Barber's death in Ethiopia fifteen months earlier. Barber was relatively new as a correspondent and may have consumed waters or foods that led to his severe kidney illness. Phillips would have never done that; he knew better and was very careful about what he ate or drank.

It is not unreasonable to suggest that there may have been foul play involved in his illness given his concerns a few weeks earlier that his life was in danger as long as he remained in Salamanca. The Franco forces did not view the correspondents with favor, particularly those who were critical of them. Arthur Koestler, a correspondent for the British *News Chronicle* was arrested, imprisoned at Seville, and sentenced to death. He probably would have been executed had the British Foreign Office not taken an interest in his case. [421] Hubert 'Knick' Knickerbocker, an American journalist who wrote for the Hearst newspapers, was arrested and imprisoned at San Sebastián for a brief time before being expelled from Spain. F.A. Rice of the London *Morning Post* was detained and interrogated, his messages back to England were heavily censored and twisted to support the Francoist viewpoint. He chose to leave Spain while he could. Another English journalist, Sefton Delmar, was expelled. John T. Whitaker of the *New York Herald Tribune* went to the front without permission and was told he would be shot if it happened again. [422] It is not at all unreasonable to believe that foul play was involved in Phillips death.

---

[420] "Sir P. Phillips Dead," *The Times of India*, January 30, 1937, p. 11.

[421] Arthur Koestler, *Spanish Testament*, London: Victor Gollancz, 1937.

[422] Paul Preston, "The Answer Lies in the Sewers: Captain Aguilera and the Mentality of the Francoist Officer Corps," *Science and Society*, Vol. 68, No. 4, Fall 2004, pp. 277-312; also Paul Preston, *We Saw Spain Die: Foreign Correspondents in the Spanish Civil War*, London: Constable & Robinson, Ltd., 2008, p. 155.

The Francoist forces were particularly brutal from all accounts and the assassination of a correspondent would not have been beyond their capability, given the tens of thousands of civilians killed by these forces.

There are numerous chemicals that can cause nephritis, but these are often overlooked as a cause of the disease. There are no indications that Phillips' body was subjected to an autopsy and if it was, there is no certainty that the cause of the nephritis would have been identified in the 1930s. Perhaps the disease was due to purely natural causes, but that seems very unlikely.

The funeral/memorial service and cremation of Percival Phillips took place on February 2, 1937, at Golders Green Crematorium in northwest London. The crematorium's buildings all have an Italian style, nearly Tuscan, and include a notable tower visible from Hoop Lane, off the Finchley Road.

The memorial service had Professor J. Hunt Bannister from the Royal College of Music as the organist and the music selected was by Bach, except that the closing was Mendelssohn's Funeral March from "Songs Without Words." The Rev. J.C. Nankivell officiated. Nankivell was an old friend of Phillips. He had been an army chaplain prior to the World War and he served in France in that capacity during the time that Phillips was there. It is hard to say if they were in the same locale at any time because Phillips' by-line usually said "with the British forces somewhere in France," or some similarly vague geographic reference. Both men had a strong interest in the theater and both were members of the Garrick Club. The reverend would later be described as "a priest who was also a man of the world without losing his devoutness or tenderness or sympathy; his friendship had a great appeal to many in whose lives organized religion played a little part." [423]

The funeral for the most part would have resembled a newspaper convention. David Darrah, London bureau chief of the *Chicago Tribune*, represented that newspaper. Webb Miller was there representing United Press, America. Miller had also been a correspondent in Europe during World War. Frank Hillier, Foreign Editor of the *Daily Mail*, was there. Sir Alfred Watson and Arthur

---

[423] "Obituary: The Rev. J.C. Nankivell," *The* (London) *Times*, December 28, 1951, p. 6.

E. Watson, the former and current Editors of the *Daily Telegraph*, respectively, were there. J.B. Wilson was there representing the *Daily Express*; he was formerly the news editor of that newspaper. J.H.B. Warden was there in place of his father, W.L. Warden, Director of Associated Newspapers Limited. [424]

There were others in attendance who had worked with Phillips in one capacity or another over the years. W.T. Massey was there; he had served as news editor for the *Daily Telegraph* from 1923 until 1935; he had also been a correspondent in France in 1914. Cyril Lakin was there. He served in France in 1914, and since 1929 he was the assistant editor of the *Daily Telegraph*. H.C. Ferraby a naval war correspondent for the *Daily Express* was also there, as was Walter Fish, editor of the *Daily Mail* from 1926 to 1929.

More personal friends were there as well. Douglas Crawford was there. He was in France in 1914 as a correspondent for *The Times* and later served as night editor, assistant editor and then foreign editor of the *Daily Mail*. Phillips knew the Crawfords well. Oscar Pulvermacher, another night editor at the *Daily Mail*, was there with his wife.

Although there were several correspondents there from the 1914-1918 war, none of the accredited correspondents from 1915 were there. Perry Robinson had died seven years earlier, and Beach Thomas and Herbert Russell were nearly seventy years of age and may have been in poor health. Philip Gibbs was losing his vision at the time and probably preferred familiar surroundings. Henry Nevinson, Phillips colleague from his coverage of the Balkan Wars, and one of the visiting correspondents with the accredited correspondents in 1918, did come to the funeral. James Grant Anderson, a stage actor and repertory theater production manager, was there. Anderson was a fellow passenger on the S.S. *Ranchi* when Phillips made a trip back to England in 1926. There was also a Miss Anderson at the funeral. She was Helena Isabel Grant Anderson, sister of James Grant Anderson, and a stage actress at the time in London.

There were numerous wreaths sent to Golders Green when Phillips died. Two of these resided on his coffin during the funeral. As one would expect, one of these was from Lord Camrose, the

---

[424] "Funerals: Sir Percival Phillips," *The* (London) *Times*, February 3, 1937, p. 17.

owner of the *Daily Telegraph*. The other was from Miss Anderson. Another wreath was sent by Sister Stemp of Tangier, Morocco, the nurse who accompanied Phillips back to London from Tangier only two weeks before his death.

Little is known of Kenneth Hatfield, who was there with his wife, Olive, and we are uncertain how Phillips knew him or the nature of their relationship. He was about ten years younger than Phillips. It is also known that he was an engineer for a shipping firm out of Yokohama, Japan. He lived at 10 Tavistock Square, W.C., when he was in London. And he had helped Phillips with his will, but beyond this nothing is known.

Hatfield turned out to be an inheritor of part of Phillips' estate. That estate was valued at more than $45,000, a substantial sum in the midst of the depression years. [425] Phillips' nephews, Wilbur and James, sons of his late brother, Smith, later brought suit against Hatfield primarily to ensure that the will was executed correctly. In February of 1938 the court ruled that the will was properly executed and had two of the nurses who witnessed Phillips signing the document verify this; the third nurse had died in the year following Phillips' death. When the will was finally executed Hatfield received part of Phillips' estate in England and the nephews received the property he held in Brownsville, which was valued at approximately $15,000.

The will was later made public in the U.S.[426] The nephews, James Knox Phillips and Wilbur Warner Phillips, "were left a trust fund with the Union Trust Company of Pittsburgh, in equal shares and in the house at 417 Church Street," the house where Phillips grew up in Brownsville. Phillips also left a fund of £1400 to be set aside "to pay Mrs. Wauman the amount as paid monthly now." She was his housekeeper. He left "Miss Helen Isabel Anderson cash and securities amounting to £ 4,000 securities and £ 5,000 cash." To each of the two sons of Douglas Crawford, he left £ 500 cash." He left his Zeiss camera to Kenneth Hatfield, and one of the Simpson etchings to Oscar Pulvermacher.

---

[425] "Former Brownsville Reporter Left Estate of More Than $45,000," *The (Connellsville) Daily Courier*, January 25, 1938.

[426] "News of the Courts," *The (Connellsville) Daily Courier*, June 1, 1944, p. 3.

Dispatches from the World

Most of these individuals were friends of Phillips. Oscar Pulvermacher was a newspaper colleague. In addition to being night editor of the *Daily Mail* for a period of time, he "later established the northern edition of the *Daily Telegraph* in Manchester."[427] He would die several years later in Johannesburg, South Africa.

Douglas Crawford was a newspaper man like Phillips. As noted above he was a correspondent in France for *The Times* in 1914 during the World War. When he returned to England, he became night editor of the *Daily Mail*. He retired in 1938 after 28 years with that newspaper. He died in 1943 at the age of 60.[428]

The mysterious heir is Miss Helena Isabel Anderson. She inherited a substantial part of Phillips' estate. Ironically, there is little evidence that she knew Phillips during his life. In fact her existence only becomes known with his death and her presence at the funeral, and in his bequest to her in his will. As noted above, we know that she was a younger sister of James Grant Anderson, the actor, producer and director of repertory theater stage productions. She was born in Richmond, Surrey, in 1906, and when Phillips died she would have been 30, about half his age.

She appeared in plays for more than a decade prior to Phillips' death. Her earliest performance may have been in "Barrier Between" at the Palace Pier, St. Leonards, in Brighton on March 9, 1925. [429] She would have been 18 years old at the time of this production by her brother and his Grant Anderson Repertory Company. Some of her London performances and one Southampton performance were reviewed in *The Times*. The plays identified were: "A Pig in a Poke," at the Embassy Theatre (London) in April of 1929; "Art and Mrs. Bottle; Or, The Return of the Puritan," at the Empire Theatre (Southampton) in November of 1929; "Great Cats Play Chess," at the Arts Theatre (London) in May of 1935; and, "We Love and Learn," at the Richmond Theatre (London) in September of 1937. [430] The reviews were neither flattering, nor overly critical. She appears to

---

[427] "Obituary, Oscar Pulvermacher" *The Times* (London), November 1, 1958.
[428] "Mr. Douglas Crawford, Journalism and Publicity," *The Times* (London), September 14, 1943, p. 6.
[429] Lionel Carson (ed.), *The Stage Yearbook*, 1926, London: The Stage Offices, p. 123.
[430] Reviews of these appeared in *The Times* on April 29, 1929, May 2, 1935, and Sept. 15, 1937.

have tried using different stage names. She tried Lena Anderson and later Isabel Anderson, but she appears to drop out of the London stage acting environment after her 1937 appearance. Lena Grant Anderson was the name she used after that time.

In between the above plays Lena did some touring with her brother and the repertory company he had set up in 1929. It is known that they were in Bombay, India, from 1929 until 1934. In the latter year she played the role of the Governor's wife in "While Parents Sleep," written by Anthony Kimmins. The play was also done in Shanghai and Tokyo as the company toured the Far East. Aidan Crawley, the former cricket player who appeared with her in the play when it was put on at the Garrison Theatre in Bombay, described Lena in his autobiography as "small and vivacious with large grey eyes and an attractive voice. On stage she was totally professional, prepared for every mistake, determined only to get through the performance." [431]

During the sixteen months that Phillips spent in Bombay, India, in 1931 and 1932, he stayed at the Taj Mahal hotel. The members of the Grant Anderson repertory theater group, James Grant Anderson, his sister Lena, and their mother Helen C. Grant, also stayed at the Taj Mahal. It was common for Phillips and others to gather in the bar of the Taj Mahal Hotel at the end of the day for chota pegs (small drinks). Harry Greenwall of the *Daily Express*, who had worked with Phillips during the war in France, would often join him there. Greenwall had stayed with the *Express*, but Phillips had moved on. Rene MacColl (of the *Daily Telegraph*) would also join them there, as would other correspondents "working" Bombay at the time. [432] It is reasonable to assume that the Andersons would also join those assembled in the Taj Mahal bar at these times.

At the same time that Lena and James Grant Anderson were in Bombay in 1934, Phillips was there. He had been asked to accompany Esmond Harmsworth on a tour of the Far East followed by a trip around the world. Esmond was the son of Harold Harmsworth (Lord Rothermere), owner of the *Daily Mail* at the time and while Phillips

---

[431] Aidan Crawley, *Leap Before You Look: A Memoir*, London, Collins, 1988, p. 109.
[432] Rene MacColl, *Deadlines and Datelines.*, London, Oldbourne Press, 1956, pp. 39-40.

went along he was not particularly happy about it referring to the tour as "a rich man's junket." [433] After leaving Bombay they went to Burma (now Myanmar) and then Bangkok, before flying on an Imperial Airways flight to Singapore. Upon their arrival in Singapore they were interviewed by the local newspaper. Phillips insisted that the trip was undertaken mainly for reasons of pleasure. Aidan Crawley, the former cricket player for Kent and Oxford, but then a *Daily Mail* reporter agreed with this assessment. Harmsworth also agreed, but pointed out they were taking every opportunity to study the problems of the countries they had visited and to interview numerous officials in these same countries. [434] After Singapore, rather than continuing on to China, Japan and North America as originally planned, they decided to return to England. Perhaps Phillips' comments were bothering Harmsworth and this is why they cut the trip short. If the comments bothered Harmsworth a great deal, it may be one more reason why Phillips left the *Mail* and moved over to the *Telegraph*.

When Phillips died in 1937, James and Lena Anderson were in England. A couple years later in 1939 Lena and her brother joined the Entertainments National Service Association (ENSA). ENSA was set up primarily to bring entertainment to British troops during World War II. This theater group performed all over the world, from London to Burma, from Ceylon to North Africa.

Following the war James Grant Anderson set up another repertory company that toured every part of the United Kingdom. Lena was a partner in this operation. In 1958 at the age of 52, Lena married a man named Alfred Holland. Little is known of this marriage, but Lena apparently kept her maiden name, which would not be uncommon for a stage actress. It is known that Aidan Crawley visited with James and Lena forty years after their India tour in London. This would have been the mid 1970s and both were still doing repertory theater. [435] At the time Lena would have been nearly seventy years of age. What became of her husband

---

[433] Ibid., p. 94.

[434] "Daily Mail Trio In Singapore. Out for Pleasure—and Copy," *The Singapore Free Press and Mercantile Advertiser*, March 7, 1934, p. 3.

[435] Ibid., p. 111.

is unknown. Her brother James died in October of 1985 in the London area; he was 88.

Both Percival and Lena were based in London most of the year and they must have met each other while traveling. We don't know what Percival Phillips' relationship was with Lena beyond being a friend or an admirer of her, or her acting. However, the placement of the wreath on his coffin and his bequest to her would suggest it was more than something that simple. It is believed that Lena moved to the north of England following her brother's death. There is a record of a Lena Anderson dying there in 1989.

An assessment of Percival Phillips talent as a journalist would give him points for his getting the facts and relaying these in a very precise way. He was not a literary journalist for the most part, but he did have some very well written "literary" pieces over the years. Falk thought that his writing was weak and sedate toward the end of his life. But this is unfair considering that he was responsible for one of the major journalistic scoops of the 1900-1950 era less than a year and half before he died.

As an individual he had certain goals in life. He wanted to be a war correspondent and he wanted to have a major scoop. He achieved both of these goals. He covered more wars than just about any other correspondent of that time. The Ethiopian oil concession scoop is still noted today as a major journalistic accomplishment.

Had Phillips survived his ailments it is interesting to ponder what he would have done for the rest of his life. World War II was about to begin and it is of interest to consider what he would have done at that time. He probably would have continued working, not as a correspondent, but as a foreign editor for the *Daily Telegraph* in London. His last two wars, the one in Ethiopia and the other in Spain, had been frustrating experiences. The level of censorship had made it nearly impossible to be a war correspondent during those conflicts. This would have been worse during the war that was coming. It is unlikely that Phillips would have retired.

It is not known who wrote Phillips' obituary for the *Daily Express*. It concludes by stating that Percival Phillips was a lonely man. This does not seem to be consistent with what we now know about him, although it may have been true of the young American who worked for the *Daily Express* decades earlier. There was no doubt he was a private person with a small circle of friends, the closest of which were not newspaper people. He loved England and being a journalist, but he had a life beyond the newspapers he wrote for most of his journalist colleagues were not aware of it.

AFTERWORD

It is now more than seven decades since the last of the events described here occurred. Newspapers can no longer afford the expense of sending reporters to all parts of the world for several months to record the events occurring there. Television networks do this and there are some outstanding reporters doing exceptional duty in different parts of the world for them, but their coverage in many instances is partial and "sound bite" oriented, nothing that would cover half of the front page of a newspaper in most cases. Newspapers have become fewer. That is unfortunate. It is only newspapers that can provide the detail that is necessary for informed decisions in any democracy. Of the major newspapers that have survived, we find far too many owned by the same interests that own national television news programs.

So far as is known none of Phillips' contemporaries mentioned in this biography have survived the seventy odd years since 1937. Two came very close. The first of these was Fay Gillis Wells. She was a reporter and wife of Linton Wells. She is noted in the biography as being in the rail passenger car with Phillips on the trip from Djibouti to Addis Ababa in 1935. She went on to have careers in broadcasting and aviation. She died in December of 2002 at the age of 94.

The second was William Deedes, a journalist who was in Ethiopia at the same time that Phillips filed his "scoop." Deedes went on to write a few books about those days. One of the most recent of these was *At War with Waugh: The Real Story of Scoop*, which was published in 2003. He also served as an editor of London's *Telegraph* for twelve years. He died in 2007, also at the age of 94.

Those who venture to Brownsville, Pennsylvania, will find the Christ Episcopal Church and "Bowman's Castle" (now called Nemacolin Castle) still standing. The family residence at 417 Church Street was sold by Phillips' nephews in the 1930s and later demolished for a parking lot.

A trip to London will reveal that Phillips' apartment and the apartments of others in the building at 60 Chancery Lane have been converted to offices.

Both of Phillips' nephews became teachers. The last of these died in 2002.

Phillips wrote an article in 1913 about families auctioning off their ancestry in the form of paintings of individuals from earlier generations and related items of value at the various auction houses in London. On May 6, 2006, all of the medals and items related to Phillips' war service and knighthood were sold by a Canadian auction house. These items brought $3,000 to the unknown seller from an equally unknown buyer.

SELECTED BIBLIOGRAPHY

Balfour, Patrick, "Fiasco in Addis Ababa." in Ladislas Farago (ed.), *Abyssinian Stop Press*, London: Robert Hale & Company, 1936

Borden, Henry (ed.), *Letters to Limbo*, Toronto: University of Toronto Press, 1971.

Brown, Charles H., *The Correspondents' War: Journalists in the Spanish American War*, New York: Charles Schribner's Sons, 1967.

Cardozo, Harold, *March of a Nation: My Year of Spain's Civil War*, London: The "Right" Book Club, 1937.

Carson, Lionel (ed.), *The Stage Yearbook, 1926*, London: The Stage Offices, 1927.

Christiansen, Arthur. *Headlines All My Life*. New York: Harper and Brothers, 1961.

Churchill, Sir Winston, *The Gathering Storm*, Boston: Houghton Mifflin, 1948.

Clarke, Basil, "Men of the Green Brassard: Some Famous Correspondents and Their Work," *The War Illustrated*, Vol. 6, No. 146, June 2, 1917, p. 368.

Clarke, Basil, *My Round of the War*, London: William Heinemann, 1917.

Cochran, Charles B., *I had almost Forgotten . . .*, London: Hutchinson & Co., Ltd., 1932.

Collins, Douglas. *The Story of Kodak*, London: H.N. Abrams, 1990.

Crawley, Aidan, *Leap Before You Look: A Memoir*, London: Collins, 1988

Crozier, F.P., *Impressions and Recollections*, London: T. WernerLaurie, Ltd., 1930

Crumrine, Boyd (ed.), *History of Washington County*, Philadelphia: L.H. Everts and Co., 1882.

Dark, Sidney, "Little Portraits. Four Journalists. Sir Percival Phillips," *John O'London's Weekly*, February 17, 1923, p. 699.

Davis, Charles Belmont, *Adventures and Letters of Richard Harding Davis*, New York: Charles Schribner's Sons, 1917.

Deedes, W.F., *At War With Waugh: The Real Story of Scoop*, London: Macmillan, 2003

Deedes, W.F., *Words and Deedes: Selective Journalism, 1931-2006*, London: Macmillan, 2006.

Desmond, Robert W. *Windows on the World: The Information Process in a Changing Society, 1900-1930.* Iowa City: University of Iowa Press, 1980

Desmond, Robert W. *Tides of War: World News Reporting, 1931-1945*, Iowa City: University of Iowa Press, 1984

Dunn, James, *Paperchase: Adventures In and Out of Fleet Street*, London: Selwyn and Blount, 1938.

Early, Eleanor, *Ports of the Sun: A Guide to the Caribbean, Bermuda, Nassau, Havana, and Panama*, Boston: Houghton Mifflin Company, 1937.

Ellis, Franklin (ed.) History of Fayette County, Pennsylvania: with biographical sketches of many of its prominent citizens,

Falk, Bernard, *Five Years Dead: A Postscript to "He Laughed in Fleet Street,"* London: The Book Club, 1938.

Farrar, Martin J., *News from the Front: War Correspondents on the Western Front: 1914-1918*, London: Sutton Publishing Company, 1999.

Forbes, Archibald, *Memories and Studies of War and Peace*, London: Cassell, 1896.

Forrest, Wilbur, *Behind the Front Page: Stories of Newspaper Stories in the Making*, New York: Appleton-Century Company, 1934.

Fyfe, Hamilton, *My Seven Selves*, London: George Allen & Unwin, Ltd., 1935.

Gallagher, Donat. "Black Majesty and Press Mischief," *The London Magazine*, October 1982, pp. 25-38.

Gibbs, Phillip, *Adventures in Journalism*, New York and London: Harper and Brothers Publishers, 1923.

Gibbs, Philip, *Now It Can Be Told*, New York and London: Harper and Brothers Publishers, 1920.

Gibbs, Philip, *The Pageant of the Years: An Autobiography*, London: William Heinemenn, Ltd., 1946.

Gibbs, Philip, *The War Dispatches* (edited by Catherine Prigg), Isle of Man: Times Press Limited, 1964.

Gramling, Oliver, *AP: The Story of News*, Ann Arbor, Michigan: University Microfilms, 1968.

Grant, Bernard, *To the Four Corners: The Memoirs of a News Photographer*, London: Hutchinson and Co., Ltd., 1933.

Griffiths, Dennis (ed.), *The Encyclopedia of the British Press 1422-1992*, New York: St. Martin's Press, 1992.

Groom, Winston, *A Storm in Flanders: The Ypres Salient, 1914-1918*, New York: Atlantic Monthly Press, 2002.

Hart, J. Percy, *Hart's History and Directory of the Three Towns: Brownsville, Bridgeport, West Brownsville*, Cadwallader, PA: J. Percy Hart, 1904.

Hastings, Sir Patrick, *The Autobiography of Sir Patrick Hastings*, London: William Heineman, Ltd., 1948.

Haverstock, Nathan A., *Fifty Years at the Front: The Life of War Correspondent Frederick Palmer*, London and Washington: Brassey's, 1996.

Hemingway, Ernest, "French Speed with Movies on the Job," *Toronto Star*, May 16, 1923.

Henrey, Robert, *A Century Between*, New York: Longmans, Green and Co., 1937

Herman, Arthur, *Gandhi and Churchill: The Epic Rivalry That Destroyed an Empire and Forged Our Age*, New York: Bantam Books, 2008.

Hochschild, Adam, *To End All Wars: A Story of Loyalty and Rebellion, 1914-1918*, Boston: Mariner Books, 2012.

Hubbard, Wynant, *Fiasco in Ethiopia: The Story of a So-called War by a Reporter on the Ground*, New York and London: Harper and Brothers, 1936.

Irwin, Will. *The Making of a Reporter*, New York: G.P. Putnam's Sons, 1942.

John, Angela V., *War, Journalism and the Shaping of the Twentieth Century: The Life and Times of Henry W. Nevinson*, London and New York: I.B. Tauris, 2006.

Jordan, John (ed.), *Genealogical and Personal History of Fayette County, Pennsylvania, Vol. I*, New York: Lewis Historical Publishing Company, 1912

Kaul, Chandrika, *Reporting the Raj: The British Press and India, c. 1880-1922.* Manchester: Manchester University Press, 2003.

Keegan, John, *The First World War,* New York: Alfred A. Knopf, 1999.

Kingman, Russ, *Pictorial Life of Jack London,* New York: Crown Publishers, 1979.

Knightly, Phillip, *The First Casualty: The war correspondent as hero and myth-maker from the Crimea to Kosovo,* Baltimore: The Johns Hopkins University Press, 2002.

London, Charmian, *The Book of Jack London,* New York: The Century Company, 1921.

MacColl, Rene, *Deadline and Dateline,* London: Oldbourne Press, 1956.

Makin, William J., *Red Sea Nights,* New York: Robert M. McBride &Company, 1933.

McCullough, David, *The Johnstown Flood,* New York: Simon and Schuster, 1968

McCullagh, Francis. *Italy's War for a Desert; Being Some Experiences of a War-Correspondent with the Italians in Tripoli,* Chicago: F.G. Brown & Co., 1913.

McCullagh, Captain Francis. *In Franco's Spain: being the experiences of an Irish war correspondent during the great civil war which began in 1936,* London, Burns, Oates & Washbourne, Ltd, 1937

McFarland, Joseph F., *20th Century History of the City of Washington and Washington County, Pennsylvania.* Chicago, IL: Richmond Arnold Publishing Company, 1910.

McMillan, James, *The Way It Was, 1914-1934: Based on Files of the Express Newspapers,* London: William Kimber,1979

Maitland, Francis Hereward, *One Hundred Years of Headlines, 1937-1937,* London: Wright & Brown, Ltd., 1938.

Manchester, William, *The Last Lion: Winston Churchill; Visions of Glory, 1874-1932,* Boston: Brown, Little & Company, 1983.

Miller, Webb, *I Found No Peace: The Journal of a Foreign Correspondent,* Garden City, NY: Garden City Publishing Co., Inc., 1938.

Monks, Noel, *Eyewitness,* London: Frederick Muller, Ltd., 1955.

Nevinson, Henry W., *In The Dark Backward,* London: George Routledge & Sons, Ltd., 1934.

Nevinson, Henry W., *More Changes More Chances*, New York: Harcourt Brace and Company, 1925.

Nevinson, Henry W., *Last Changes, Last Chances*, London: Nisbet & Co. Ltd., 1928.

Palmer, Frederick, *My Second Year of the War*, New York: Dodd, Mean and Company, 1917

Phillips, Percival, "A Race in the Air," *Outlook*, May 28, 1910, pp. 145-148.

Phillips, Percival, "Out in the Cold: the tragedy of the war correspondent," *The Saturday Evening Post*, February 1, 1913

Phillips, Sir Percival, *Mesopotamia: The Daily Mail inquiry at Baghdad*, London: Carmelite House, 1922.

Phillips, Sir Percival, *The Prince of Wales' Eastern Book: a pictorial record of the voyages of H.M.S. "Renown", 1921-1922*, London: Hodder & Stoughton, 1922

Phillips, Sir Percival, *The Red Dragon and the Black Shirts; how Italy found her soul; the true story of the fascisti movement*, London: Carmelite House, 1922

Phillips, Sir Percival, "Bagdad: City of Returning Glory by the Tigris", in J.A. Hammerton (ed.), *Countries of the World: Described by the Leading Travel Writers of the Day*, London: Amalgamated Press, Ltd, 1924, pp. 497-516.

Phillips, Sir Percival, "Belgrade: Progressive Capital of the New Serbia," in J.A. Hammerton (ed.), *Countries of the World: Described by the Leading Travel Writers of the Day*, London: Amalgamated Press, Ltd, 1924, pp. 693-702.

Phillips, Sir Percival, *The Daily Mail Trade Union Mission to the United States*, London: Carmelite House, 1926.

Phillips, Sir Percival, "American Wins the Marathon," in Sidney Dark and Walter Wilson Cobbett (ed.), *Fleet Street: An Anthology of Modern Journalism*, London: Eyre and Spottiswoode, 1932., pp. 85-94.

Phillips, Percival, *Far Vistas*, London: Methuen, 1933.

Phillips, Percival, "The War and the Walker," in George Lynch and Frederick Palmer (eds.) *In Many Wars by Many War Correspondents*, Tokyo: Tokyo Printing Company, 1904, pp. 149-153.

Preston, Paul, *We Saw Spain Die: Foreign Correspondents in the Spanish Civil War*, London: Constable and Robinson, Ltd, 2008.

Pugh, B.W. and P. R. Spiring, *Bertram Fletcher Robinson: A Footnote to the Hound of the Baskervilles*, London: MX Publishing, 2008.

Rankin, Nicholas, *Telegram from Guernica: The Extraordinary Life of George Steer, War Correspondent*, London: Faber and Faber, 2003.

Rey, C.F., *In the Country of the Blue Nile*, London: Duckworth, 1927.

Reynolds, Reginald. *The White Sahibs of India*, Secker and Warburg, Ltd., 1937.

Roberts, Cecil. *Half Way: An Autobiography*, New York: D. Appleton and Company, 1931.

Roth, Mitchell, *Historical Dictionary of War Journalism*, Westport, CT: Greenwood Press, 1997.

Russell, Herbert, *With the Prince in the East*, London: Methuen, 1922.

Shirer, William L., *Gandhi: A Memoir*, New York: Simon and Schuster, 1979.

Shirer, William L., *The Nightmare Years 1930-1940, 20th Century Journey. Vol. II*, New York: Bantam Books, 1985.

"Sir Percival Phillips 'The Imperturbable,'" *The Newspaper World*, No. 2323, July 18, 1942, p. 8.

Snow, Edgar, *Journey to the Beginning*, New York: Random House, 1958.

Smith, Ernest, *Fields of Adventure: Some Recollections of Forty Years of Newspaper Life*, Boston: Small, Maynard and Company, 1924.

Strauss, Monica, *Cruel Banquet: The Life and Loves of Frida Strindberg*, New York: Harcourt, 2000.

Taylor, S.J., *The Great Outsiders: Northcliffe, Rothermere and the Daily Mail*, London: Weidenfeld & Nicolson, 1996

Thomas, William Beach, *A Traveller in News*, London: Chapman and Hall, Ltd., 1925.

The Three Towns: A Sketch of Brownsville, Bridgeport and West Brownsville, published from *The Three Towns* (newspaper) of September, 1883, Second edition, Brownsville: Brownsville Historical Society, 1976.

Thurman, Judith, *Isak Dinesen: The Life of a Storyteller*, New York St. Martin's Press, 1982

Von Stutterheim, Kurt, *The Press in England*, translated by W.H. Johnson, London: George Allen and Unwin, Ltd., 1934.

Walker, Dale L., *Januarius MacGahan: The Life and Campaign of an American War Correspondent*, Athens, OH: Ohio University Press, 1989.

Waugh, Evelyn, *Scoop*, Boston: Little, Brown and Company, 1937.

Waugh, Evelyn, *Waugh in Abyssinia*, London: Longmans, Green and Co. Ltd, 1936.

Weintraub, Stanley, *Silent Night: The Story of the World War I Christmas Truce*, New York: Penguin Putnam, Inc., 2001.

Wells, Linton, *Blood on the Moon: The Autobiography of Linton Wells*, Boston: Houghton Mifflin Company, 1937.

Williams, Valentine, *World of Action*, Boston: Houghton Mifflin Co.,1938.

Wilson, Keith (ed.), *The Rasp of War: The Letters of H.A. Gwynne to the Countess Bathurst, 1914-1918*, London: Sidgwick & Jackson, 1989.

Ziegler, Philip (ed.), *The Diaries of Lord Louis Mountbatten, 1920-1922*, London: Collins, 1987.

NEWSPAPERS

There were several newspapers examined during the research for this biography. Some of these were on microfilm and others in electronic format. These are listed below:

Pennsylvania Newspapers:

Brownsville Clipper 1889-1907
Clipper Monitor (Brownsville) 1907-1912
Charleroi Mail 1824-1930
Daily Courier (Connellsville) 1902-1930
Evening Democrat (Warren) 1893-1900
Evening News Standard (Uniontown) 1893-1940
Monesson Daily Independent 1902-1935
Morning Herald (Uniontown) 1924-1940
Philadelphia Inquirer 1900-1940
Pittsburgh Dispatch 1892-1935
Pittsburgh Post 1895-1940
Pittsburgh Press 1895-1938
Rural Notes (Canonsburg) 1979-1885
Scranton Times 1900-1930
Valley Independent (Monesson) 1960-1970

Other U.S. Newspapers

Atlanta Constitution (Georgia) 1890-1900
Chicago Daily Tribune 1900-1940
Daily Picayune (New Orleans) 1890-1894
Fort Wayne Daily Gazette (Indiana) 1890-1894
Lima News (Ohio) 1920-1940
Lincoln Sunday Journal and Star (Lincoln, Nebraska) 1920-1935
Los Angeles Times 1900-1940

William R. Black

Post Standard (Syracuse, New York) 1900-1940
The Times (New York) 1890-1940
Washington Post (Washington, D.C.) 1895-1940

United Kingdom Newspapers

Daily Express (London) 1900-1925
Daily Mail (London) 1920-1940
Daily Telegraph (London) 1930-1937
Sunday Times (London) 1900-1940
The Times (London) 1900-1940

Other International Newspapers

Evening Times (Wellington, New Zealand) 1925-1940
Globe and Mail (Toronto, Canada) 1936-1940
Singapore Free Press and Mercantile Advertiser 1920-1940
Straits Times (Singapore) 1925-1938
Times of India (Bombay, India) 1920-1940
Toronto Star (Canada) 1900-1940

INDEX

A

A.B.C. newspaper 249
Acquitania 215
Addis Ababa, Ethiopia   51, 204, 227, 229-230, 232-242, 250, 269
Admiral Dewey 48
aeroplane 53-4, 127, 180
African Exploitation and Development Corporation 231
Alexandra, queen of England 44, 77
Alliance, Ohio 12
Amanullah, king of Afghanistan 199-200
Amelia, queen mother of Portugal 87
Amelia, queen of Portugal 87
Amiens 115, 142
Anderson, Capt. 24
Anderson, Helena Isabel Grant, also Lena Anderson 261-266
Anderson, James Grant 194, 261, 263-265
anti-Semitic views 162-163
Antwerp, Belgium 83, 104, 113, 149
Arno 76
Ascania 196
Australia 62, 73, 192-3

B

Balderston, John 129
Baldwin, Stanley, prime minister of Great Britain 181, 194

Balkans 29, 55, 93, 97, 99, 156, 226
Baltic 188
Bannister, Professor J. Hunt 260
Barber, Will 230, 240, 259
Barcelona, Spain 78, 250
Barcelona Rebellion of 1909 246
Barry, Robert 134
Barzini, Signor 226
Bathurst, Lady 121-2, 146
Battersby, H.F. Prevost 122
Battle of Loos 114
Battle of Ypres 115, 121
Beaverbrook, Lord, also William Maxwell Aiken 177
Belfast 61, 131-3
Belgenland 52
Berlin 77, 79, 199, 254
Beron, Leon 84
Biarritz, France 80-81
Bidon, Henri 226
black fog 44
Blevins, John 39
Blixen, Bror 201
Blumenfeld, Ralph D. 60, 79, 95-7, 104-9, 122, 128, 131-3, 136-7, 143-4, 163, 177, 222
Boer War 59, 225
Bolin, Luis , also Captain Don Luis Bustamente de Torquemada 248-50
Bombay, now Mumbai, India 52-3, 171, 173, 199, 209-10, 254, 264-5
Bone, James 243

Borden, Sir Robert Laird 184
Bowman, W. Scott 71
Bowman, Jacob 14
Britain's General Medical Council 192, 253
British Empire Exhibition 188
British fleet 77-8
British intelligence 127-8
Browning, Mrs. Jessie 175
Brownsville Clipper 12-3, 19, 21, 25, 26-7, 30, 35, 40-1, 43, 45-7, 60, 62, 69, 70-1, 75
Brownsville, Pennsylvania 3-7, 11-6, 19, 30, 45-8, 57, 60-4, 69-71, 83, 132, 157-8, 165, 189, 202, 211-12, 253, 262, 269
Brownsville Seminary 11
Brussels, Belgium 101. 108, 199
Buchan, John 111-112, 114
Buckley, Henry 246
Bulgaria 97-8, 111, 116

C

Cain, David H. 137
Calcutta 97
Camrose, Lord 261
Canada 44, 51, 83, 112, 156-7, 189, 192-3, 197, 203, 245
Canary Islands 242, 245, 249
Canonsburg, Pennsylvania 4-7, 10, 13
Capa, Robert 237
Capetown, South Africa 201-2
Cardozo, Harold 249
Carlos, king of Portugal 87
Carlton Hotel 45
Carmania 195
Carnegie, Andrew 15, 45, 48
Caronia 158

Carroll Township 5
Castle, Ivor 97
Castle Shannon, Pennsylvania 164
Catalonia, Spain 78
Catalonian rebellion 78
Cawnpore, now Kanpur, India 97
Cecil Hotel 45
Cecil Township 3
censorship 65-7, 98, 106, 109-10, 112, 115-18, 125-7, 146, 154-6, 172, 240-1, 248-50, 259, 266
Chalfant family 13
Chamberlain, Neville 192
Champagne riots 88
Champagne district 88
Chatham College 6
Chiang Kai-shek 199
Chicago Inter-Ocean, The 30
Chicago Record Herald 30
Chicago Times Herald 30
Chickamauga 35
China 53, 64, 69, 90, 177, 183, 193-4, 197-200, 203, 213-5, 255-6, 265
Chinese-Russian railway conflict 202-3
cholera belt 90, 253
Christmas truce 123-5, 277
Church, Haydn 50, 165-6
Churchill, Winston 61, 84, 183, 211, 239
Cipolla, Signor Arnaldo 257
Clarke, Basil 107, 111, 118-9
Claybaugh, Alfred 19-20, 25-6, 57
Cologne, Germany 125-6, 151-2, 187
Communist Party of China 198
Communists 183, 188, 197, 199-200, 202-3, 245
Connellsville, Pennsylvania 5, 11, 22
Constantine, king of Greece 170
Conus 193

Coolidge, Calvin 12
Coronation in Ethiopia 190, 204, 214, 229, 236
Coulters family 13
Crane, Stephen 61
Crawford, Douglas 261-3
Crawley, Aidan 264-5
Crete 30
Crippen, H.H. 83-5
Cross of the Legion of Honor 158
Cuba 33-7, 62, 80, 225
Cummings, Caroline 8
Cunningham, Miss Mary 175

D

Daily Chronicle 98, 102, 111-12
Daily Express 35, 59 61, 65, 68-70, 76-81, 88-90, 99, 102-3, 105-6, 108-13, 121-2, 126, 131-2, 135-7, 151-8, 163-70, 177, 210, 222-3, 233, 235, 254-5, 261, 264, 266-7
Daily News, The 113
Daily Picayune, The 27
Damascus 158-9
Dark, Sidney 50, 57
Darrah, David 260
Davis, Frances 249
Davis, Richard Harding 32
Davis, O.K. 64
Delmar, Sefton 259
Deutschland 246
Dick, Alan 246
Dillinger, John 216
Djibouti, French Somaliland 204, 227, 229, 236, 241-2
Donora, Pennsylvania 5
Dos Passos, John 246

Doyle, Arthur Conan 59, 61
Dr. Pershing's Pittsburg Female College 6
Dragon, H.M.S. 156-7
Draper, Arthur S. 134
Drexel University 6
Duchess of Cornwall 44
Duke of Cornwall 44
Duke of Gloucester 200-01
Dunn, Robert L. 64
Dunn, James 123-7
Durbar Coronation of 1911 93-97

E

Early, Eleanor 77
Earthquake in Jamaica 75-7
Edinburgh 43
Edward VII, king of England 44, 46, 61, 77, 79, 81
Elgar, Sir Edward 188
Emperor of Japan 66
Empire Nursing Home 257
Empress of Asia 197
Empress of France 193
Entebbe, Uganda 201
Essen, Germany 186-7
Etaples, France 135-6
Ethiopia 51, 184, 204, 214, 227-33, 235, 239-41, 246, 250, 259, 266, 269
Etruria 61
Europa 222
Evening Democrat, The 38

F

Falk, Bernard 254-6, 266
Far Vistas 213-5, 219, 236
Far East tour 57, 171-4

Fayette County, Pennsylvania 5, 11, 18, 22, 24-5, 72, 165
Fee, D.H. 7
Feibelman, Rene H. 108-9
Ferguson, Sir James 75
Ferraby, H.C. 261
Ferson, John L. 5, 6, 8
Finch-Hatton, Captain Denys 201-2
Fish, Walter 261
Fleet Street 45, 164, 255-6
Forbes, Archibald 29-30
Formosa, now Taiwan 199
Forrest, Wilbur 134
Fort Wayne Gazette, The 27
Foster, Stephen 27, 30
Francis, James 11
Franco, General Francisco 1, 224, 245, 247-51
Franco-Prussian War 29-30
Frick, Henry Clay 12, 15
Fulton, Robert 3, 13

G

Gaekwar of Baroda 94-6
Gallagher, O.D. 235-8
Gallipoli 114, 170
Gandhi, Mahatma 172-3, 207-11, 219
Gandhi's demands 208, 211
Gandhist rioters 172
Garrick Club 53, 260
Geneva 168-70, 230
George, Annie 40
George V, king of England 81-2, 93
German black list 125-6
Gibbons, Percival 107, 111, 134
Gibbs, Philip 50, 56-7, 102, 111-17, 119, 143-4, 148, 151-2, 164, 226, 242, 261

Gibbs, Tony 56
Gibraltar 2, 87, 171, 246, 251-3
Gilmore School 5
Globe, The, periodical 113
Golders Green Crematorium 260-1
Golitho, Joseph 22
Goring, Hermann 248
Gottberg, German correspondent 98
Graff, Mary 12, 48
Grant, Bernard 83
Graziani, General Rudolfo 241
Great War, also see World War 57, 72, 101-130, 139-150
Greco-Turkish War 30-2
Greenwall, Harry 264
Gwynne, H.A. 109, 121-2, 146

H

Hahnemann Medical College 6
Haig, Field Marshall Douglas 121, 146, 151
Hands, Charlie 224-5
Hankow, China 197-8
Harding, Warren G. 12
Hare, John H. 64
Harmsworth, Esmond 264
Haruna Maru 194
Hastings, Patrick 186-7
Hatfield, Kenneth G.S. 257, 262
Havana, Cuba 32-3
Hawaii 64, 215
Hazzard, Colonel Chill 25-6
Hemingway, Ernest 238, 246
Henrey, Robert 191
Hesdin, France 115
Hillier, Frank 260
Hinrichs, Louis 66-7

284

Hitler, Adolph 183-5, 219-20, 239, 245
Honolulu, Hawaii 64, 215
Hoover, Herbert 12, 215
Huxham, Frances G. 70-3
Huxham, Lieutenant Percy J.B. 70, 73

I

Il Messaggero 257
Imperial News Conference 192-3
Iraq 177-82, 185, 230, 232
Ireland 3, 11, 61, 128-9, 131-5, 167, 177, 246
Irvine, John 135-6
Irwin, Will 104
Italian invasion of Ethiopia 184, 239-41
Italy 88-91, 158, 170, 177, 182-5, 200-1, 220, 226-7, 230, 239, 241, 245, 247

J

Jaffa, Palestine 159, 161
Jaime I 245, 247
Jamaica 71, 75-7, 214
James, Colonel Lionel 64
Japan 31, 51, 61-2, 64-7, 69, 89-90, 156, 171, 215-16, 262, 265
Jefferson Academy 4
Jerusalem 159, 162-3
Johnstown Flood 18

K

Kaiser Wilhelm Der Grosse 82
Kampala, Uganda 201
Keenan, Thomas J. 27, 30
Key West, Florida 37
King, Dr. W.D. 6

Kingston, Jamaica 75-6
Kisinger, family 13
Kitchner, Lord 102, 107, 109
Klu-Klux-Klan 222
Knickerbocker, Hubert 'Knick' 259
knighthood 163-8, 198, 223, 258
Knightly, Phillip 235-8
Knox & Reed 12, 15, 17
Knox, Alfred 48
Knox, Caroline 11
Knox, David S. 11
Knox, Harriette 11-12, 48
Knox, Isabella 11
Knox, Mary 11
Knox, Narcissa 11
Knox, Philander Chase 11-12, 15, 17, 48, 63, 80, 88, 175
Knox, Richard 11-12
Knox, Samuel 11, 48
Knox, Sarah Francis 11
Knox, Thomas 11, 48
Knox, Rev. William 11-12
Knox, William Francis 11, 175
Koestler, Arthur 259
Kohlsaat, H.H. 30
Korea 61, 65-6
Kuomintang, the Chinese National Party 198-9

L

Lakin, Cyril 261
Lanaway, Lieutenant F.C. 72
Law, Bonar, prime minister of Great Britain 181
League of Nations 17, 168-9, 190, 239, 241, 254
Ledoux, Phillip 216-217

Lenhart, George W. 16, 19, 21
Lenin, Nikolai 188
Lewis, Sir Wilmott 243
Liege, Belgium 102-3
Lisbon, Portugal 87, 128, 252
Lizard, Cornwall, UK 51, 189
Lloyd, William 191-2
London, Jack 60-61, 64
London, UK 2, 43-8, 50-3, 62, 65-7, 69-71, 76-81, 88, 94, 96, 98-9, 102, 104, 107, 109, 111, 113, 118, 123, 127, 129-31, 133-4, 136-7, 148, 153, 158, 163-5, 167, 172, 186-7, 189-90, 194, 196-7, 199-201, 207, 212, 215-16, 221-2, 227, 229-30, 232, 235-6, 242-3, 249-50, 254-6, 259-66
Lucknow, India 97, 173
Lynch, George 31
Lytton, Major Neville 109-10, 225-6

M

Maasdam 32-3
MacColl, Rene 264
MacGahan, Januarius 29, 156
Mackenzie, Dewitt 166
MacKenzie, George 174
Madrid, Spain 78, 248-250
Maine 33
Manchester, UK 46, 80
Manchuria 61-2, 64, 66, 202
Manuel, king of Portugal 87
Marconi, Guglielmo 45
Marella 193
Marlowe, Thomas 186-7
Massey, W.T. 261
Mathias, Isaac 174
Mauretania 197

McAndrews, Barney 22
McCullagh, Francis 1, 91-2, 223-4, 226, 246, 250-2
McKeesport, Pennsylvania 11, 47-8
McKinley, William 12, 40, 48
McPherson, Fenton 194
Mellon, Andrew 12
Menominee 189
Mesopotamia, now Iraq 178-181
Methodist Episcopal Church 8, 47, 132, 212
Miller, David Knox 11, 211-12
Miller, James Smith 11, 13
Miller, Sarah Knox 11, 13, 17, 21, 46
Miller, Webb 246, 260
Mills, James 227, 229
Monks, Noel 223-4, 233, 237, 246
Monongahela River 3, 13, 22, 24, 48
Monongahela Republican 25-6
Monongahela, Pennsylvania 25
Montrevil, France 115
Montrose 83
Moretti, Giuseppe 27
Morning Post, The 109, 111, 118, 121-2, 146, 259
Morrison, Stinie 84
Mount Union College 12
Mountbatten, Lord Louis 167
Mussolini, Benito 182-4, 200, 219-20, 227, 231, 239, 245
Mustafa Pasha, now Svilengrad 98

N

Nanking, China 199
Nankivell, Rev. J.C. 260
National Recovery Act 212
National Road 3, 212

Nehru, Jawaharlal 207, 210
Nevinson, Henry 98-9, 111, 114, 116, 147, 226, 261
New Castle, Pennsylvania 39
New Deal 221
New Delhi, India 93, 97, 167, 208
New York City 30, 33, 40-1, 44, 47, 61-2, 64, 83, 113, 158, 189, 195-7, 215, 221-2, 228, 242, 250
New York Herald 64, 104, 228
New York Herald Tribune 228
New York Times 30, 125, 195, 232, 255
New Zealand 75, 192-3
Nizam of Hyderabad 95-6
Normandie 221
Northcliffe, Lord, also Alfred Harmsworth 113, 132, 177, 219
Northern Rhodesia, now Zimbabwe 201

O

Olson, Sidney 243
Olympia 204
Olympic Games 81, 200
Omiskey, miner 22
Orwell, George 163, 246
Outlook 80, 113

P

Page, Rebecca 11
Palestine 158-63, 200
Palmer, Frederick 31, 64, 111, 147-8
Parliament 44, 131, 192
Passchendaele 115, 121
Paulhan, Louis 80
Pearson, C. Arthur 59-60

Philadelphia, Pennsylvania 6, 47, 65, 221-2
Philadelphia Inquirer 65
Philippine Islands 33
Phillips, Anne C.M., also Annie Phillips 3-7, 10-11, 13, 16-18, 21-2, 41, 46-8, 69-71, 83, 137, 174-5, 177, 193, 202, 211-12
Phillips, Fulton 3, 7, 18, 26
Phillips, Hibbard Samuel 3-10, 13, 16, 18, 21, 26, 201-2
Phillips, James Knox 71, 262
Phillips, Percival 38-41, 80-4, 88-91, 96-9, 101-11, 125-9, 132-7, 139-44, 157-9, 165-6, 168-70, 190-1, 238-42, 255-8
  China coverage by 193-9, 203, 213-15
  Coronation Durbar coverage by 93-97
  Daily Express years of 59-175
  Daily Mail years of 177-217
  Daily Telegraph years of 219-55
  early reporting in Pennsylvania 22-7
  engagement in London 69-73
  Ethiopian Invasion coverage by 227-42
  Gandhi and India coverage by 207-11
  illness and death 253-67
  Irish Rebellion reporting by 131-7
  Jamaican earthquake coverage by 75-7
  Pennsylvania family of 1-21
  Pennsylvania youth of 12-27
  Pittsburg Dispatch reporting of 37-58
  Spanish Civil War coverage by 245-52
  Western Front coverage by 111-30, 139-50
Phillips, Robert Fulton 3, 13
Phillips, Samuel 3-4
Phillips, Sarah Fulton 3
Phillips, Smith, also James Smith Miller Phillips 11, 15-17, 46-8, 71, 73, 79, 104, 174, 212

Phillips, Wilbur Warner 71, 262
Pierard, Louis 108-9
Pierre, Emile 228
Pittsburg, Pennsylvania 6, 24, 26, 70
Pittsburg Post 33, 35, 37, 164
Pittsburg Press 28, 30, 164
Pittsburg Dispatch 37-40, 45, 60-1, 67, 104, 129
Pittsburgh, Pennsylvania 3, 5-6, 8, 10-16, 20, 22, 24, 27, 29, 32-3, 37, 39-40, 45-6, 48, 50, 53, 72. 85, 157, 193, 195, 211, 222, 229, 253, 262
Pittsburgh Press Club 157-8
Port Arthur, now Lüshan 64-5
Portugal 2, 87, 251
Portugal revolution 87
Post, Wiley 228
President Hoover 215
Press Club 41, 53, 158
Prince of Wales, later Edward VIII 156-8, 167, 171-4, 200-02, 210
Pryor, S.J. 59
Puerto Rico 33, 35
Pulitzer, Joseph 34
Pulvermacher, Oscar 261-3

Q

Quebec 83
Queen Mary 214, 242-3

R

Railway Age 113
Ramasen, Mohammed 97
Ranchi 194, 254-5, 261
Rankin, Nicholas 238

Ras Taffari, prince regent of Abyssinia 189-90
Reed, David 12
Reed, James Hay 12
Reichspost 99
Reinoehl, George S. 34
Renown, H.M.S 156, 171-2
Republican National Convention of 1936 243
Reuters News Service 111-14, 164, 197, 250
Rey, C.F. 236
Rice, F.A. 259
Rickett, Francis M. 227, 230-4, 239
Robinson, Bertram Fletcher 59-60
Robinson, Henry Perry 107, 111, 113, 147-8, 151-2, 164, 167, 261
Rogers, Will 228
Rolls, Charles 54
Roosevelt, Franklin D. 212, 221-2
Roosevelt, Theodore 12, 17, 48, 63, 79-80, 99
Rothermere, Lord, also Harold Harmsworth 177-8, 183-4, 216, 219-20, 249, 264
Rotterdam, Holland 107, 123
Royal Aero Society 53
Royal Automobile Society 53
Royal Bombay Yacht Club 53
Royal Geographic Society 53, 174
Russell, Herbert 111, 113, 148, 164, 167, 172, 261
Russia 56, 61, 64-7, 156, 177, 188, 190 197, 200, 202-3
Russo-Japanese War 1, 31, 62-5, 76, 79, 111
Russo-Turkish War 29-30

S

safari of the Prince of Wales 200-02
sailing permit 222-3
Salamanca, Spain 1, 247-8, 250-1, 259
Salter, Cedric 246
San Francisco 64, 75, 215
San Francisco Examiner 64
Saturday Evening Post 98
Savage Club 53, 136
Savoy Hotel 45, 49, 51, 104
Saxton, George 40
Scio, Ohio 37-39
Scoop in Ethiopia 227-233
Scoop, a novel 219, 233-4
Scotland Yard 83
Scovel, Sylvester 32
Scranton, Pennsylvania 9-10, 18
Selassie, Haile, emperor of Ethiopia 190, 204, 214, 229-31, 236-241
Shanghai, China 67, 197-9, 203, 264
Shanghai Club 53
Shunk, William 13
Siberia 64, 228
Smith, Ernest 163
Smith, John B. 21
Sofia, Bulgaria 98-9, 128
Soraya, queen of Afghanistan 199-200
Southern Rhodesia, now Zambia 201
Spanish American War 32-7, 80
Springer family 13
St. Omer, France 114-15, 154
St. Vincent's Monastery 39
Stallings, Lawrence 228
Steer, George L. 238
Stemp, Daphne 254
Stemp, Maud Florence 254, 262
Stephens, Pembroke 246, 254

Stickle Hollow riots 22, 24-7, 58
Stockholm, Sweden 79, 81, 11, 127
Strand 45, 236
Strattman, Brother Herman 39-40
Stuart, Major A.G. 105, 107, 114

T

Taft, William Howard 13, 88
Taj Mahal Hotel, Bombay, now Mumbai 264
Tanganyika, now Tanzania 201
Tangier, Morocco 2, 253-5, 262
Thatched House Club 53
Third Home Rule Bill 131
Thomas, W. Beach 107, 111, 113, 115, 147, 151-2, 164, 261
Tientsin, China 199
Times, The 64, 66, 94-6, 112-13, 172, 183, 192, 197, 221, 238, 243, 255, 261, 263
Times Literary Supplement 213
Times of India, The 258
Tokyo 1, 31, 65-6, 215-16, 264
Tribune of New York 134, 228, 259
Tripoli, now Libya 88 92, 159, 223, 246-7
Troy, John 22
Tuohy, James 134
Turkey 30, 88-9, 156, 163, 199
Tyd, The 125

U

U.S. Steel Corporation 15
Uganda 200-1
Ulster Volunteer Force or UVF 131-2
Union Monitor 25
Uniontown, Pennsylvania 5, 71
United Associated Presses 15

V

Victoria, queen of England 44, 167
Vienna 99, 220
Vimy Ridge 121, 135, 245
Vost, Lieutenant Colonel William 97

W

war service honors 163
War Office 104-5, 128, 131, 164
Warden, J.H.B. 261
Warden, W.L. 261
Warner, Lucille 71
Warner, Rev. W.G. 71
Washington & Jefferson College 4
Washington College 4
Washington, D.C. 13, 48, 62-4, 222
Washington County, Pennsylvania 2-5, 8, 165
Washington, Pennsylvania 4, 211
Washington Post, The 27, 243
Watson, Sir Alfred 260
Watson, Arthur E. 260-1
Waugh, Evelyn 219, 227, 229-30, 233-4, 236
Wauman, Mrs. 256, 262
Waverly Hotel 44
Wells, Fay Gillis 228, 269
Wells, Linton 228, 236, 269
Wembley rodeo 189
West Virginia University 12
Western Front 111-130, 139-50

Westernland 43
Whitaker, John T. 259
White, Graham 80
Wignall, Trevor C. 242
Wilhelm II, kaiser of Germany 77, 126, 191
Williams, Douglas 111-12, 114, 148
Williams, Valentine 111-12, 114, 154
Wilson, Colonel Hutton 107
Wilson, Woodrow 168
Wilson, J.B. 261
Winn, Roland 250
World, The , also the *New York World* 34-5, 40, 91, 134, 247
World War , also The Great War 49-50, 56-7, 72, 101, 107, 109, 123, 127-8, 133, 156-8, 168, 178 182, 185, 191, 200, 209, 223, 225-6, 238, 242, 245, 255, 260, 263

X

Xenia Torchlight and Examiner 40

Y

Yokohama, Japan 64, 216, 262
Young Europeans meeting 210

Z

Zionist movement 162